SLIGO

For the next generation,
Ayda Rose, Conor, Cian and Donnacha

The Irish Revolution, 1912–23

Sligo

Michael Farry

FOUR COURTS PRESS

This book was set in 10.5 on 12.5 point Ehrhardt by
Mark Heslington Ltd, Scarborough, North Yorkshire for
FOUR COURTS PRESS
7 Malpas Street, Dublin 8, Ireland
www.fourcourtspress.ie
and in North America for
FOUR COURTS PRESS
c/o ISBS, 920 N.E. 58th Avenue, Suite 300, Portland, OR 97213.

A catalogue record for this title
is available from the British Library.

ISBN 978-1-84682-301-5 hbk
ISBN 978-1-84682-302-2 pbk

Printed in Great Britain
by Antony Rowe Ltd, Chippenham, Wilts.

Contents

Illustrations

28 Frank Carty and Martin Brennan with the Rolls Royce armoured car *Ballinalee* in Tubbercurry, Sept. 1922.
29 Two of the six anti-Treaty IRA killed on Benbulben in Sept. 1922.
30 The funeral of the anti-Treaty IRA killed on Benbulben in Sept. 1922.
31 Charles Phibbs inspecting the grave dug in front of his residence, Doobeg House, in May 1922.

Credits
Illustrations 1, 6: Sligo County Library; 11: Foley/Kilgannon collection, Sligo County Library; 2: Sister Elizabeth, Sligo; 3 *left*: Owen Tansy; 3 *right*: Michael Dyar; 4: Veronica Landet; 5, 7: Kilgannon, *Sligo and its surroundings*; 8: Joe Hunt; 9, 10, 12, 13, 14, 15: Capt. A.L. Dunnill, 'A summary of events during the period in which the 1st Battalion Bedfordshire & Hertfordshire Regiment was stationed in Ireland, 1920, 1921, 1922', Bedfordshire and Luton Archives and Records Service, Bedford; 16: Madeleine Bradley; 17: Aisling McTiernan; 18, 19, 20, 30: Padraic Kilgannon; 20, 21: Alan Finan; 22, 23, 24, 25: Independent Archive, National Library of Ireland; 26: Ena Gawley; 27: Pat McDermott; 28: Matthew Brennan; 31: Mrs Judith Newbury: Archives and Special Collections, Bangor University.

MAPS

Abbreviations

3WD	Third Western Division
4WD	Fourth Western Division
Adj.	Adjutant
AG	Adjutant General
AOH	Ancient Order of Hibernians
ASU	Active Service Unit
Batt.	Battalion
Bde.	Brigade
BMH	Bureau of Military History
CDB	Congested Districts Board
CI	County Inspector, RIC
CM	*Connachtman*
CS	Chief of Staff
CSO	Chief Secretary's Office
DÉCC	Dáil Éireann Courts (Winding Up) Commission
DÉLG	Dáil Éireann Local Government
DI	District Inspector, RIC
DJ	District Justice
HML	His Majesty's Lieutenant
IB	*Irish Bulletin*
IGC	Irish Grants Committee
II	*Irish Independent*
IMA	Irish Military Archives
INAAVDF	Irish National Aid Association and Volunteer Dependents Fund
I/O	Intelligence Officer
IPP	Irish Parliamentary Party
IRA	Irish Republican Army
IRB	Irish Republican Brotherhood
IT	*Irish Times*
ITGWU	Irish Transport and General Workers Union
IUA	Irish Unionist Alliance
IV	*Irish Volunteer*
IWFL	Irish Women's Franchise League
JP	Justice of the Peace
LGB	Local Government Board
MP	Member of Parliament
NAI	National Archives of Ireland
NLI	National Library of Ireland

O/C	Officer Commanding
PR	Proportional Representation
PRONI	Public Records Office of Northern Ireland
QM	Quartermaster
RDC	Rural District Council
RH	*Roscommon Herald*
RIC	Royal Irish Constabulary
SC	*Sligo Champion*
SCL	Sligo County Library
SF	Sinn Féin
SI	*Sligo Independent*
SN	*Sligo Nationalist*
ST	*Sligo Times*
TD	Teachta Dála, member of Dáil Éireann
TNA	The National Archives, London
UCDAD	University College Dublin Archives Department
UIL	United Irish League
WS	Witness Statement
WUA	Women's Unionist Alliance

Acknowledgments

This book is the culmination of thirty years' interest in and study of the revolutionary period in County Sligo. It would be impossible to list all those, who over the years either contacted me or were contacted by me on the subject. Their help in answering queries and sourcing photographs has been invaluable. Aidan Mannion and Paul Gunning have been especially helpful in recent years.

I was lucky in being able to meet some Sligo veterans of the War of Independence and Civil War and wish to record my gratitude to those who shared their experiences with me.

I completed a doctoral dissertation at the Department of Modern History in Trinity College, Dublin on the Civil War in Sligo and the support and interest I received from that department, fellow students and in particular from my supervisor, Professor David Fitzpatrick, was vital.

UCD Press published *The aftermath of revolution: Sligo 1921–1923*, based on my thesis, in 2000 and I am especially grateful to the then executive editor at that press, Barbara Mennell, for her input and support. The 1921–3 sections of this book are largely based on that volume.

I am grateful to the friendly and efficient staffs of the National Library, the National Archives, the Military Archives, UCD Archives, the Valuation Office, the Representative Church Body Library, the Orange Order archive, the Grand Lodge of Freemasons Archive, the Institute of Celtic Studies and Historical Research, the Garda Museum, Sligo Town Hall and the National Archives, London. Donal Tinney, the Sligo County Librarian, and his colleagues were particularly helpful as were Nigel Lutt and the staff of the Bedfordshire and Luton Archives and Records Service.

The maps in this volume were created by Dr Mike Brennan whose professionalism, expertise and cooperation made for an enjoyable and successful collaboration.

It has been a pleasure to work with my editors, Professor Mary Ann Lyons and Dr Daithí Ó Corráin, who first convinced me to undertake the book and then guided me expertly through the process.

My late parents, brothers and sisters, close friends and fellow workers all deserve thanks for their interest and encouragement over many years.

My wife Winifred and children Fiona, Oisín, Sinéad and Aisling have been unfailing in their support of, and interest in, my preoccupation with Sligo's history over the past three decades.

Trim, Co. Meath
May 2012

The Irish Revolution, 1912–23 series

Since the turn of the century, a growing number of scholars have been actively researching this seminal period in modern Irish history. More recently, propelled by the increasing availability of new archival material, this endeavour has intensified. This series brings together for the first time the various strands of this exciting and fresh scholarship within a single coherent, overarching interpretative framework, making available concise, accessible, scholarly studies of the Irish Revolution experience at a local level to a wide audience.

The approach adopted is both thematic and chronological, addressing the key developments and major issues that occurred at a county level during the tumultuous 1912–23 period. Beginning with an overview of the social, economic and political milieu in the county in 1912, each volume assesses the strength of the home rule movement and levels of labour and feminist activism. The genesis and organization of paramilitarism from 1913 are traced; responses to the outbreak of the First World War and its impact on politics at a county level are explored; and the significance of the 1916 Rising is assessed. The varying fortunes of constitutional and separatist nationalism are examined. The local experience of the War of Independence, reaction to the Truce and the Anglo–Irish Treaty and the course and consequences of the Civil War are subject to detailed examination and analysis. The result is a compelling account of life in Ireland in this formative era.

Mary Ann Lyons
Department of History
NUI Maynooth

Daithí Ó Corráin
Department of History
St Patrick's College, Drumcondra

Foreword

This series of county histories of the Irish revolution is a bold and imaginative venture, which may recast our understanding of how and why the two Irish states came into being. Since the 1970s, various scholars have used the materials of local history to add flesh and blood to the great movements for and against Home Rule and the Republic. By investigating key actors and organizations at parish, town, or county level, it has proved possible to challenge once-dominant assumptions about the rationale, conduct, and impact of political and military campaigns in the period of national and revolutionary turmoil between 1912 and 1923. The attempt to write history 'from below' has significantly undermined the 'grand narrative' (still favoured by many latter-day republicans) of national awakening leading to moral victory, betrayal by perfidious Albion or her Irish allies, and uncompleted decolonization.

By looking closely at the workings of communities, the careers of local activists, and the ways in which national issues were reduced to provincial practicalities, historians have discovered how little changed in the lives and attitudes of many who experienced the revolution. While political and state structures were transformed, 'ordinary' people tried as before to minimize disruption, avoid alienation from their neighbours, and grab whatever opportunities revolutionary turmoil offered. In short, local studies have helped to restore the force of rationality and adaptability in Irish revolutionary history, and thus to call into question the primacy of the romantic idealism often attributed to the 1916 rebellion or republican resistance in the civil war.

In general, the deeper one delves into local and personal sources, the more tenuous seems the control exerted by leaders, central institutions, and agencies of enforcement. This applies just as much to revolutionary organizations as to the instruments of government, which were more conspicuously disintegrating under the pressures of revolution. The weakness of central authorities is something that almost all scholars familiar with local sources have noted, and that impression has only been accentuated by the release of further personal testimony, especially the recently digitalized 'witness statements' collected by the Bureau of Military History. Immersion in local documentation also encourages an almost anthropological approach to the history of communities, reminiscent of the *Annales* 'school' of French historians who began to turn history on its head half a century ago.

Such generalizations discount numerous differences of approach and interpretation among historians who have documented Irish revolutionary history at local level. Even today, studies of the IRA's military campaign are published that

portray each local ambush or 'engagement' as just another local manifestation of
a national 'war of independence' sanctioned by the popular will. These studies,
however valuable in assembling local documentation of participants and events,
typically ignore or skate over the complex psychological, political, social, and
economic contexts in which conflict occurred. Likewise, military specialists
investigating the performance and (mis)behaviour of the Crown forces only
occasionally probe the mentality and assumptions of those involved (a welcome
exception is David M. Leeson's recent study *The Black and Tans: British Police
and Auxiliaries in the Irish War of Independence, 1920–1921* (Oxford, 2011).

At its best, local history helps us to identify and reassert the socio-economic
origins and influences that shaped political and military events. The effect is to
complicate, enrich, or unravel conventional narratives based on propagandist
assertions by revolutionary protagonists and their modern apologists. Yet no two
local studies, however sophisticated and deeply documented, concur in all
aspects of interpretation. As an early contributor to the field, I have noted with
interest, even alarm, that almost every study of similar design has taken issue
with one or more of my key negative findings. In 1998, for example, Peter Hart
controversially imputed sectarian motives to republican killers in Cork; Marie
Coleman (2003) reasserted the importance of local leadership in Longford; and
Fergus Campbell (2005) affirmed the radical roots of the revolution in Galway.
The outcome has been enhanced understanding of local variations, coupled with
the eruption of intricate and sometimes bitter debates on emotive issues such as
'ethnic cleansing' and the alleged hypocrisy of prominent revolutionaries. Yet all
of these studies broadly confirm the primacy of local factors in forging alliances,
and the resistance of local communities to radical changes imposed by outsiders.

Needless to say, no uniform 'rules of engagement' have hitherto been applied
to local studies of the Irish revolution. Each scholar has independently determined the appropriate region of study, the period to be covered, the balance
between national and local contexts, and the range of protagonists under investigation. Even so, the very multiplication of studies has informally encouraged
greater compatibility, as those joining the field try to relate their findings to
previous work by analyzing similar sources and adopting similar techniques of
analysis. Scholars have thus begun to develop a common language whereby
conflicts of interpretation may be analyzed more incisively. This series promises
to accelerate the process of convergence by generating county-based studies,
covering the entire period between the introduction of the third Government of
Ireland Bill in 1912 and the ostensible cessation of hostilities in 1923.

Some may be uneasy with the chosen unit of analysis, given the great varia-
tion between counties in population and intensity of conflict, and also the
obvious superficiality of county as against parochial or 'communal' allegiances.
Yet the county unit has already been applied with great success in many projects,
especially the impressive volumes of interdisciplinary essays published by

William Nolan's Geography Press. By aiming to cover the entire island, the series will encourage scholars to dissect 'loyalism' as well as nationalism at local level, so helping us to understand how diehard opponents of Home Rule for Ireland in 1912 became equally implacable defenders of Home Rule for Ulster after 1920. The editors' decision to incorporate the period of civil war is particularly welcome. Whereas many earlier works, including my own, excluded the period after 1921 because of the paucity of available records and the sensitivities of surviving witnesses, these impediments have no relevance today. By commissioning concise yet fully annotated studies, the editors have made it possible for a wide range of emerged and emerging scholars to digest and interpret the ever widening range of accessible sources. The series should not only illuminate the history of each county, but also help to build up a much needed comparative framework for broader debates about Irish revolutionary history.

The first volume shows how much can be achieved by a disciplined expert within the chosen format. Michael Farry, already the leading historian of revolutionary Sligo, contributes a succinct yet detailed narrative of the county's political evolution between 1912 and 1923. Deploying a wide range of primary documents, he shows that military activity in the county was far more intense during the early months of the civil war than during the Anglo–Irish conflict, and almost unsullied by sectarian attacks or the killing of civilians. Dr Farry's explanations for these apparent anomalies will surely be explored and tested in future contributions to the series.

David Fitzpatrick
Trinity College, Dublin
August 2012

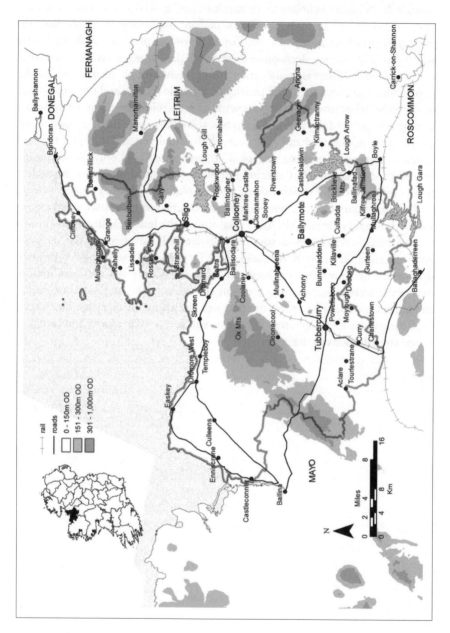

1 Places mentioned in the text

1 County Sligo in 1912

In advance of the 1918 election, the Catholic bishop of Achonry, Patrick Morrisroe, refused to give advice to his flock, which included the Catholic population of a large area of County Sligo. He and his clergy were ready to lead their people, the bishop assured them, as soon as the people had indicated the direction that they intended to take.[1] One can understand why Morrisroe, who had tried to respond sympathetically to the twists and turns of popular politics during the previous six years, had decided to abstain from offering advice. County Sligo had, in 1913, been the fourth-best organized Irish county in terms of United Irish League (UIL) membership but on the eve of the 1918 election was the fourth-best organized Sinn Féin (SF) county. The bishop might have been even more confused had he known what was in store. At the 1922 general election the Sligo–Mayo East constituency was the only one to return an anti-Treaty majority and during the Civil War Sligo proved to be a continuous source of trouble to the Provisional and Free State governments.

Sligo was a maritime county with an important port, a county of lowlands and mountains. The Ox Mountains, wider towards the west, divided the county with the Collooney gap serving as a vital communications link. To the south a large area of fertile and well-drained lowlands stretched as far as the Curlew Mountains near Boyle and the limestone ridge along the Leitrim border on the east. Coastal lowlands bordered the ocean to the north of the Ox Mountains and north of Sligo town. An extensive range of limestone uplands including the Benbulben Mountains lay along the border with Leitrim to the north of Sligo town. The road network was extensive but designed primarily for horse and cart rather than mechanized transport.

In 1911 Sligo ranked twenty-second among Irish counties as regards land area and nineteenth in terms of population. The latter had fallen from a high of 180,886 in 1841 to a low of 79,045 in 1911. This represented a 6.2% fall from the 1901 population, the fifth-largest population drop among Irish counties and above the Connacht average of 5.7%. When we consider that the population of Sligo town increased by 2.7% during the same period, the decline in the county's rural population was one of the highest in Ireland.[2] The rate of emigration from Sligo was decreasing, 21% emigrated between 1881 and 1891, 14% between 1891 and 1901, and 11% between 1901 and 1911.[3]

Notwithstanding the growth of Sligo town, the county was still overwhelmingly rural with just under 70% of those employed in the county engaged in agriculture.[4] Farms were small: in 1901 almost 50% were fifteen acres or less, and only 3.5% were over 100 acres, though this was close to the Connacht average.[5] Using the proportion of residents on holdings valued at £15 or less as

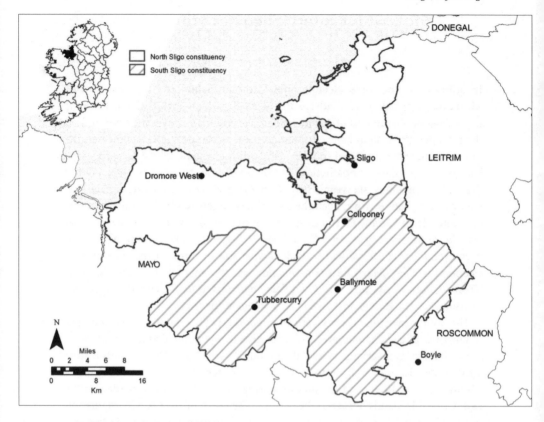

DONEGAL

North Sligo constituency

South Sligo constituency

Sligo

LEITRIM

Dromore West●

Collooney

MAYO

Ballymote

Tubbercurry

N

Miles
0   2   4   6   8

0   8   16
         Km

ROSCOMMON

Boyle

2 Parliamentary constituencies

a rough index of the prevalence of poverty, Sligo was the least poor county in the province, but far poorer than the national average.[6] In Sligo town just over 27% of the working males were general labourers and of the 1,274 females with occupations, there were 438 domestic servants, 127 nuns and 277 seamstresses and dressmakers.[7]

Improved transport links during the second half of the nineteenth century contributed to the development of Sligo town. Railways connected it to Dublin, Belfast, Limerick and Galway. The smaller urban centres – Tubbercurry, Ballymote and Collooney – also had access to the rail network. Sligo port, the most important in the north-west, was linked to Liverpool, Glasgow and Derry and exported annually large numbers of cattle and agricultural produce from the surrounding districts. The growing prosperity of Sligo town was reflected by the erection of new public and commercial buildings such as the town hall, the courthouse, the Bank of Ireland and Ulster Bank during the latter part of the nineteenth century. The emergence of the Catholic middle class resulted in new Catholic buildings – the friary, the cathedral, Summerhill College and convents

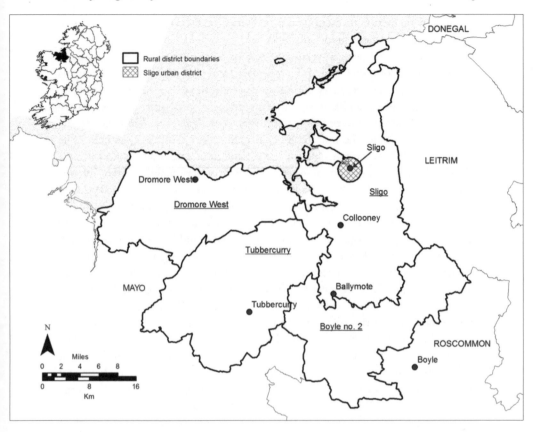

Rural district boundaries
Sligo urban district

DONEGAL

Sligo

LEITRIM

Dromore West●

Sligo

Dromore West

Collooney

Tubbercurry

MAYO

Ballymote

Tubbercurry ●

Boyle no. 2

ROSCOMMON

Boyle ●

N

Miles
0 2   4   6   8

0   8   16
Km

3 Local government divisions

– and the change of street names to honour Grattan, O'Connell and Teeling.[8] By
the end of the nineteenth century the installation of a modern sewerage system
and piped water ensured that the town had a clean, affluent appearance.[9]

    Despite these developments, Sligo Corporation's finances were in an impecu-
nious state and workers' housing as well as the streets and roads were in poor
condition. In 1915 the Corporation Medical Officer for Health warned that 'the
housing accommodation of the town is very bad. There are several streets in
which there is scarcely one house fit for human habitation. The majority of these
houses constitute a grave risk to the public health'.[10] Daniel O'Donnell, the
mayor, and the Corporation spent a considerable amount of time during 1912
and 1913 trying to obtain a grant and a loan to steamroll the streets.[11] They
blamed the crisis on previous Conservative-controlled Corporations, the lax
attitude to paying rates and the strictures imposed by two acts of Parliament.[12]
A random Local Government Board (LGB) audit found that some Corporation
members themselves were in arrears of rates. This, and the general state of the

borough, were frequently cited by unionists as a foretaste of the probable fate of local government under home rule.[13]

The reforming Local Government Act of 1898 established Sligo County Council, Sligo Borough Council (Corporation) and four Rural District Councils (RDCs) of Sligo, Tubbercurry, Dromore West and Boyle No. 2 (see map 3). The extension of the franchise meant that members elected were predominately nationalist. Each of nineteen electoral divisions returned one councillor to the County Council and the four RDC chairmen were ex-officio members. The County Council was responsible for the collection of rates and maintenance of roads and other essential services while the RDCs were mainly responsible for sanitation and public health. The RDC councillors also served on the Boards of Guardians, which were responsible for workhouses and hospitals. County Council elections were held every three years and many councillors were returned unopposed, though elections when held could be robustly contested. Allegiance to the IPP was a pre-requisite for success. Sligo Corporation had twenty-four councillors representing three wards and each January two councillors had to stand for re-election. These annual elections could be bitterly contested with representatives of labour, ratepayers, UIL and AOH in opposition despite the fact that all claimed allegiance to the IPP.

The Protestant tradition remained strong in Sligo comprising 15% of the population of Sligo Borough (the highest of any Connacht town) and 10% of the county with sizeable numbers in every part but especially in Riverstown and some coastal parishes in the north and north west.[14] Although the great landlords of County Sligo – Wood-Martins, Gore-Booths, Coopers and O'Haras – lost their political power as a result of the Local Government Act and sold much of their estates as a result of the Wyndham Land Act of 1903, Protestant businessmen continued to make significant contributions to the life of Sligo town. Belfast-born Arthur Jackson married into the Pollexfen family, managed the Sligo Steam Navigation Company and served as chairman of Sligo Harbour Commissioners. Harper Campbell Perry came to Sligo in the 1880s to join the large provision and curing business of Harper Campbell and became its chairman, a director of the Sligo Steam Navigation Company and a harbour commissioner.[15] Sligo Protestants had a vibrant network of social outlets including the County Club, the Constitutional Club, described as 'the headquarters of conservatism in Sligo', and clubs such as Sligo United YMCA, County Sligo Golf Club, Sligo Boating and Rowing Club and the County Sligo Cricket Club.[16] There were two Sligo Freemason lodges: one attracted the merchant class while the other had a membership of clerks and shop assistants. Three Orange lodges appear to have existed in the county at least until 1921, in Sligo town, Ballymote and Riverstown.[17]

Sligo did not play a leading role in any of the great political movements of the nineteenth century. In terms of agrarian outrages between 1879 and 1882, it ranked fourth in Connacht and tenth in Ireland.[18] The county had been divided in 1885 into two parliamentary constituencies, North Sligo and South Sligo (see map 2), and both seats were held by nationalists. The 1891 North Sligo by-election, at the height of the Parnell controversy, saw a bitter contest in which the anti-Parnellite, Bernard Collery, prevailed by a narrow margin. The Catholic clergy were split and the bishop of Killala was said to have supported Parnell. Unionist candidates contested both Sligo seats in 1892 and 1895 but were easily defeated. These were the last contested parliamentary elections for Sligo constituencies until 1918.[19]

In the first decade of the twentieth century Sligo demonstrated its loyalty to the re-united Irish Parliamentary Party (IPP) under the chairmanship of John Redmond. The UIL played a decisive role in reunifying the party and became its constituency organization. Founded at Westport in January 1898 as a radical agrarian organization, it spread quickly through Connacht and the rest of Ireland. By December 1898 there were 15 UIL branches in Sligo, 36 a year later and 46 by 1901, a figure which remained constant until 1913.[20] Sligo was one of the best organized counties and at the end of March 1913 its UIL membership ranked fourth in Ireland.[21] Key organizers were *Sligo Champion* owner Patrick A. McHugh and John O'Dowd. Leitrim-born McHugh had been MP for North Leitrim from 1892 to 1906 and for North Sligo from 1906 until his death in 1909. He was also mayor of Sligo from 1888 to 1900. Born in 1857 near Tubbercurry, O'Dowd spent some years in the US. On his return home in 1876 he joined the IRB and took part in Land League agitation. He was returned unopposed as North Sligo MP in March 1900 and for South Sligo in the general election seven months later. Thomas Scanlan, a farmer's son from Drumcliff who emigrated to Glasgow, became North Sligo MP on McHugh's death in 1909. He was called to the bar in 1912. Both MPs were unopposed until 1918. This was not unusual. In the December 1910 general election only 41 of the 101 Irish constituencies were contested.[22] Membership of the UIL was essential for anyone seeking office as it controlled all public bodies. Weekly columns of UIL branch reports in the local press detailed their concerns which were often agrarian and local, and included regular motions of confidence in the party and the leadership. In many cases local clergy were involved, usually as branch presidents.[23]

The land question remained a key political issue in Sligo throughout this period. The UIL continued to agitate to force landlords to sell estates and give up grazing ranches. The 1907–8 ranch war had involved widespread boycotting and cattle driving. Michael Wheatley's figures for cattle drives indicate that Sligo was very active in 1908 after which activity declined until 1914. The only fatality of the ranch war occurred at Riverstown, Sligo in October 1908 when a small force of RIC exchanged fire with a large group of cattle drivers, killing one of them. The Birrell Land Act (1909) granted the Congested Districts Board (CDB) compulsory purchase powers and increased its budget substantially, leading to accelerated land purchase. It also extended the areas classified as 'congested' to include all of County Sligo.[24] As Wheatley has shown, land purchase in Sligo was well below the national average by 1912, lagging significantly behind neighbouring Leitrim and Roscommon.[25]

A Sligo Trades Council existed since the late 1890s and had campaigned for fair labour conditions and local industry. The UIL supported it from the beginning. In September 1911 a Sligo ITGWU branch was founded at a public meeting chaired by the mayor, Daniel O'Donnell, and addressed by Walter Carpenter, an ITGWU organizer. Dock worker and sailor, John Lynch, became the secretary of the branch, which was soon one of the most active in the country.[26]

There is no reference to any Sligo involvement in support of Sinn Féin (SF) in the 1907 North Leitrim by-election apart from a claim by Alec McCabe that he had written articles for the SF election newspaper. When C.J. Dolan, the unsuccessful SF candidate, thanked those who had assisted from outside counties he did not include Sligo. The Tubbercurry 'Sinn Féiner' who sent a pound to help with election expenses was presumably Patrick Dyar, who, according to McCabe, was the only other SF supporter besides himself in Sligo. McCabe was born in 1886 in Keash, south Sligo, where his mother was a primary teacher; his father was a Longford-born RIC man. Educated at Summerhill College, Sligo, McCabe became a primary teacher and was appointed principal of Drumnagranchy National School, Keash in 1910. Dyar, a native of the St James's Well area of south Sligo, worked as a foreman in Cooke's of Tubbercurry.[27]

There was a small but important Fenian legacy in the county with John O'Dowd MP often stressing his past involvement. P.J. Sheridan, who had lived in Tubbercurry, had been a key Fenian organizer and a prominent Land League official. He fled to the US to escape arrest and was involved with the Invincibles, who were responsible for the 1882 Phoenix Park murders. He died in the US in 1918.[28] There was an IRB circle in Sligo town but it appears not to have been active.[29] Here and there in the county there were supporters of more radical politics. Two creamery employees in south Sligo corresponded with the Irish-American physical force republican Joseph McGarrity in 1911 and 1912 but appear not to have been actively involved in the IRB until McCabe, a member of the supreme council, organized the area in 1914.[30] In 1911 a group already involved in Sligo Wanderers GAA club, including teacher, John R. Treacy, founded the Sligo Gaelic Club, with the aim of developing Irish ideals through lectures, concerts and debates. Some lectures attracted large audiences such as that by Major John MacBride on the Manchester Martyrs in 1911, which was chaired by the mayor.[31]

A branch of the Gaelic League had been operating in Sligo since the early years of the twentieth century. Activists included two teachers, Galway native

Pádhraic Ó Domhnalláin and Mayo-man Seán Ó Ruadháin.[32] Fr Brian Crehan, a Galway native, who was at Grange in 1912, was also involved. Prominent politicians stressed the importance of the Irish-Ireland movement and the *Sligo Champion* published a weekly column in Irish. However, there is little evidence that the organization was making much headway in the county. The 1911 Sligo Gaelic League AGM sounded a note of disappointment: 'As far as teaching Irish to adults was concerned the work of the branch had been practically nil. Adult Sligo had shown as little disposition as in the past to learn the language of their country'.[33] Ó Domhnalláin sounded a similarly sour note at the 1914 meeting to form the Sligo Volunteers when 'he hoped the Irish Volunteer movement would be taken up more enthusiastically in Sligo than the language movement was'.[34]

The Royal Irish Constabulary (RIC) occupied thirty-four barracks in County Sligo in 1914 (see map 4). A County Inspector (CI) was based in Sligo. Limerick-born Robert Ievers Sullivan occupied this post until he retired in June 1920 and was succeeded by Clare-born Thomas Neylon. Five District Inspectors (DIs), based at Sligo, Tubbercurry, Easkey, Ballymote and Collooney, reported to the CI. When the Collooney position became vacant in 1914 it was not filled and barracks in that area were supervised by adjacent DIs. In 1914 there were 216 policemen in Sligo, a ratio of 365 persons to one policeman; Sligo was thus in the lowest third nationally in terms of police strength by county.[35] The force was under strength, morale was low, recruitment was dropping and there was discontent over levels of pay. In general the force had become well integrated into local communities and operated more like a civil than a colonial police force.[36] As regards indictable offences for the period 1908 to 1912 Sligo was second highest in Connacht but only ranked twenty-fourth nationally.[37]

Four local newspapers were published in Sligo town in 1912. The *Sligo Champion* had the largest circulation. It was a loyal IPP supporter and during the early years of this study a confident, aggressive voice in support of Catholic Sligo and the home rule cause. As the political climate changed, however, it became more tentative in its judgments and took no side at the 1918 election. It welcomed the truce and strongly supported the Anglo-Irish Treaty. Shortly after P.A. McHugh's death, Bernard McTernan, who had been editor and managing director of the *Sligo Champion*, left it and founded the *Sligo Nationalist* which was similar in political stance and tone. Taken over by SF supporters and renamed *The Connachtman* in April 1920, it became a strong SF voice and opposed the Treaty but collapsed during the early days of the Civil War. Two unionist newspapers were published in Sligo: the long-established, solidly conservative *Sligo Independent* and the more recently founded *Sligo Times*. Both attempted to avoid political controversy by stressing their commitment to the betterment of Sligo and only occasionally responded to provocation by the *Sligo Champion*. Glasgow-born Robert Smyllie was founder and editor of the *Sligo Times*, a generally brighter publication than the *Sligo Independent* which Smyllie called 'our staid

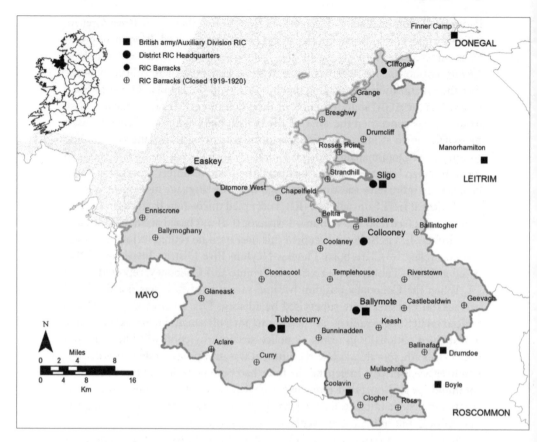

4 Police and British army distribution, 1912–21

contemporary'. Nevertheless it closed in 1914.[38] The *Western People*, published in Ballina in County Mayo, circulated in north-west Sligo and reported news from that area while the *Roscommon Herald*, published in Boyle, County Roscommon, was read in south Sligo. The latter was an exceptional newspaper, nationalist but anti-IPP; its independent line and use of political cartoons set it apart.

The newspapers mentioned above were valuable sources for this study as were the multitude of reports and records from the British government, the RIC, the IRA, the Free State army and government. The reports of the RIC CI in Sligo show the officer responding month by month to the developing situation. The 'summary of events' written by Captain A.L. Dunnill of the Bedfordshire and Hertfordshire Regiment, stationed in Sligo in 1920–1, provides a valuable insight into the activities, tactics and attitude of the British forces in the county. Written afterwards in the form of a daily diary, it is in the nature of an official history with many incidents being factually recorded and no more. Dunnill's accounts of the

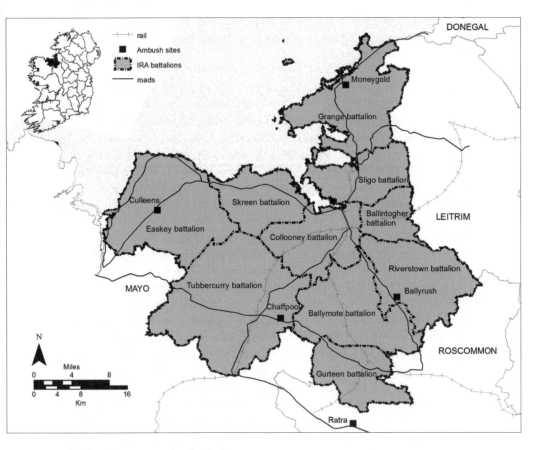

5 IRA battalion areas and ambush sites, 1919–21

Crown forces' response to police killings at north Sligo, Tubbercurry and Bally-mote make no mention of reprisals. His and the troops' respect and sometimes even admiration for the activities of the IRA breaks through occasionally.[39]

On the IRA side the opening of the Bureau of Military History (BMH) witness statements collected in the 1950s has made available accounts of the activities of sixteen Sligo participants. These statements are short and in general concentrate on the military aspect of the revolution with little mention of personal motivation, republican administration or political activity. However, they do cover most of County Sligo and should ensure that no significant military engagement is neglected. All Sligo statements stop at the truce. The statements by two female Sligo-born witnesses concern activities generally carried on outside the county; hence Cumann na mBan within the county is not well represented there. This is corrected to a large extent by the questionnaires in the Sighle Humphreys papers in the UCD Archives which contain material from Sligo town and south Sligo. Likewise, the interviews with veterans recorded by Ernie O'Malley are replete with details not found in the more official Bureau statements.

The wealth of material, sifted and analyzed, provides the basis for this study of County Sligo, 1912–23, the years of 'extraordinary convulsion'.[40] The story begins with the IPP apparently about to achieve its goal of home rule in spite of the confident, vociferous opposition of Sligo unionists. It charts the effect of the outbreak and continuation of the World War on the popular mood and the political situation. With the postponement of home rule and the IPP's support for an increasingly unpopular war, a group of younger Sligo politicians, allied with a smaller group of more extreme activists, asserted their independence. Reaction to the Rising in Sligo mirrored the rest of the country and the North Roscommon by-election forced the Sligo opposition to assert openly their independence and eventually take the SF side and make Sligo one of the best-organized counties in Ireland. It returned two SF TDs by large majorities in December 1918. Armed activity developed much more slowly in the county and Sligo was never to the fore in this regard. Sligo IRA did carry out some rescues, raids and ambushes but lack of arms and poor leadership resulted in few impressive operations. There were different levels of activity in different areas as a result of the arrest of leaders and distribution of enemy forces. The attempts to establish a republican counter-state in Sligo were moderately successful but the involvement of the IRA in policing, courts and local government allowed that body to claim a success beyond what had been achieved and to regard themselves as the natural rulers of the county during the truce period. The freedom that the IRA had during this period led to the Sligo leaders being appointed to the leadership of the newly formed 3rd Western Division and to assert control of local government bodies. The Treaty threatened this control and most of Sligo IRA opposed it, though large numbers in south Sligo, influenced by local leaders, took the pro-Treaty side. While the anti-Treaty IRA was strong militarily in Sligo it had no plan for a detailed offensive response to the outbreak of war. It quickly adopted familiar guerrilla methods which, without widespread popular support, were bound to fail. The difficulties in organizing the National army meant that anti-Treaty activity survived, albeit with dwindling numbers, until the end of the war. By then most of the people of County Sligo welcomed the return to something approaching normality. Since late 1918 law and order had been partisan and uncertain, transport had been disrupted and normal life upset. Sligo unionists also welcomed this despite seeing a form of self-determination implemented which went far beyond the home rule they had so vigorously opposed. They had lamented the departure of the British army and the RIC but the majority of them settled down and made the most of their new situation.

2 Home rule at last?

The year 1912 opened in a flush of nationalist optimism. The long struggle for home rule for Ireland, which began in the 1880s and had seen the highs of the Parnell years and the lows of the subsequent split, seemed to be coming to fruition. John Redmond's alliance with the Liberals had resulted in the 1911 Parliament Act which had removed the House of Lords' right to veto bills passed in the Commons and limited its ability to delay such bills to two years. This meant that Unionists could no longer depend on the upper house blocking a home rule bill. There was little discussion nationally about the possible contents of the bill being drafted during 1911 although the financial clauses did generate some debate. The consensus was that the IPP leadership should be trusted.[1] This was also the case in Sligo where the *Sligo Champion* was certain that it would be a good bill but showed little interest in its provisions. Both Sligo MPs, Thomas Scanlan and John O'Dowd, rallied constituents for what Scanlan called 'the last battle for Home Rule'.[2] He was anxious that UIL branches show unionist and English public opinion that there was no apathy on the issue and urged contributions to the home rule fund.[3] O'Dowd believed that all other questions were subsidiary and promised that home rule would bring with it the final division of the land and even the drainage of the Owenmore River. He warned South Sligo UIL executive that 'Executives are formed not for the purpose of deciding little points as to who should be the owner of a cabbage garden', a remarkable admonition in an area noted for agrarian concerns.[4] The *Sligo Champion* lectured UIL branches on the 'parochialism of their outlook', criticized their reports, 'we are trying to find out what they are doing, and though they write us long reports we are trying in vain' and asked them to collect for the home rule fund.[5]

When the third home rule bill was introduced in April 1912 the same newspaper welcomed it as: 'far and away the best Home Rule measure that Ireland has ever had a chance of obtaining'.[6] However, the two Sligo unionist newspapers reflected the growing disquiet among their readers. The *Sligo Times* claimed that the bill would disappoint nationalists while not allaying unionist fears. The *Sligo Independent* hoped that the great fight against it would be successful and agreed with a Church of Ireland Synod resolution that 'the proposed measure would bring turmoil and strife, and would inflict vast harm on the country's economic progress'.[7]

During 1913 a UIL organizer helped restructure Sligo branches and the *Sligo Champion* continued to urge branches to affiliate and collect for the home rule fund.[8] Sligo nationalists responded well to the appeals of MPs, the IPP and the *Sligo Champion*. A series of Sunday home rule meetings was held during

September. 'We Must Have Home Rule' proclaimed the banner over the Sligo meeting (see plate 2). Scanlan expressed satisfaction that 'Sligo has done better this year than it has for many years past' and had given the lie 'to the assertion … that the Nationalists are apathetic about Home Rule'.[9] Membership of Sligo UIL branches remained consistently high during these years but funds raised were significantly larger in 1912 and 1913 than in previous years.[10]

There may have been unity in nationalist Sligo as regards home rule, but there was bitter political rivalry in Sligo town during 1912 and 1913 between the mayor, Daniel O'Donnell, and fellow Sligo businessman John Jinks.[11] O'Donnell was the older man, 59 in 1912, born in Enniskillen, owner of the Imperial Hotel and, significantly, head of Sligo AOH, Connacht Provincial Director and a national trustee. He developed the AOH as his power base, helped by the 1911 National Insurance Act under which it had become a recognized organization. He boasted of its phenomenal growth in Sligo in June 1912 and in December the Sligo CI, Robert Ievers Sullivan, believed it threatened to supersede the UIL.[12] Wheatley's analysis of the *Sligo Champion*'s AOH reports shows a fifty per cent increase from 1911 to 1912 and an eighteen per cent increase from 1912 to 1913.[13] By contrast, the UIL was Jinks's power base. Aged 42 in 1912, he was a native of Drumcliff. A publican, auctioneer and funeral director, he was first elected to Sligo Corporation in 1898 at the age of 25.[14] Both Jinks and O'Donnell courted the powerful Trades Council and Transport Union, with O'Donnell apparently the more successful. Sligo Corporation had twenty-four councillors elected from three town wards, North, East and West. Robert Smyllie's election in 1911 as the only conservative member generated some agitation with Jinks being accused of supporting him. There was a small group of more recently elected, younger nationalist councillors including chemist, T.H. Fitzpatrick, and builder's merchant, Dudley M. Hanley. This set was outside the Corporation's ruling elite and at times clashed with it, but its members showed no early signs of being 'advanced nationalists'.[15] O'Donnell was re-elected for a second term as mayor in 1912 and whereas his programme included improved housing for the workers and steamrolling the streets he stressed that the Corporation's finances had first to be placed on a sound basis.[16] It was common knowledge that Jinks intended to oppose O'Donnell for the mayoralty in 1913 but Jinks withdrew when it became clear he did not have a majority.[17] O'Donnell died in March 1914 leaving Jinks unopposed as mayor later that year.[18]

Notwithstanding O'Dowd's 'cabbage garden' appeal, agrarian agitation continued in Sligo in 1912. Although it received little coverage in the press, it featured in monthly police reports with CI Sullivan recording a 'strong agitation against the grazing system' in the Easkey and Collooney districts which only abated at the end of the year. At the beginning of 1912 three Sligo people, including veteran nationalist councillor Peter Cawley, served short jail sentences for agrarian campaigns but there were few comments on this by local nationalists.[19] Sligo MPs made regular representations to the CDB and asked numerous parliamentary questions about Sligo properties. Agitations usually ceased when farms were bought by the CDB. However, during 1912 and 1913 the CI reported only five 'important purchases' by the CDB or the Estates Commission. In some cases large farms were bought by individuals, resulting in agitation to force new owners to give up the land.[20] The *Sligo Champion* gave substantial publicity to a case in the Ballymote area where the UIL supported two Church of Ireland ladies who resisted eviction by a relative; the case was used to assert the UIL's non-sectarian character.[21]

Impending home rule resulted in a determined campaign by the Irish Unionist Alliance (IUA) to demonstrate that unionist opposition was not confined to Ulster.[22] Bryan Cooper of Markree Castle, Collooney was the main figure in mobilizing such opposition in Sligo. He had been educated at Eton, joined the British Army but resigned his commission a few years later. In January 1910 he was elected Unionist MP for South Dublin but lost his seat at the December election the same year. He and fellow Protestants and former substantial landowners, Malby Crofton of Longford House, Beltra and Charles O'Hara of Annaghmore, Collooney, were Sligo members of the IUA executive committee; Cooper attended regularly, the others less often.[23] Cooper also hosted a meeting in Markree Castle in January 1912 to organize a branch of the Women's Unionist Alliance (WUA) in which the wives and daughters of Protestant businessmen were active.[24] Sligo unionists argued that they had the right to assert publicly their objections to home rule, that they did not wish to break the connection with the British Empire and that home rule would be injurious to the prosperity and peace of Ireland. They rarely alleged intolerance in Sligo. Indeed Colonel James Campbell said at the 9 March meeting of the WUA 'there is not a county of Ireland where I think we live in better accord'.[25] However, at a June meeting Cooper claimed it would be impossible for them to live in Ireland if the bill was passed, 'We distrust the policy of the United Irish League and we dread the Ancient Order of Hibernians'.[26] The *Sligo Champion*, determined to raise the tolerance issue, claimed that unionist meetings in districts with nationalist majorities demonstrated the latter's tolerance and questioned why no speaker addressed intolerance towards the Catholic minority in Ulster. It challenged the *Sligo Independent* to confirm how tolerantly Protestants were treated in Sligo and accused some Sligo Protestant firms of recruiting almost exclusively from loyalist Ulster.[27] The Sligo WUA's work included posting publicity material to homes in the marginal Cricklade constituency in England and two members went on 'mission work' there to explain the Irish unionist position. These were Westmeath-born Nina Eccles, who lived in Wine Street, Sligo and Margaret Zaida Ffolliot, owner of Hollybrook House, Aghanagh in south-east Sligo.[28]

The *Sligo Champion* claimed that the June Sligo IUA meeting was attended

mainly by landlords and 'their underlings' but the *Sligo Independent*'s boast that
it was representative of every district in the county and included farmers, clergy,
businessmen and merchants was closer to the truth. Businessmen Arthur
Jackson, Henry Lyons and P.C. Kerr were on the platform and speakers
included Crofton, Cooper and south Sligo farmer and shopkeeper Charles
Graham.[29] A Sligo branch of the Irish Junior Unionist Alliance was formed in
August 1912 with P.D. Perceval of Hazelwood as president. Bryan Cooper, the
group's national secretary, chaired the meeting and outlined objections to home
rule including UIL control of police, double taxation, and the nationalist
concept of administration as getting jobs for as many of their friends as
possible.[30]

   One example of apparent intolerance towards a non-Catholic in Sligo
received a degree of publicity but few comments on its sectarian nature. A
coordinated attack on George Henry Smith, an English-born, Protestant
principal of Sligo Municipal Technical School, began with an anonymous letter
in the *Sligo Nationalist* in January 1912 and climaxed when the mayor made a
rare appearance at a Technical Committee meeting to state: 'It is time he [Smith]
found some tolerance for the co-religionists of the people here'. Smith defended
himself vigorously and there was lukewarm support from Councillor Edward
Foley. Eventually Smith resigned on obtaining a principalship in Wales.[31]

   County Sligo belonged to two Church of Ireland dioceses. The contrasting
attitudes of the two bishops reflected not just their ages and upbringing but also
the different natures of their dioceses. The east and north of the county,
including Sligo town, belonged to the united diocese of Kilmore, Ardagh and
Elphin and its bishop from 1897 to 1915 was the Trinity College Dublin
educated Rt Revd Albert Elliott (1828–1915) whose attacks on home rule at the
1913 diocesan synod led to much negative comment in the nationalist press.[32]
The rest of Sligo was part of the western Tuam, Killala and Achonry diocese.
John Plunket, born in Bray and educated at Harrow and Cambridge, was elected
bishop in April 1913. His statement that 'happy relations' existed between his
people and their Catholic neighbours was welcomed by nationalists.[33]

   Sligo's proximity to Ulster and a direct rail link facilitated the attendance by
some Sligo non-Catholics at anti-home rule events in Ulster. In January 1912
Presbyterians from Sligo, Ballymote and Dromore West took part in the
Presbyterian Church demonstration in Belfast.[34] Over one hundred Sligo unionists received a great welcome in Portadown en route to an April demonstration
in Belfast.[35] The Solemn League and Covenant was signed on Ulster Day, 28
September 1912, as a popular protest against home rule. On the previous
Sunday intercession services were held in the main Protestant churches in Sligo
town and some Sligo unionists attended an Enniskillen Ulster Covenant meeting
a week before Ulster Day.[36] Twenty-six covenant signatories gave Sligo
addresses. No prominent Sligo unionist was listed, though Arthur Jackson's

daughter signed in Belfast. The English-born Church of Ireland rector and the Tyrone-born court clerk signed the covenant in Easkey, County Sligo.[37]

Anti-home rule activity continued during 1913. Sligo WUA and the Junior Unionists held successful AGMs and regular meetings during the year.[38] In November 1913 P.D. Perceval and Bryan Cooper presented addresses on behalf of Sligo at a unionist meeting in Dublin attended by Bonar Law, Conservative Party leader, and Edward Carson. A number of Sligo Protestant merchants and shopkeepers signed a petition against the home rule bill's financial clauses at the same time and the *Sligo Champion* published the petition and their names. Jinks asked nationalists to 'take particular note' of the signatories. Public bodies as well as UIL and AOH branches passed motions of censure which provided ammunition for Sligo unionists, two of whom complained of intolerance in the *Daily Express* and the *Glasgow Herald*. The *Sligo Independent* protested at alleged threats but did not actually state that traders were being boycotted. The whole affair, it remarked, 'furnishes a powerful commentary on the freedom of thought which these bodies ... are prepared to allow the Unionists of Sligo' and it expressed the hope that 'wiser counsels will prevail'.[39] Nothing more was heard of this matter and it appears that no boycotts were actually implemented. In autumn 1913 suggestions for a conference on the basis of the exclusion of Ulster were rejected by Redmond and Bonar Law. The *Sligo Independent* claimed that these overtures were a sign that all was not well with the Liberal coalition but the *Sligo Champion* mocked the exclusion proposal as 'very hard lines on those who have joined hands and hearts with their brethren in Ulster'.[40]

Unionist women were more politically active than nationalist women. The IPP did not allow females to join, did not include female suffrage in their demands and helped defeat the 1912 Parliamentary Franchise (Women) Bill.[41] The AOH did not permit female membership but did facilitate the formation of ladies' auxiliary branches such as those in Sligo town and Maugherow. The Sligo town 'lady Hibernians' were represented on the platform at Thomas Scanlan's September 1912 meeting, the only reference to such female involvement.[42] Olga Crichton, wife of Church of Ireland landowner Alex Crichton, was involved in a Sligo branch of the Irish Women's Franchise League (IWFL) in 1912, which held outdoor meetings, poster parades and talks. She organized a horse and car week-long suffragette tour of north Sligo and south Donegal in July with five others, including Margaret Cousins, one of the League's founders. Lady Louisa Crofton, wife of Malby Crofton, formed a Sligo Propaganda Society for Women's Suffrage which distributed literature.[43] In May 1913 Olga Crichton left the IWFL and founded a Sligo Suffrage Society which affiliated with the non-militant Irishwomen's Suffrage Federation. This may have been in response to militant action by the IWFL, including window smashing and attacks on Prime Minister Asquith during his visit to Dublin in July 1912. Olga was secretary and Lady Crofton president of this society, which held a series of

Wednesday outdoor meetings at Rosses Point during summer 1913 featuring prominent speakers from Ireland and Britain. Olga herself sold the *Irish Citizen*, the Irish suffrage newspaper, on Saturdays in Sligo town. The Crichtons took no part in the anti-home rule campaign but Lady Crofton was president of the Sligo WUA. The Protestant leadership and IPP opposition resulted in little support for the suffrage movement from nationalist newspapers or organizations. The *Sligo Times* and *Sligo Independent* regularly reported the Sligo group's activities and complimented them on their non-violent actions, contrasting it with the more sensational actions of other Irish and English suffragettes.[44]

Labour in Sligo was strong in the industrial and the political life of the town. Sligo Trades Council had been supported by the UIL from its foundation against what was perceived as the common enemy, 'the Protestant, unionist, commercial establishment' which dominated much of Sligo's trade and employment.[45] Many labour activists were also members of Sligo UIL and AOH and regularly stood for election as nationalist/labour candidates.[46] The nationwide growth of the ITGWU and a wave of strikes during 1912 made James Larkin a household name, often vilified by the press.[47] When a Sligo meeting was to be addressed by Larkin in March 1912, the Catholic bishop of Elphin, John Joseph Clancy, denounced Larkin and socialism and expected that no 'faithful member of the Church' would take part in the meeting. A large crowd did attend, out of curiosity rather than disrespect the *Sligo Champion* suggested, but no local non-labour politician appeared on the platform. The *Sligo Champion* took an anti-Larkin, pro-labour line, claiming that Larkin's harangue at the meeting showed no appreciation of local conditions and asked Sligo labourers to state their grievances so that they might be redressed.[48] Control of employment at Sligo quay was the priority for Sligo Transport Union. In February 1912 John Lynch was jailed for threatening a labourer, who was reputedly part of a gang 'monopolising all the works at the quay'.[49] When a quay strike began in early June, P.T. Daly, ITGWU organizer and republican, was sent from Dublin to manage it. He complained of unfair work practices and exorbitant stevedore fees. The *Sligo Champion* blamed the dispute on irregular practices by middlemen, complimented the strikers on their admirable conduct but warned about possible harm to Sligo port. Both Jinks and O'Donnell were active on behalf of the strikers. The strike was settled in less than two weeks with an entirely new system in place on the quays, the stevedores now being appointed by the dockers.[50] Later in the year Transport Union members took some former stevedores to court, successfully in some cases, for arrears of wages. It was said that those who had been part of the old regime had no work since the strike.[51] Charges of assaults in September and letters to the *Sligo Champion* in November 1912 about work on the quay suggest that the stevedores who had been replaced and had not joined or were not allowed to join the union were likely to be the source of more trouble.[52]

Labour power in Sligo was consolidated when John Lynch was elected to the Corporation in January 1913, heading the poll in the north ward.[53] In March a dispute about unpaid bonus money escalated into a major strike which again paralyzed the port and much of Sligo town. Strike breakers from Liverpool and ousted stevedores worked on the ships and a striker was killed in clashes with strike breakers. P.T. Daly again ran the strike. The *Sligo Champion* continued to refuse to blame Union members, claiming disturbances were caused by 'rowdies who are using the strike as an opportunity for the gratification of their own low instincts'.[54] Business premises' windows were smashed and traders who dealt with 'scab' labourers were boycotted. Jinks and O'Donnell again supported the strikers. After fifty-six days they achieved their closed shop demand but details of the settlement were withheld to avoid either side claiming victory. Subsequently some strike breakers had letters published expressing regret and promising to be loyal union members.[55]

In September Sligo Corporation and the Transport Workers joined in the widespread support for workers involved in the Dublin lockout.[56] This changed when plans to take Dublin children to England made headlines. Sligo County Council, AOH and UIL branches praised the action of J.D. Nugent, AOH general secretary, in preventing this, though the *Sligo Champion*'s editorials continued to avoid antagonizing the local Transport Union. No non-Union politician attended a November ITGWU public meeting in Sligo in support of the Dublin strikers.[57] At the beginning of 1914 the Trades Council and Transport Union nominees were unopposed at the Corporation elections; in the view of the *Sligo Champion* 'The Council is now principally composed of Labour representatives'.[58]

Although there was considerable general political consensus, local government meetings were by no means dull affairs. 'Veritable pandemonium' broke out at a Tubbercurry RDC meeting in June 1912 as a result of a co-option dispute. In a subsequent court case a councillor was convicted of assault.[59] An outbreak of typhoid in Tubbercurry in summer 1912 resulted in a number of deaths, accusations of medical neglect and demands from residents and the LGB for a safe water supply. This led to endless debates with motions being passed and rescinded depending on which guardians attended.[60] In early 1913 an LGB auditor's report on Tubbercurry Board of Guardians was very critical of the state of its books and rate collection.[61] Patronage was at the root of many disagreements. In May 1912 John O'Dowd MP chaired a meeting at which his son unsuccessfully sought the position of County Council clerk. When charged with neglecting his duty at Westminster to attend the meeting, O'Dowd claimed that he had been at home because of illness and was defended by south Sligo UIL branches. In July the same son was appointed accountant to the County Council amid scenes of discord.[62] In September 1912 the election of workhouse master led to animated scenes at Dromore West Board of Guardians.[63] The *Sligo*

Times was critical of the *Sligo Champion* and *Sligo Independent*'s monopoly on advertising and printing contracts from public bodies. The *Sligo Champion* defended itself against an accusation of overcharging: 'We charge more than others because our circulation far exceeds all theirs put together'. The LGB auditor investigated the awarding of the contract to the *Sligo Champion* and members of the council who had accepted that newspaper's tender were surcharged, though this was quashed on appeal.[64]

The local elections in early June 1914 generated very little interest in Sligo. The *Sligo Champion* called for 'no unnecessary contests' and only nine divisions were contested. Outgoing members were re-elected in five, two outgoing members were defeated and in the remaining two, outgoing members did not stand. John O'Dowd was opposed by James Wynne, whom he called a 'nonentity and factionist', and won easily. Women could be candidates and vote in these elections and Catherine Brennan was elected for the Glendarragh electoral area in Tubbercurry Rural District, the first woman elected to a public body in Sligo.[65]

The Irish Volunteers were founded in Dublin at the end of November 1913 as a counterweight to the Ulster Volunteers. Though the IPP did not support or encourage this new force, the *Sligo Champion* supported its formation and development.[66] In Sligo Jinks seized the initiative, perhaps regarding the Volunteers as a vehicle for promoting his leadership of Sligo nationalism. When he suggested that the Corporation should take the lead in starting a corps, Councillor Hanley disagreed, saying that the initiative should come from the people.[67] After some preliminary consultations a corps was formed at a public meeting on Sunday 1 February 1914 at which Jinks presided. Also on the platform were Gaelic Leaguers, Fr Brian Crehan, Ó Domhnalláin and Ó Ruadháin, AOH Corporation members Henry Monson and Henry Depew, and E.J. Harte and P. Farrell of the Trades Council. Neither Sligo MP attended. Monson, a Sligo furniture merchant, had succeeded O'Donnell as Sligo AOH leader and had been elected to the Corporation for the first time in January 1913. His involvement reflected local circumstances rather than the national antipathy of the AOH towards the Volunteers.[68] The CI recorded that the formation 'caused great apprehension among the better classes of both sides of politics' indicating the official non-involvement of the UIL.[69] The first public parade of the Sligo Battalion took place on Sunday 15 March with an impressive 500 men marching around the town.[70] There is little evidence that the Sligo town corps thrived with subsequent reports in the *Sligo Champion* often containing references to poor attendances. In July the Sligo town battalion was reorganized into three companies, one per ward, and the *Sligo Champion* suggested that 'it would be a very regrettable thing if Sligo town … was not in a position to show an example not only in the country districts but to every county in Ireland'.[71] The Volunteers developed slowly in the rest of the county and by the end of April only four companies, all founded by Jinks and Foley, were in existence.[72] The first south Sligo corps was formed in early May at a meeting in Keash presided over by Fr P.J. O'Grady PP. An inaugural meeting in Tubbercurry a week later heard veteran nationalist Luke Armstrong claim: 'They had tried the effect of speechmaking long enough. It was now time they should consider some more effective policy'.[73] Four new corps were formed in Sligo during May, a reflection of the nation-wide increase in response to the Curragh mutiny and Larne gun-running. By the end of May the AOH and UIL were cooperating with the Volunteers. In early June the Ballisodare & Corhownagh UIL branch formed a corps and Thomas Scanlan MP inspected a route march of the Sligo town Volunteers. The county had fifteen corps at the end of June. The increase in Sligo was the lowest of the five counties studied by Wheatley.[74]

On 25 May the home rule bill passed its third reading despite the government's intention to introduce another bill to allow some Ulster counties to remain outside home rule. 'Home Rule at last', the *Sligo Champion* proclaimed and the AOH band led a parade in Sligo town which culminated with the burning of an effigy of Carson.[75] Both Sligo MPs were given enthusiastic receptions on returning to their constituencies with Scanlan claiming: 'It is the victory of the Fenians, it is the victory of the Land League, it is the victory and the triumph of the people over persecution and oppression'.[76] In June Redmond demanded twenty-five nominees on the Volunteers' governing committee. To avoid a split this was agreed to and John Jinks was among Redmond's nominees.[77] The IPP take-over gave a new impetus to the Volunteers and by the end of July Sligo had twenty-seven corps. The movement reached its peak in Sligo at the end of September when it had forty-four branches and 4,951 members.[78]

At this same time Alec McCabe, who had joined the IRB as a trainee teacher in Dublin, helped organize the IRB in Sligo in conjunction with some Volunteer corps. He established circles in south Sligo at Keash, Tubbercurry and Cloonacool and in north Sligo at Cliffoney with local activist William Gilmartin. Seán Mac Diarmada (Seán MacDermott) visited the county as an IRB organizer. Father Michael O'Flanagan, who was appointed to Cliffoney parish in August 1914, may also have been involved.[79]

July saw intense interest in Volunteers and volunteering. Local and national newspapers were full of rumours of gun-running and arms landing on the Irish coast. The *Sligo Champion* reported that the mayor had secured 300 rifles for local volunteers from an American boat on the Sligo coast. A Maugherow Volunteers report stated: 'The rifles are safe. They were removed from Ardgoran Wood, Lissadell on last Sunday night by a strong escort of Volunteers … Long live the Mayor of Sligo'. There is no other evidence of such a landing.[80] On 26 July a Volunteer review was held in conjunction with the annual Keash Feis. Major James Crean from headquarters inspected eight Volunteer companies from south Sligo and two each from Leitrim, Mayo and Roscommon, a grand total of about 1,600 men.[81] During the last week of July 5,000 Volunteers marched to Sligo town hall to protest about the Bachelors Walk killings. Speakers included Jinks, Foley and Monson. The latter said: 'The alliance between John Redmond and the Liberal government must be broken because they in Ireland would not tolerate one law for the Nationalists and one law for the Ulster Volunteers'. Sligo-born Michael O'Mullane declared that the time for talking was done. If home rule was denied he urged the Volunters to 'let the rifle speak at last'.[82]

By early August 1914 public opinion in Sligo, as in the rest of the country, was concentrated on home rule. Sligo nationalists had mobilized politically to support Redmond and the IPP. They had contributed impressive financial support and robustly defended home rule against their Protestant fellow county-men. The passing of the bill was celebrated in the belief that nothing could now prevent its implementation. However, the apparent success of the Ulster Volunteers in manpower and arms and the contrasting weakness and uneven official attitude towards the Irish Volunteers upset their confidence. While the nationalists of Sligo had flocked to the ranks of the Volunteers only after the approval of the IPP, as the crisis developed, rhetoric in Sligo, as elsewhere, became more violent and bellicose. The IPP and their local leaders sometimes led but were more often swept along by this wave. Even John Jinks, at a Bachelors Walk protest meeting in Sligo, joined in saying that if there was to be a war the men and women of Sligo would be at the front.[83] The war that started in August 1914 was not the potential civil war he was referring to but it changed profoundly the political landscape in Sligo, in Ireland and in Britain. The First World War relegated the home rule question from the forefront of political life. At the very moment when the cherished goal of the IPP seemed to be within its grasp, the political environment was transformed. The challenge confronting Redmond was to formulate a policy on the war which would allow his party to remain polit-ically relevant. Over the next two years the IPP's failure in this difficult task created a political vacuum for others to fill.

3 'Our place is ... on the side of the allies'[1]

Britain's declaration of war on 4 August 1914 transformed Irish politics with both nationalists and unionists offering loyalty in the expectation of political rewards. Redmond immediately committed to the British war effort by offering the services of the Irish Volunteers to defend Ireland from invasion and the *Sligo Independent* praised his declaration: 'Ireland is the one bright spot in such a time of gloom and suspense'. The *Sligo Champion* was much more cautious and reflected the gamble inherent in Redmond's offer. It hoped that England 'has learned the lesson ... that if Ireland is to be her friend in time of stress she must treat Ireland with confidence and justice in times of peace'.[2] Redmond's strategy did not pay off. The failure of the British government to respond quickly and generously to his gesture, the postponement of home rule, the prolonged nature of the war, the unpopularity of recruiting and the spectre of conscription led to a sharp decline in support for the IPP and in activity by local UIL branches and Volunteer corps.

Redmond's stance brought a warm response nationally from Irish unionists, with several ex-officers offering their services to the Irish Volunteers.[3] Bryan Cooper joined the Volunteers and promised to 'urge every Unionist to do the same'. On 4 August he attended Collooney company drill, took charge of a section and offered the use of part of his demesne for drilling.[4] On 9 August Major R.W. Hillas of Templeboy offered his services to the Volunteers and was immediately appointed Sligo Inspecting Officer. His 'Call to arms to the manhood of Sligo', published on 15 August, explained that it was 'the bounden duty of every man fit to bear arms to enrol himself in the Irish Volunteer force to protect his home and family from the foreign invader'.[5] Unionist involvement did not, however, meet with universal approval. A Tubbercurry Volunteer told headquarters: 'We want no British Unionist officers ... We are for Ireland and for Ireland alone'. Colonel Maurice Moore, Inspector General of the Volunteers, replied that the choice in Sligo was between unionist officers or none.[6] Jinks informed Moore that the appointment of Hillas would be generally welcomed and Alec McCabe was 'delighted to have some responsible person placed at head of affairs in the county'.[7] Hillas wrote to fifteen Sligo corps for details of officers and arms but claimed to have received only five replies by 2 September. Interpreting this as personal opposition, he resigned: 'It is too evident that people of my class are not required by certain supporters of the movement'.[8] The *Sligo Independent* reported the establishment of a Sligo unionist Volunteer corps, which at the end of August had about seventy members.[9] There is no further mention of these Volunteers until early 1915 when meetings to organize regular drill practice and elect officers were held. By May 1915 half their members were said to have joined the colours.[10]

In spite of Redmond's offer, the government made no immediate move on home rule. The *Sligo Champion* warned of 'soft talk': 'Unionist warriors joining the ranks must be given to recognize that despite their ability to pay large subscriptions they are not to be allowed to dominate the movement'. Until home rule was on the statute book, it said, there should be 'no hurry on the part of Irishmen to enlist'.[11] On 18 September home rule was finally placed on the statute book but suspended for the duration of the war with the question of Ulster unresolved. 'Home Rule at last!' the *Sligo Champion* editorial proclaimed (again) but the *Sligo Independent* called it a betrayal of unionists.[12] On the following day Thomas Scanlan MP arrived in Sligo and was taken by torchlight procession to the Imperial Hotel. There he claimed that 'Ireland is now and shall be for all times a nation once again … The Statute which was yesterday enacted makes Ireland free but this same statute binds Ireland indissolubly to the British Empire'. A group of protesters from the Trades Council and Transport Union, led by John Lynch and including Councillors Gibbons and Harte, heckled Scanlan. There were shouts of 'To hell with the Empire' and the meeting ended with 'a spirited bout of fisticuffs'.[13] At a subsequent Trades Council meeting a resolution condemning the protesters was carried in Lynch's absence.[14] Lynch attended the next meeting at which the motion was expunged and a motion of confidence in Lynch passed unanimously.[15] This represents the end of the Jinks/Lynch, nationalist/labour, alliance in Sligo town. It was surely no coincidence that in subsequent months the *Sligo Champion* gave prominence to criticism of the Transport Union for a work-stoppage at a Rosses Point hotel and allegations of financial irregularities by a former officer.[16]

On 20 September Redmond made his Woodenbridge speech urging Volunteers to be ready to serve in the British army wherever needed which split the movement. The majority sided with Redmond and were styled the National Volunteers. The rump that went with Eoin MacNeill retained the name Irish Volunteers. Both Volunteer groups produced eponymous newspapers. Sligo nationalist newspapers supported Redmond and Tubbercurry Corps was the only Sligo unit to support MacNeill publicly. A correspondent to Volunteer headquarters claimed that apathy had reduced the active membership in Tubbercurry to seventeen, all Sinn Féiners, all 'strangers employed there'.[17] It was reported in the *Irish Volunteer* that Sligo town Volunteers supported MacNeill but this proved untrue.[18] As a result of dissention in Sligo the AOH formed a separate National Volunteer corps with Henry Monson and Michael Nevin, a grocer's assistant in Sligo town and secretary of Sligo AOH, as officers. Nevin told headquarters that 'the Volunteers in Sligo had been smashed up' and many members of the old Sligo Corps 'were disgusted at the bad management and lack of discipline existing therein'.[19] Monson and Nevin in time became SF activists but in autumn 1914 were fully behind Redmond. At the end of September a meeting supporting Redmond was attended by delegates from twenty-five Sligo corps, the two MPs, and Jinks and Monson. On the same day a conference of Achonry diocesan clergy under Bishop Morrisroe thanked Redmond and the party for obtaining home rule.[20] On 10 October the Sligo AOH county board expressed confidence in Redmond and reports from Sligo National Volunteer corps in late September and early October contain numerous similar expressions of support.[21] At the end of October, CI Sullivan estimated that only 280 of the over 4,000 Volunteers in Sligo were Sinn Féiners. He reported that only Keash, Tubbercurry and Grange corps were pro-MacNeill. Delegates from these three attended the Irish Volunteers convention in Dublin on 31 October 1914.[22]

At the end of August Sullivan recorded that 'people in general are taking an active interest in the war, their sympathies being entirely with the British forces'.[23] In the opening months of the war this was reflected in a local and national press full of war-related stories.[24] Olga Crichton of the Sligo Irish Women's Suffrage Federation announced that they were giving up active suffrage work for the duration of the war. Increases in food prices led to public meetings and a Sligo War Distress Fund committee included Protestant and Catholic clergy, the mayor, Alderman Lynch, P.D. Perceval and Henry Monson.[25] By the end of November enough had been subscribed to an ambulance fund to purchase and equip the vehicle for the front.[26] Five families of Belgian refugees were welcomed and housed in Sligo military barracks.[27]

There appears to have been general support for recruiting in the early months in Sligo with large groups accompanying called-up reservists to the railway station. This support did not translate into large numbers enlisting.[28] Immediately after the passing of home rule, Charles O'Hara, who held the honorary title of His Majesty's Lieutenant (HML) for County Sligo, published an Appeal to the Manhood of Sligo 'to uphold the interests of our Empire'.[29] Bryan Cooper chaired an 'enthusiastic' meeting in Collooney 'to explain why Britain was at war and to encourage recruiting'. Fr Michael Doyle, the local PP, told the meeting that the war was just and that if Germany won 'The old age pension would disappear and land reform would cease'.[30] In November the *Sligo Independent* noted 'a very marked enlisting spirit' and the *Sligo Nationalist* said that over 700 from Sligo and vicinity 'are now in the firing line or ready to take their places before the German hosts'.[31] Both Sligo MPs supported the war effort in line with the general IPP stance. At a National Volunteers re-organization meeting in September, Scanlan stated that 'our place is with the freedom-loving people on the side of the allies'.[32] At the November South Sligo UIL executive meeting John O'Dowd promised that 'Ireland would nobly and willingly do her part in defence of that Empire of which she was now an integral part'.[33] The local press named locals who had enlisted, including Patrick Jinks, eldest son of the mayor, who joined in early November.[34] Reports of the deaths of Sligo-born soldiers were given prominence.[35] Many Sligo natives were members of the 1st and 2nd Battalions of the Connaught Rangers involved in the late 1914 battles in northern France.

The initial enthusiasm did not last and at the end of September CI Sullivan complained that 'Recruiting generally in this County is very slack'. Although SF and the Transport Union in Sligo were against enlistment, he believed their influence was slight.[36] P.T. Daly gave a strong anti-recruiting speech at an October Transport Union meeting in Sligo and at the end of the month anti-recruiting posters appeared in Sligo town.[37] In the 1915 Corporation elections Councillors Gibbons and Harte, who had protested at Scanlan's return, were defeated by two independent candidates, Samuel Tarrant and Jordan Roche, who claimed to represent the ratepayers' interests.[38] Jinks was unanimously elected mayor. Councillor Smyllie praised him, previously 'an advanced Nationalist', for having become very loyal and mentioned having seen him applaud the national anthem. John Lynch said he wanted no loyalty of that kind; he wanted an Irish Republic.[39]

During the second half of 1914 there was a dramatic country-wide fall in National Volunteer activity.[40] This was also true in Sligo and was accompanied by a marked decline on the part of the UIL. In December the CI wrote: 'In this county the movement is practically dead' and attributed the decline to 'The idea that if they were drilling they would be the first sent to the front'. This was certainly one factor but others included the IPP's support for the war effort and the indefinite postponement of home rule. Sixteen Sligo Volunteer corps held drills during November, six during December but only two during January 1915.[41] A meeting in Sligo in early November to put the Sligo Corps 'on a practical footing' had only 'a fairly good attendance' and at the end of December only seven Sligo corps were affiliated including three town corps, Sligo Temperance, National Foresters and Sligo AOH. Nothing more was heard of the first two.[42] In April 1915 the CI reported that 'Drilling among the Irish National Volunteers is practically at an end'.[43]

Difficulties in establishing a National Volunteers Sligo county board typified this decline. In February 1915 Maurice Moore appealed to Scanlan to help form a board but the MP was too busy and asked the mayor to call a meeting. In March a Volunteer organizer in Sligo reported: 'there are too many conflicting elements and each is jealous of the other'.[44] The *Sligo Champion* pleaded for the sinking of 'all petty differences' and on 23 March a Sligo Volunteer county board was finally formed at a meeting attended by O'Dowd. Jinks referred to friction in Sligo Volunteers but said 'that little bit of spleen did not long exist'.[45] However, the existence of this board did nothing to give the Volunteers new vitality. Only a 'fair representation' from Sligo attended the monster National Volunteers review in Dublin on Easter Sunday.[46] In April and May 1915 there were attempts to revive corps and form battalions. Branches showing activity included Sligo town AOH corps, Skreen & Dromard, and Maugherow, described in May as the 'one company in Sligo which is really alive'.[47] The CI reported at the end of September that efforts to revive the UIL had not been successful, though at the end of October he did say that 'some of the UIL branches have been reorganized by local efforts'.[48]

The rival Irish Volunteers survived but did not prosper during the same period.[49] The RIC estimated in January 1915 that there were 275 Irish Volunteers in Sligo.[50] Small units remained in Keash, where McCabe was active, Tubbercurry, where Patrick Dyar was active, Mullinabreena, where Frank Carty continued to organize and Gurteen, where Owen Tansey was a leader.[51] According to Carty, after the split

> in all but a few places in South Sligo Volunteer companies disappeared altogether ... During the latter part of 1914 and the whole of 1915 we did our best to keep together the scattered units of the Volunteers, to organise new units, to discourage recruiting for the British army and to collect arms.[52]

In the Cliffoney/Grange area the Volunteers were backboned by IRB men with William Gilmartin and Seamus Devins prominent. Towards the end of 1915 they bought about twenty single-barrelled shotguns and a few revolvers in Dublin. McCabe procured a number of revolvers, sometime before the 1916 Rising, which he distributed among IRB members in his area.[53] McCabe was principal of Drumnagranchy National School near Keash and an altercation with a curate, Fr Felix Burke, led to an enquiry in June 1915. The outcome was seen as a victory for McCabe but the following month Revd P.J. O'Grady, PP, gave him three months' notice, calling him: 'A recognised associate and leader of an objectionable and political society in the parish'. It seems that the bishop was about to agree to McCabe's reinstatement because of parental pressure when McCabe was arrested in Sligo in early November with gelignite in his possession.[54] At his February 1916 trial, defence witnesses testified to the use of explosives for fishing and he was found not guilty.[55] A company of Irish Volunteers was started in Sligo town in late 1915 by Seamus MacGowan who had come to Sligo from Dublin to work as a reporter on the *Sligo Nationalist*. This small group also included Billy Pilkington, James Keaveney and Jim Kirby who was the first captain.[56]

In spite of the support of prominent nationalists for recruiting there was continued dissatisfaction with the numbers enlisting in Sligo, especially in the rural areas. Charles O'Hara chaired a Sligo recruiting committee set up towards the end of 1914 that comprised unionists and nationalists, among them Jinks, Foley, Hanley and Monson.[57] Jinks and Foley supported recruiting throughout the war and Monson was prominent at least until August 1915. Hanley was less to the fore, though he did allow his motor car to be used in at least one Sligo recruiting tour.[58] There was also clerical support. Bishop Bernard Coyne of Elphin, who became bishop in March 1914, sent a letter of welcome to the April recruiting campaign and Revd Canon Batty Quinn, PP, presided at the Ballymote meeting. Bishop Coyne told the Roscommon CI that he would 'oppose and condemn any pro-German conduct on the part of his clergy' in response to a complaint about a priest using anti-recruiting language.[59] The *Sligo Champion* countered complaints about nationalist enlistment by claiming in December 1914 that unionists were slow to enlist and in January that 'The few unionists who did volunteer took good care beforehand that their place would be in the back of the army. Most of them are attached to the veterinary department'. It hoped more Sligo unionists would 'follow the noble and self-sacrificing example set them by the nationalists'.[60] P.D. Perceval said he believed that both sides had done their best with about 1,200 Sligo men having responded to the call.[61]

Farmers' sons were targeted in recruiting campaigns but with little success. On 8 April Jinks and Scanlan were on the platform of a recruiting meeting in Sligo courthouse. Chairman Charles O'Hara praised the men of Sligo town and Ballymote for their response but said he was disappointed with the rest of the county. Scanlan defended Sligo's record, particularly Sligo town, claiming that practically 1,000 recruits and reservists from Sligo had joined the colours. W.R. Fenton, clerk of the Crown and Peace in Sligo, said that 'The labouring and other classes had done very well' but criticized the poor response from the farmers' sons.[62] Advertisements for an Irish Guards' recruiting tour in April asked Sligo farmers to lay down their spades and listen. The CI reported a warm welcome everywhere but 'few recruits have volunteered as a result'. He complained: 'Farmers are getting big prices for their stock and produce but no class in the community has done less for recruiting'.[63] There were recruiting tours in the county in June, September and November: 'The results as regards as enlisting farmers' sons was disappointing but as usual men were forthcoming from the towns'.[64]

Throughout 1915 the local press continued to report the deaths of Sligo natives, including two sons of Colonel William G. Wood-Martin, the historian, antiquarian and landowner. Five Sligo Connaught Rangers died on 26 April 1915 at the second battle of Ypres.[65] Connaught Rangers took part in the Sulva Bay landings at Gallipoli in August and at least seven Sligo-born members were killed during that month.[66] Well-known Sligo footballer, Bobby Burnside, badly injured at the Dardanelles, died of wounds at Southampton and was given an impressive military funeral in Sligo on 19 September.[67]

In spite of the poor returns, there was little public opposition to recruiting in County Sligo. In late 1915 a recruiting 'personal letter' sent to all men of military age in Ireland and full-page recruiting advertisements in local newspapers fuelled fear of conscription. The *Sligo Independent* claimed that farmers' sons from the Ballymote and Tubbercurry areas had left for America. At a meeting in Sligo in early October, Canon Edward Doorly, Sligo administrator, defended the county's recruiting record: 'Almost every available man was now in one capacity or another in the army. The Irish farmer had not all the sons they read about in the papers at the present time'.[68] In response to the recruiting circular, a Tubbercurry meeting of thirty-three men 'composed mainly of shop assistants' signed an anti-recruiting document that stated they would resist with their lives any attempt to enforce compulsory military service. Patrick Dyar, one of the organizers, was arrested and sentenced to one month hard labour. When he returned to Tubbercurry at the end of December he was greeted by a brass band and a bonfire and presented with an address of welcome.[69]

The outbreak of war, followed by Redmond's offer of Irish Volunteer assistance in the war effort and the indefinite postponement of home rule, led to a rapid decline in the numbers and activity of the UIL and Volunteers in County Sligo. The IPP and its local MPs found themselves without a meaningful war-time role apart from encouraging enlistment. Early enthusiasm for the war waned as it became obvious that the conflict would be protracted. Repeated recruiting appeals, tours, posters and speeches did little to encourage enlistment but rather increased the unpopularity of the IPP MPs and incited anti-recruiting elements in the county to become more vocal. In Sligo town the anti-recruiting stance of the labour element resulted in the fracture of its alliance with the Jinks camp. The group of younger independent-minded councillors on the Corporation, led by Dudley Hanley, began to distance themselves from the IPP, the local MPs as well as from Jinks and his followers. The first hint of this came at the 1916 mayoral election. In January Jinks asked O'Hara for his help to have two council-lors, who were in the army, allowed home to vote for him. Both attended the meeting and their votes ensured that Jinks became mayor for 1916. He had been opposed by Hanley, who was proposed by Monson and supported by John Lynch and the majority of labour councillors. In his post-election speech, Hanley said that he had not stood in the interest of opposing recruiting but as a protest against the way Corporation affairs were being managed, suggesting that recruiting had indeed become an issue. This new alliance between Lynch and his labour followers and the anti-Jinks nationalists soon took control of Sligo Corporation. Almost all of these were later to side with Sinn Féin but at that juncture were content to maintain an independent stance and await develop-ments.[70] Their reaction to the momentous events of the next two years proved vital in the development of Sinn Féin and the revolution in Sligo.

4 'How is the future of Ireland to be served?'[1]

The years 1916–17 were pivotal in Sligo and indeed throughout the country as the IPP was supplanted by SF as the predominant political party. This process was completed nationally in October 1917 when the SF convention 'ratified and consolidated the new united party which had developed during the previous six months'.[2] Before the 1916 Rising there were only small groups of SF supporters in Sligo town but their anti-recruiting stance and activities attracted publicity and their numbers gradually increased in the county. The Rising itself saw no action in Sligo and resulted in few arrests and internments there. However, as in the rest of the country, sympathy with the executed, opposition to the government's overreaction and the inadequacy of the IPP's response resulted in a transformation in Sligo public opinion. There was still no viable political alternative and 'Sinn Féin' was used as a blanket term for all those who were anti-IPP. The crucial event for Sligo was the North Roscommon by-election in early 1917 when most of the group of younger independent Sligo town councillors joined with SF supporters and campaigned for Count Plunkett against the IPP candidate. Subsequent developments in the first half of that year forced them to declare openly for SF; two high-profile meetings in Sligo to confer the freedom of the borough on Plunkett and Countess Markievicz generated much publicity. By the time SF was reorganized nationally, Sligo was ready and SF clubs were quickly formed in every parish in the county.

The increase in support and activity in County Sligo for advanced nationalism before the Rising was noticed by the CI who reported that 'The Sinn Fein party were very active prior to the rebellion and were gaining adherents'.[3] Frank Carty recalled that 'In the early part of 1916 we had increased our membership over the southern part of the county' though it was still no more than a 'skeleton organisation'.[4] Sligo unionist A.M. Lyons said that although there was a negligible number of Sinn Féiners in Sligo town in early 1916, their following was growing in some of the smaller towns and W. Russell Fenton, clerk of the Crown and Peace, thought that Sinn Féiners in the county were 'more numerous than people think'.[5] In March the *Sligo Independent* said of Tubbercurry that 'Sinn Feinism is fairly prevalent in the district'.[6] In April Robert G. Bradshaw, a Church of Ireland member and Tipperary native who came to Sligo the previous year, warned against Sinn Féinism in a letter to the *Sligo Champion*, claiming that 'the realisation of our National Hopes' depended on allied victory. He later became a prominent Sinn Féiner and highly influential anti-Treaty IRA member. At the same time Keash UIL expelled three members 'for identifying with the Sinn Féin policy'.[7] South Sligo MP John O'Dowd called SF 'a gang of non-entities' at the April County Council meeting. John Hennigan, a nationalist councillor from the Drumcliff area, refused to condemn SF, saying they had done more against conscription than any other body in Ireland. This caused uproar.[8]

In March CI Sullivan reported that unnamed new Irish Volunteer branches were in the process of being formed and detailed Irish Volunteer public activity on St Patrick's Day. Fifty uniformed Cliffoney Volunteers were led by William Gilmartin and Andrew Conway who carried revolvers. McCabe led sixty-nine unarmed 'Sinn Feiners' in Ballymote and at Mullinabreena IRB member, J.J. Berreen, led a parade of fifty-two unarmed Volunteers.[9] A police report on the 1916 Rising estimated that at the time of the Rising, there had been a total of 307 anti-Redmond Volunteers at Keash, Tubbercurry and Cliffoney holding a total of fourteen firearms.[10] South Sligo Volunteers had eight or ten effective rifles, thirty to forty revolvers and a 'pretty large assortment' of shotguns.[11] Cliffoney Volunteers had about twenty single-barrel shotguns and a few revolvers.[12]

It is difficult to ascertain the extent to which Sligo IRB and Volunteers were aware of the impending Rising but Volunteers in the three active areas mobilized in response to the original order. Prior to MacNeill's countermanding order, up to sixty Cliffoney Volunteers had plans to march on Sligo.[13] When Sligo town Volunteers heard that the Rising had started, they tried to contact Cliffoney but their messenger was arrested and no action was taken. Representatives of Volunteer units met in Tubbercurry town hall but dispersed when no orders were received. Keash IRB mobilized on the night of Sunday 23 April with the intention of attacking the local police barracks but in the absence of McCabe the attack was called off.[14] In Dublin on Easter Saturday and Sunday, McCabe was instructed by the Military Council to return home and cause as much disruption to communications as possible. He eventually arrived in Keash on Tuesday and claimed to have been planning military operations with a small group of south Sligo Volunteers, including Carty, when news of the Dublin surrender came.[15]

Among Sligo unionists there was some anxiety but little sense of crisis. Sligo magistrates only met on the Saturday and decided that if the Rising spread to Sligo the public would be asked to enrol as volunteers. The surrender and the imposition of martial law meant that this was never implemented. On Wednesday 26 April Thomas Cryan, described by police as 'the local organiser of the Keash branch of the Irish Volunteers', was arrested in Ballymote and sent to Wandsworth detention centre in England.[16] One week after the Rising about sixty men of the North Staffordshire Regiment arrived in Sligo. They arrested fifteen Volunteers in the Cliffoney district, who were interned in Wandsworth, making a total of sixteen Sligo internees. Six were released at the end of May; the others were sent to Frongoch internment camp, north Wales.[17]

A Sligo native, 25-year-old Constable James Gormley of Ballintogher, was killed at Ashbourne during the Rising when his RIC patrol from Navan was attacked by Volunteers under Thomas Ashe. In Ballintogher 'nearly all the people, including the local Volunteers', attended a requiem Mass for the dead constable.[18]

Popular reaction to the Rising was influenced by the executions and subsequent searches, arrests and internments.[19] Sligo UIL was quick to support Redmond. On 7 May the North Sligo executive meeting passed a resolution of confidence in him and the IPP. On 14 May, two days after the last of the executions, Keash UIL branch coupled a similar motion with one congratulating themselves on recent stern action against 'factionists'. On the same day Ballisodare & Corhownagh UIL branch added a resolution condemning the executions to one of support for Redmond. The *Sligo Champion* claimed 'a sickening thud went through the heart of Ireland with each fresh announcement [of executions]' and said that the searches and arrests in Sligo and Leitrim were causing 'a good deal of dissatisfaction'. The *Sligo Nationalist* suggested that these searches were regarded 'with amused contempt'.[20] Seamus MacGowan of Sligo Gaelic Club contributed a profile of Seán Mac Diarmada to the *Sligo Champion* of 27 May; the *Sligo Nationalist* printed a profile of Pearse on 1 July and, in subsequent weeks, profiles of Connolly and Clarke.[21] 'The feeling of the people was generally against the rebels at the time', CI Sullivan reported later, but added that 'subsequent feelings of the people was [sic] opposed to the executions, arrests and internments'.[22] In late June Bunninadden UIL passed a comprehensive resolution:

> That we demand the immediate release of our countrymen and women who are held without trial in prison on suspicion of complicity in the late revolution. The brutal execution of the leaders of the revolution who surrendered had alienated a great deal of sympathy from the government and the continued persecution of these people who were deported and imprisoned will certainly aggravate that feeling and breed feelings of resentment and revenge in the minds of thousands who had no connection or sympathy with the rising. We call on Mr Redmond to insist on their prompt release and request our representative Mr O'Dowd to continue to exert himself in their interest.[23]

Scanlan MP visited the Sligo prisoners in Wandsworth and demanded their release in the House of Commons.[24] When Charles McGarrigle, who had just been released, attended a Sligo Board of Guardians meeting in June, the mayor, John Jinks, welcomed him saying that 'while they all did not approve of the recent rebellion in Dublin' he was proud that a man who had been in Wandsworth Detention Barracks was present and he proposed a resolution calling on the authorities to release the remaining Cliffoney prisoners.[25] Seven more Cliffoney prisoners received a warm welcome in Sligo on their release in July and the last arrived home on 3 August 1916.[26]

Following the Rising, the Irish National Aid Association and Volunteer Dependents Fund (INAAVDF) was set up to help dependents of those killed and imprisoned. The mayor presided at a Sligo meeting called by the Corporation in July. Those in attendance included UIL councillors Jinks, Foley and Fitzpatrick, and Sligo Gaelic Club members Denis A. Mulcahy, John R. Tracey and J.J. Clancy. Stating that he knew some of those executed and acknowledging the national change of mood, Jinks, nonetheless, regretted that 'recruiting had been injured'. Foley and Clancy were appointed secretaries of the fund in Sligo. Clancy, a native of Ballygrania, Collooney and a nephew of a former Catholic bishop of Elphin, John Joseph Clancy, was educated in Summerhill College, Sligo and worked on the staff of the CDB before becoming secretary to the Sligo County Committee of Agriculture.[27]

In the summer Lloyd George proposed bringing the postponed home rule bill into effect at once but with the exclusion of six northern counties. Redmond and the IPP participated in negotiations believing that exclusion would be temporary.[28] The *Sligo Champion* took the official party line: 'though the proposed settlement is not all that Irishmen could wish [for], it is we believe the best that at present England could give. Three-fourths of Ireland in the hands of Irishmen will not be bad for a start'.[29] At a Kilcreevin UIL meeting, chairman Canon Batty Quinn, PP Ballymote, stated: 'It is great to have Home Rule even for twenty-six counties'.[30] However, this was not a popular view and resolutions against partition were unanimously passed by Sligo and Tubbercurry Boards of Guardians, Sligo Corporation and Sligo District Council.[31] In his report for June the CI warned that 'The sudden concern shown by the Government for home rule after the rebellion has strengthened the Sinn Fein party which in my opinion is growing in numbers and influence ... No one seems pleased at the proposed partition of Ireland'.[32] North Sligo UIL executive directed Jinks to vote against exclusion at the July National Directory meeting but he was under no obligation to comply.[33] In the event, he voted with Redmond.[34] Jinks did not attend the next executive meeting but by letter asked delegates 'to stand with your leader, his party and your representative'. He was roundly condemned. Chairman Revd P. Butler's call for a resolution of confidence in the IPP brought a torrent of scorn: 'Glory be to God we are tired of supporting them ... We are tired of passing resolutions'. A compromise resolution condemning the British government for deceiving Redmond and the IPP was passed.[35] Redmond had withdrawn his support for the proposed scheme by then on learning that the northern Unionists had been assured that exclusion of six counties would be permanent. At the very time when the IPP needed to show the value of constitutional nationalism, it failed.[36]

In September at Sligo Borough UIL branch, Scanlan demonstrated awareness of growing SF sympathy while advocating 'common sense' methods:

There has been a rebellion (applause) and the men who fought in that rebellion fought as nobly as it is possible for men to fight in any cause. (Loud and continued applause). They fought a good fight but gentlemen it was a foolish fight. (Several voices – No!) ... They fought not only against the British Empire but against the national interests of Ireland ... If I quarrel with them, do not take me as despising their courage or determination. On the contrary I acknowledge it and am proud of it. (Cheers). But here in sober common sense we talk and discuss the future of our country. How is the future of Ireland to be served?[37]

Redmond visited Sligo on 29 October for the unveiling of a memorial to P.A. McHugh.[38] The CI's claim in his September report that efforts were being made to reorganize Sligo UIL may be based simply on these visits by MPs.[39]

Sometime in the latter part of 1916 a SF club officially started in Sligo town but this appears to have involved renaming the Gaelic Club, already popularly referred to as the SF club. Founding members included John R. Treacy, Denis A. Mulcahy, Seamus MacGowan and Jim Keaveney. There were also a significant number of female club members. The CI reported the club's inauguration in November estimating that it had thirty members.[40] These did not include the prominent Sligo town councillors who had not yet made up their minds which side to support. By the end of 1916 the popular mood in Sligo, as elsewhere, had changed and the IPP had lost support but as yet there was no satisfactory alternative organization.[41] This was reflected in the unanimous selection of Dudley Hanley as mayor of Sligo in January 1917. Although he and the younger councillors were now in a position of strength on the Corporation, it was yet unclear where their allegiances lay. Events in the early part of 1917 forced them to decide.[42]

Nationally, the release of the remainder of the internees in December 1916 and the series of by-elections in 1917 were turning points. The first made little difference in Sligo as few prominent Volunteer leaders had been arrested. However, the North Roscommon by-election on 3 February 1917, on Sligo's doorstep, proved crucial. Former Cliffoney curate, Fr Michael O'Flanagan, played a major role in the campaign to elect Count George Plunkett. Alec McCabe assisted in the campaign with a south Sligo group as did a Sligo town group including Treacy, Mulcahy, Monson, Henry Depew and Fitzpatrick and some of O'Flanagan's former parishioners from Cliffoney. Plunkett's victory was celebrated at Sligo, Tubbercurry, Mullinabreena and Gurteen, where the proceedings were serious enough to be reported to the Competent Military Authority for possible prosecution.[43] The *Sligo Champion* claimed that the election result was 'Ireland's verdict on the executions, the idiotic arrests of innocent persons, the blundering of military despots' but made its usual plea for unity behind Redmond. Sligo Corporation unanimously passed a resolution, proposed by the mayor, congratulating Plunkett on his victory. However, members stressed that this was not meant as criticism of Scanlan or Redmond. T.H. Fitzpatrick's proposal that they offer the freedom of the borough to Plunkett was initially questioned but then carried without opposition.[44] South Sligo UIL executive declared their 'unaltered confidence' in the IPP, though the proposer did venture that Redmond was 'too ready to accept statements of British ministers'.[45]

Attendance by Sligo councillors at a ceremony granting the freedom of Sligo to Count Plunkett on St Patrick's Day 1917 and at a subsequent banquet was seen as decisive declarations for SF. A letter to the *Sligo Champion* claimed that the mayor had burned his boats by presiding at the meeting but noted that despite having canvassed for Plunkett in North Roscommon Alderman Foley did not attend. Speakers included Arthur Griffith, Michael O'Mullane and the mayor.[46] Mary Mulcahy, Denis's wife, and Brighid O'Mullane of Sligo SF club helped organize the event and as a result of discussions with Countess Plunkett they formed a branch of Cumann na mBan in Sligo with Brighid O'Mullane as secretary.[47] Mary Mulcahy also represented Sligo at the INAAVDF executive meeting in Dublin in April 1917, a rare mention of nationalist female involvement at this level in Sligo.[48] Sligo Cumann na mBan branch, with fifteen members according to the CI, appears to have been the only one in the county at the end of 1917.[49] When Count Plunkett invited delegates from public bodies to an April conference in Dublin, Jinks opposed a proposal by Depew that Sligo Corporation send two delegates. Hanley praised the IPP and the local MP but said that the party had not achieved very much in the previous ten or twelve years. The resolution was carried by twelve votes to three, the dissenters included Jinks and Foley. The *Roscommon Herald* and the *Sligo Champion* ridiculed the attempts of some councillors to avoid giving offence to one side or the other.[50] The conference was attended by two representatives of Sligo Corporation and Mayor Hanley. Some delegates from Sligo SF also attended as did Henry Monson, head of Sligo AOH.[51]

There were only two SF clubs in Sligo by the end of March but after Plunkett's convention real growth occurred, part of the 'dramatic advance' noted throughout the country.[52] Seán Milroy of the SF leadership spent the last week of May organizing SF clubs in County Sligo: by the end of July fifteen clubs with a membership of 773 had been established.[53] South Sligo was more advanced than the rest of the county and on 29 April delegates from eight parishes met in Tubbercurry to form the South Sligo SF Alliance. Pádhraic Ó Domhnalláin, the Irish teacher and Gaelic League activist, presided. Its June meeting heard that more clubs had been formed, some with the 'active cooperation of the clergy'. One of the most significant clerical supporters was Fr P.J. O'Grady, PP Keash, previously a staunch IPP supporter, who became president of Keash SF club.[54] From July the *Sligo Champion* printed a column of SF club reports and the *Sligo Nationalist* published a similar column from mid-August.[55]

The by-elections in 1917 helped consolidate SF support. After the victories in South Longford and East Clare, returning Sligo election workers were paraded to the Sinn Féin Hall where meetings were held. These celebrations were sometimes interrupted by protests from serving soldiers' wives – separation women – and by soldiers invalided home. Victory celebrations at Gurteen resulted in arrests after revolver shots were fired as the parade passed the police barracks. The resulting arrests, remands, trials and imprisonments provided SF with invaluable publicity during summer and autumn 1917.[56] The significance of the East Clare by-election result was not lost on the *Sligo Champion*: 'If something is not done and done promptly to conciliate Irish sentiment, Sinn Féin will take the place of constitutionalism and the fires which flared on the hills of Clare will be ablaze in every part of Ireland'.[57]

CI Sullivan reported attempts to reorganize Sligo UIL branches during early 1917: 'An organiser has been appointed and the local MPs have attended the executive meetings'. He also commented that actions, including expulsion, had been taken against UIL officials suspected of leaning towards SF.[58] Councillor Henry Monson, president of the Sligo AOH County Board and Connacht Provincial Director, had publicly supported SF. In April he was replaced by Jinks as the North Sligo UIL representative on the national directory and soon afterwards was suspended by the AOH national executive. When Sligo AOH County Board supported Monson it was also suspended. At the end of July James J. Bergin from the AOH national body attended meetings of the Sligo branch and of Sligo County Board. When the board disregarded Bergin's advice and re-elected Monson president, the AOH national board declared these proceedings null and void. At a Sligo division meeting at the end of August Monson's suspension was endorsed and the division returned to the fold. It appears that SF supporters had decided to leave the AOH by this time, having made their point and embarrassed the national leadership.[59]

Yet control of most Sligo public bodies was still in IPP hands and O'Dowd was unanimously re-elected chairman of Sligo County Council in June. Jinks's son secured a position as a relieving officer for Sligo Board of Guardians, defeating (among others) ex-Frongoch prisoner McGarrigle, who had declared for SF. *Nationality* asked why Jinks, the advocate of recruiting, was seeking a position rather than a khaki uniform for his son.[60]

The conferring of the freedom of Sligo on Countess Markievicz after her release in June occasioned further publicity for SF.[61] The ceremony took place on Monday 23 July and the preceding weekend was marked by SF celebrations in the town and surroundings. The Countess was greeted on the Saturday by the mayor, a brass band and almost 300 Volunteers armed with sticks as protection against Union Jack-waving separation women who heckled the Sinn Féiners and sang pro-British songs. On Sunday Markievicz, the mayor and his wife, John Hennigan and Darrell Figgis toured north Sligo and addressed fourteen SF meetings. Several SF notables, including Eamon de Valera, Joe and Frank McGuinness, Laurence Ginnell, Seán Milroy and Count Plunkett, arrived on Monday for the meeting and banquet. The Countess told the huge crowd, 'I became a rebel because the older I grew ... the more I realised that nothing could help Ireland only get rid of England bag and baggage'. The following weekend SF held meetings at Ballymote and Keash at which Milroy and Harry Boland spoke. However, the CI reported that an attempt to hold a SF meeting at Easkey had to be abandoned owing to the hostility of the crowd.[62] The spread of SF in the county worried Charles O'Hara and on 19 August he suggested to Sir Bryan Mahon, commander-in-chief British forces in Ireland, that troops should be posted to Sligo: 'Things appear peaceful here at the present but the new organization is spreading rapidly'. Whether it was as a result of this representation or not, about 100 members of the 6th Cameronian Scottish Rifles were stationed in Sligo Barracks in the last week of November. 'Their presence has given great satisfaction' commented the CI.[63]

Bishop Morrisroe's frequent words of advice to his flock on political matters showed independence and flexibility. His 1917 Lenten pastoral tread warily but learnedly through the questions of the day – the war, resulting shortages, the aftermath of the 'domestic tragedy' of the Rising and the rise of SF. Morrisroe refused to blame the 1916 leaders, claiming not to know their motives. He also criticized the heavy-handed official response to the Rising and acknowledged the current mood. The bishop attempted to 'point out how far man may go ... in the endeavour to redress recognised wrongs affecting the country'. The bishop stressed that the government was lawful and must be obeyed but commended efforts to secure liberty as long as they were just. This pastoral contrasts with that of Bishop Bernard Coyne of Elphin who, perhaps remembering his predecessor's inability to prevent the establishment of socialism, as he saw it, in Sligo, advised about fasting and avoiding occasions of sin. Later in 1917 Morrisroe spoke publicly in favour of the Irish Convention and against the use of force but at the same time was critical of the IPP and of Unionist calls for stronger measures in Ireland.[64]

In early September delegates from twelve north Sligo clubs formed a SF executive and appointed J.J. Clancy president. At the beginning of December South Sligo SF Alliance was reconstituted as a comhairle ceantair (district executive) for the constituency with twenty-four clubs represented. Pádhraic Ó Domhnalláin was elected president, Alec McCabe and Thomas Murricane vice-presidents, and Owen Tansey and Séamus Marren secretaries.[65] There was little sign of life in Sligo UIL with very few branch meetings reported in the local press. At a meeting of the North Sligo UIL executive early in September, Jinks claimed that the 'political hurricane' passing over the country was only a passing storm.[66]

The remainder of the year saw a consolidation of SF's position in Sligo. Meetings, lectures and aeraíochtaí (open-air concerts) were held regularly and widely reported. The death of Thomas Ashe on 25 September was marked by black flags, parades and public prayers. On 7 October 'the largest meeting seen within the memory of the oldest resident' was held by SF in Tubbercurry with an attendance of over 5,000, including ten bands and representatives from twenty-one SF clubs.[67] In October and November Milroy, Griffith and W.T. Cosgrave gave lectures in Sligo town hall on aspects of SF policy.[68] When a vacancy arose in October in the Ballintrillick area of Sligo RDC, the local SF club nominee was co-opted councillor, unopposed.[69]

A measure of the strength of SF in the county was its willingness to challenge opponents publicly, even Catholic clergy. SF boycotted an entertainment organized by Killaville clergy and nationalists in December, possibly because the SF club had not been allowed use the local hall. Roads were blocked, shots fired and windows broken. The parish priest complained to SF headquarters about the incident.[70] In January 1918 a Red Cross dance in Collooney was deemed pro-war and those attending were pelted with mud and broken bottles by Sinn Féiners. When the parish priest and his curate denounced the attackers from the altar, SF demanded an apology. This was refused. Bishop Morrisroe informed a public meeting supporting the clergy's position of his dissatisfaction at 'a series of incidents more or less against religion' that had been committed in his diocese during the past year. He cited the 'profanation' of churches by flying republican flags above the cross, 'The battering and smashing of school houses that were not given for purposes forbidden by ecclesiastical law', and persons being prevented by 'bludgeon and revolver' from going to a concert in aid of the local church. Typically, he did not entirely blame those who had carried out these deeds: 'Their noble natures and their generous enthusiasm have been played upon by designing men who have an object to gain and care not how they get there'.[71] The SF convention in Dublin on 25 October, which completed the transformation of the SF movement into 'an organised political force', received little publicity in Sligo and no subsequent increase in the number of clubs was apparent.[72]

By the end of 1917 the SF take-over in County Sligo was complete and comprehensive. The group of younger nationalist councillors in Sligo town, including labour members, had joined the small group associated with Sligo Gaelic Club to form a strong SF Club. The continuation of annual elections to Sligo Corporation during the war allowed SF gain control of that body. In rural Sligo few UIL or AOH club officials or elected representatives had converted and so SF club officials were drawn from a younger generation of activists including a few also associated with the Irish Volunteers. The absence of elections since 1914 allowed the IPP to maintain nominal control of the County Council and rural councils. The once mighty IPP proved powerless to withstand the rise of SF. With home rule off the agenda, the party had lost the central plank of its platform. Its support for recruiting was becoming increasingly unpopular as the war dragged on and in Sligo, as elsewhere, its reaction to the Rising was considered inadequate. The local IPP organization, which had been unchallenged for years, and whose activities had been confined to passing pro-Redmond resolutions, collecting funds for the IPP and engaging in local agrarian disputes, found itself unable to counter the enthusiasm and idealism of the younger activists who were not bound by previous policies. The IPP's local organization, however, did provide the pattern and example for the new SF party which took their place and often their meeting places, halls and even musical instruments. In December 1917 County Sligo ranked sixth in Ireland as regards SF membership, taking population size into account.[73] Reporting forty-three Sligo SF clubs with a membership of 2,762 at the end of the year, CI Sullivan recognized that 'Sinn Fein is the only live political organisation in this county'.[74]

5 1918 – Sinn Féin: 'the only political organisation in the county'[1]

Although SF had established its political ascendancy by the end of 1917, it nonetheless encountered the challenge, previously faced by the IPP, of how to maintain momentum in the absence of a general election or normal political activity. In December 1917 CI Sullivan believed that much of SF's energy in Sligo had waned and notably in early 1918 some SF clubs were warning 'milk and water members' to attend regularly.[2] The IPP defeated SF in three by-elections in early 1918, though SF could claim that none of the three constituencies was representative of the country as a whole.[3] Just when it appeared that SF's supremacy might be seriously threatened, the British government proposed extending conscription to Ireland. SF's leadership of the anti-conscription campaign and the arrest of many of its leaders as a result of the so-called 'German Plot' enabled it to re-affirm its pre-eminent position and score a comprehensive victory in the East Cavan by-election, the last contest before the 1918 general election. In Sligo SF maintained its momentum in the early months of 1918 by taking over what had been a cornerstone of the UIL's appeal to small farmers – an agrarian campaign. This controlled campaign of land seizures was followed by participation in the nationwide drive against conscription. These two campaigns, one local, the other national, secured SF's dominance in the county providing a perfect lead-in to the well-organized, successful December 1918 general election campaign.

SF's agrarian campaign took advantage of the nationwide concern about wartime food supplies and the knowledge that farmers had not complied with compulsory tillage orders. Sligo SF comhairle ceantair set up food committees and attempted to secure potato supplies but the main activity was what the *Sligo Champion* called a 'wave of unrestrained lawlessness', in fact an opportunistic, well-organized conacre-taking campaign led by Alec McCabe, vice-president of South Sligo SF. The organizers set the price for conacre on residential land at £4 per acre.[4] Large crowds, accompanied by bands with republican flags and banners, entered selected properties and divided them for conacre at the set price among small farmers, usually SF club members. Most seizures took place in south Sligo but there were also incidents in north Sligo at Cliffoney, Skreen and Dromard.[5] In at least some cases, written demands were first made and many farmers and agents accepted the terms offered. Land agent Henry (Hal) R. Wood–Martin, a landowner himself, accepted terms on behalf of a client from 'conacre people' who 'were carrying two Sinn Fein flags on poles'.[6] The British military intelligence officer reported that over one hundred farms were visited in Sligo during February and 'that practically no resistance has been offered'. Sligo

RIC were augmented by an additional fifty men and assisted by the military on numerous occasions. No attempt was made to prevent seizures but twenty-four prosecutions involving about 150 identified leaders resulted.[7] Forty-eight of the fifty indictable offences in Sligo in February were related to this agitation. The figure for the previous month had been eight. A number of landowners secured injunctions in superior courts against trespassers.[8]

SF headquarters was concerned that this campaign, confined to the west and in particular to Sligo and Roscommon, might cause them to lose the support of medium and larger farmers. They issued a circular on 23 February requiring clubs to obtain the prior sanction of their comhairle ceantair and, in special cases, that of headquarters, for cattle drives, though no mention was made of tillage-related land seizures.[9] McCabe's letter to the *Irish Independent* at the end of February was intended to calm fears:

> As the impression seems to have got abroad that the SF Executive gave unqualified licence to land commandeering … let it be known that the South Sligo SF Ceanntair rules that no residential farm under forty acres is allowed to be entered on. Lands devoted to the feeding of milch cows, or the production of other necessaries, are also exempted.[10]

The *Sligo Champion* suggested that the campaign, notwithstanding its acceptable aim, had spun out of control and brought more discredit than credit on SF.[11] The speed and comprehensiveness with which the campaign ceased at the end of February testified to the control exercised by the SF clubs. The CI reported that 'Cattle driving has already ceased and so has the commandeering of lands'; there were no cases in March.[12]

Prosecutions arising from the campaign gave SF and their supporters further opportunities to challenge authority. McCabe and seven others made headlines when they refused to remove their caps, smoked and sang 'songs referring to Ireland and freedom' during their trial in Sligo. As they were removed from Sligo courthouse, soldiers with fixed bayonets faced a hostile crowd including Volunteers armed with hurleys. McCabe and Bernard Brady, captain of Kilcreevin Volunteers, were sentenced to three months' hard labour, others to one month.[13] Charles Gildea recalled that Volunteers had been instructed to create scenes in court in the event of arrest.[14] Similar cases involving SF activists from Cliffoney, Skreen & Dromard, Cloonacool, Sooey, Collooney and Ballintogher continued until May.[15] Clubs organized farm work for prisoners and welcome home demonstrations for released men. Constable Jeremiah Mee wryly commented: 'In many cases the prisoners had very little interest in politics [when] going to jail but after the torchlight processions there was no turning back and they became dedicated republicans'.[16] The presence of troops in Sligo, together with the increased excitement of the agrarian campaign, meant that friction was inevitable. A soldier was attacked and beaten in Sligo town in late February.[17] At the end of March some soldiers travelling by train manhandled civilians flying a SF flag at Ballisodare station. SF supporters, welcoming released prisoners at Sligo railway station, sang rebel songs and jeered soldiers who replied with 'patriotic ditties' before charging and dispersing the crowd.[18]

The conacre campaign and its aftermath ensured that SF continued to grow in Sligo, particularly in the south of the county. Twenty-three clubs were represented at the South Sligo comhairle ceantair meeting in January and thirty in April 1918. Representatives of ten clubs attended the North Sligo comhairle ceantair May meeting.[19] After the SF South Armagh by-election defeat on 1 February 1918 there were nationalist celebrations in Sligo town and returning SF election workers were heckled by separation women. Sligo AOH and Tubbercurry RDC congratulated South Armagh nationalists but Grange AOH decided to dissolve 'on account of the action of Mr J. Devlin [AOH leader] in joining hands with Sir Edward Carson at the South Armagh election' and funds in hand were sent to the SF election fund.[20] On St Patrick's Day SF held meetings and parades at Ballymote and Sligo town. The Sligo meeting, attended by contingents from fifteen districts, passed a resolution that Ireland was a distinct nation with a right to sovereign independence.[21]

After the conacre campaign the CI believed that people were 'apprehensive of some new move on behalf of the Sinn Féiners' and such a move came in response to the threat of conscription.[22] The British army was under severe pressure on the western front and the House of Commons passed the Military Service Bill on 16 April, which proposed extending conscription to Ireland. The *Sligo Champion* made it clear that the nationalist position on conscription was identical to that of SF and warned it would have to be enforced 'at the point of a bayonet.'[23] The IPP returned to Ireland to fight conscription and took part in an all-party conference in the Mansion House with SF and Labour representatives. The conference formulated an anti-conscription pledge, which was approved by the Catholic hierarchy and was to be taken in every parish after Mass throughout the country. 'The passing of the conscription act, the fear of which has been Sinn Fein's trump card had drawn the county into a state of consternation', CI Sullivan wrote, perceptively adding: 'Passive resistance will be the order and this must very soon merge into violence … The police will be thoroughly boycotted.' SF took the lead in Sligo since neither MP was at home for the first weekend of the anti-conscription campaign. Hanley, the SF mayor, presided over an anti-conscription meeting at Sligo town hall. A letter from Bishop Coyne assured them of his support. Speakers included Fr P. Butler, J.J. Clancy, president of North Sligo SF, and John Lynch. O'Dowd was not at home to chair that weekend's County Council meeting which protested against conscription. CI Sullivan reported that 'the control of the money collected [for the National Defence Fund] and the general management are with the Sinn Fein party'.[24] On the following weekend both Sligo MPs took their places alongside SF and clerics at a further anti-conscription meeting. Sligo Trades and Labour Council, Sligo Corporation, Sligo County Council and Sligo Board of Guardians, all local UIL, AOH and SF clubs expressed their opposition to conscription.[25] A large anti-conscription meeting was held in Sligo on 23 April to coincide with the Irish Trades Union Congress' general strike. Clergy were prominent in the campaign and many anti-conscription meetings were chaired by priests whose language was at times noticeably mild. At Mass in Sligo people were advised to be cautious and if the worst came to the worst to adopt a policy of passive resistance. Similar guidance was said to have been issued at many churches throughout the county. Fr Michael Doyle, PP Collooney, counselled the people to be guided by 'recognised leaders'. Bishops Naughton of Killala and Morrisroe of Achonry asked the people to unite against conscription.[26] The anti-conscription campaign proved a significant boost to SF's prestige and support. At the end of May the Sligo CI reported forty-seven SF clubs in the county with a membership of almost 4,000. He was further troubled by a new development: 'people are beginning to hold themselves aloof from the police'. In June he called Sinn Féin 'the only active political force in this county'.[27]

In the event, the British government, taken aback at the level of opposition, did not enforce conscription but instead asked that Ireland supply 50,000 recruits voluntarily. Sligo's quota would have been 1,000 men but the CI believed there was 'little prospect' of raising this number.[28] Recruiting continued to languish. When Major Murphy, who was in charge of recruiting in the Sligo/Roscommon/Leitrim area, moved headquarters from Boyle to Sligo in August, Charles O'Hara told him that they should expect very little support from previously helpful nationalists. The *Sligo Champion* described recruiting meetings in early September as 'Variety Entertainments', reporting incessant interruptions in Sligo, Ballymote and Strandhill. The Sligo meeting ended prematurely when chairman Charles O'Hara was heckled with remarks such as 'Up the rebels', 'Let the men out of jail', 'Three cheers for the German plot'.[29] Private Martin Moffatt of the Leinster Regiment, a native of Sligo town, was awarded the Victoria Cross in late 1918 and there was a well-attended reception and presentation at Sligo town hall (see plate 6). The mayor and the SF councillors did not attend and the presentation was made by Charles O'Hara.[30]

The re-organization of the Volunteers in Sligo lagged behind the growth of SF. In August and September 1917 proposals by the two Sligo SF executives that Volunteer corps be started in association with each club appear to have had limited effect. On his release from Lewes gaol in mid-1917, J.J. 'Ginger' O'Connell came to Sligo, where his father was a schools inspector, and became O/C Sligo Volunteers. His officer classes were attended by many of those later prominent in Sligo IRA.[31] The election of Frank Carty as commandant of Tubbercurry Battalion early in 1918 and the officer classes he arranged gave the organization a boost there. He claimed to have organized Volunteer companies 'in practically every parish in south Sligo'. Many who joined during the conscription campaign dropped out soon afterwards but, according to Carty, 'those who remained on formed the bulk of the men who participated actively in the subsequent armed conflict'.[32] At the end of January 1918 CI Sullivan reported the existence of five Sligo Volunteer companies with 225 members. By July this had increased to eight with 429 members. Sullivan returned the same number each month throughout the remainder of the year.[33]

The Volunteers in Sligo were poorly armed and early activity concentrated on raiding houses for arms. In early February 1918 a group led by Michael J. Marren, a carpenter from Mount Irwin in Killaville parish and O/C of the local Volunteer company, seized one shotgun, two revolvers and eight rounds of ammunition in the house of Graham Shaw near Bunninadden. Three Gurteen men were arrested, charged with the raid and convicted at Derry Assizes in early July.[34] In the same month Sligo Volunteers stole three rifles from the steamship SS *Tartar* at Sligo quay.[35] On 21 February Alec McCabe led an IRB group from the Ballymote-Gurteen-Boyle area in a raid on Rockingham House near Boyle in which 3 rifles, 15 shotguns and 2,000 rounds of ammunition were taken.[36] In April over 700 rounds of sporting ammunition was taken from a Ballymote shop. The RIC responded by removing arms and ammunition from local shops in Sligo town and the county was added to the list of those where carrying arms was prohibited unless authorized by a county inspector.[37] In June Sligo was also one of thirteen counties deemed 'proclaimed districts'. Persons charged in these counties could be tried by special jury in a different location.[38] The Volunteers developed slowly in Sligo during 1918 but were still seen as complementary to the political wing and assisted in SF-led campaigns about conacre-taking, anti-conscription and the general election.

In mid-1918 there was a significant increase in the number of Cumann na mBan branches in Sligo. As part of a nationwide recruiting drive in April 1918 Brighid O'Mullane and Mrs Flanagan from the Sligo town branch helped start branches in Sooey, Coolera, Ballintogher, Tubbercurry and Collooney and the organization spread from there.[39] At Ballintogher the organizers pointed out ways 'in which we can best help our brothers' in 'the struggle for national existence'. Sooey branch saw its task 'To help the young men, and stand by those who have sacrificed so much in defence of the rights of the country'.[40] By late summer there were at least twenty-two branches in the county, two-thirds of them in the southern constituency. Initial activities included instruction in first aid and the holding of dances, socials, bazaars and flag days to raise funds for SF election expenses. Cumann na mBan also played a significant role in the 1918 election campaign.[41] The branches were active in organizing anti-conscription women's day events in June at Sligo, where the mayoress, Mrs Margaret Hanley, was a leading figure, as well as in Tubbercurry, Collooney, Curry and

Grange. A number of these events had religious elements including the reciting of the rosary and pilgrimages to holy wells. The Sligo protest marched to the cathedral.[42]

Developments throughout the rest of 1918 helped keep SF in the public eye in the county. Within a few days of Lord John French becoming viceroy in May 1918, Dublin Castle announced that it had evidence of SF collusion with Germany. This so-called 'German Plot' saw seventy-three SF leaders arrested and deported, among them Sligo-men J.J. Clancy and J.J. O'Connell. Sligo County Council and Sligo Board of Guardians condemned the arrests; Alderman Foley warned: 'If the Government go on this way ... blood will be shed' and public meetings were held to demand the release of the prisoners.[43] The conferral of the Freedom of the Borough of Sligo on Fr Michael O'Flanagan on Sunday 23 June was another opportunity for a show of SF strength, the CI estimating the attendance at 2,000.[44] Sinn Féin had been banned on 4 July and its national executive arranged that a public statement would be read throughout the country on 15 August in protest. John R. Tracey read the statement outside Sligo town hall as did John Hennigan in Cliffoney. Both were arrested and imprisoned. At Collooney, police warned a group gathered for this purpose that they would be prevented, by force if necessary, from holding a meeting. The crowd regrouped outside the town where they held a meeting. Similarly when a group of military and police under CI Sullivan arrived to prevent a planned meeting in Skreen, the statement was instead read at a gathering some distance away. Meetings were also held at Calry, Drumcliff and Ballintrillick.[45] The successful outwitting of the police at such gatherings added to the growing sense of defiance of law and order. Two men went on the run in Sligo as a result of speeches at anti-conscription meetings and there were numerous searches for them. R.B. (Bertie) Anderson from Calry was a Protestant Sinn Féiner who had spent the pre-war years teaching in Europe. He returned to Sligo at the outbreak of war and joined the Irish Volunteers; after 1916 he became active in SF and the Volunteers. James Hayes was a Tipperary native working in Sligo. Anderson was arrested in December but Hayes was still free at the end of the year.[46]

In spite of the predominance of the national question, labour attempted to expand its organization during 1918. There was a drive in Sligo and neighbouring counties to develop the Transport Union and in March William Reilly, councillor and local tailor, was appointed full time secretary of the Sligo branch. There were existing branches in Sligo itself, Ballisodare based on the flour mills, and Maugherow based on Gore-Booth estate workers. In 1918 new branches were founded at Geevagh, Riverstown, Ballymote and Tubbercurry. Membership of the Sligo branches in June 1918 was: Sligo town 504, Maugherow 130, Ballisodare 75, Geevagh 37, Collooney 43, and Riverstown 21, the last three being deemed 'uneconomic'.[47] There was some strain in the Sligo labour movement between those who put labour first and those who prioritized national independence, although it did manage to hold together until the Treaty split. At a Trades Council meeting in May 1918 William Reilly proposed that the Council ask SF to ensure that one of its members who worked in the asylum join the Asylum Attendants Union. He threatened that if SF's attitude did not change, labour would put up a candidate at the general election. A member asserted 'that Sinn Féin was Labour and Labour was Sinn Féin'.[48] In September there was disagreement at a Trades and Labour Council meeting as regards putting forward a Labour candidate at the election and it was decided to hold a plebiscite of the membership to decide the issue. At their next meeting, however, the Council was informed of the TUC's decision not to contest the election.[49]

In Sligo town in mid-1918 disagreement among SF club members resulted in a group of younger members, led by Seamus MacGowan, breaking away and forming a Young Republican Club. This became popularly known as the Hottentots, a common nickname for SF at the time.[50] The main focus of SF activity for the remainder of 1918 was preparation for the expected general election following the end of the First World War.[51] SF was still poorly represented in local government outside of Sligo Corporation but received a boost in June when the outgoing officers of Tubbercurry RDC and Board of Guardians were replaced by members who had embraced SF. On Sligo's UDC and Board of Guardians, however, the outgoing officers who remained loyal to the IPP were re-elected and O'Dowd was re-elected Sligo County Council chairman, with only John Hennigan and a Tubbercurry representative dissenting.[52]

In February 1918 the Representation of the People Act had given the vote to all males over 21 years and most women over 30. This increased the North Sligo electorate from 8,126 to 18,448 and that of South Sligo from 6,929 to 18,003. In June the CI reported that SF was in the process of 'perfecting their organisation' and ensuring their supporters were on the electoral register.[53] South Sligo comhairle ceantair was told by headquarters that the candidate should be selected locally and four candidates went forward: McCabe, Pádhraic Ó Domhnalláin, Owen Tansey and Séamus Marren. The last two withdrew and McCabe was selected on a vote of 21 to 19. An appeal found McCabe's selection irregular but he was properly selected at a subsequent convention. North Sligo comhairle ceantair selected J.J. Clancy, then in prison, as their candidate on 15 September. At the end of the month O'Dowd and Scanlan, the outgoing MPs, were selected to contest the election.[54] Bishop Morrisroe, with unusual circumspection, stated that it was not for him to say what would satisfy the people but while he refused to support any side, he announced his preparedness to lead his flock once it had made up its mind: 'Only when the people were united would the priests give a lead, and not when the people were wrangling'. Many priests did take sides. Among Scanlan's proposers was Fr P. Butler, Sligo administrator. In South Sligo Canon James Daly, PP Mullinabreena, and Fr Thomas Quinn,

PP Toulestrane, were among John O'Dowd's proposers while remarkably one of McCabe's proposers was Fr P.J. O'Grady, PP Keash, who had once dismissed him from his teaching post. CI Sullivan recognized that SF was better prepared than the nationalists: 'Their canvassers are more active and their flags and election addresses appear everywhere'.[55]

Thomas Scanlan arrived in Sligo on 20 November, started his election campaign with a meeting in the town hall and attended the AOH County Board and Sligo County Council meetings at the weekend. On Monday evening a SF meeting in Sligo town hall, presided over by the mayor, was addressed by Fr Michael O'Flanagan who had returned 'to fire the first shot'. There was little trouble at Sligo election meetings. In the last week of November there were some interruptions from Sinn Féiners at Scanlan's meetings at Calry and Drumcliff but he received an enthusiastic reception at Maugherow. He was also well received in Kilglass but not so cordially at Easkey on the same Sunday.[56] The Sligo centre of the IUA advised unionist electors not to vote:

> A unionist who supports Sinn Fein votes for the people who rebelled in 1916 thus assisting the Germans whom they called their 'gallant ally' ... If you vote for the Nationalist you support a party pledged to Home Rule ... a party who during the major part of the greatest struggle in History maintained an attitude of callous indifference to the success or failure of the allied cause.[57]

In South Sligo, where the result was regarded as a foregone conclusion, there was even less excitement at meetings. On the eve of polling day, however, O'Dowd was assaulted while canvassing in Ballinacarrow. His car was pelted with stones and when he got out and reminded his attackers that he had given the best years of his life fighting for his country, he was knocked to the ground and kicked. Four young men from the area were later found guilty of disturbing the peace.[58] At Ballymoghany, near Easkey, an RIC sergeant was wounded in the back a few days before the election by a shotgun blast. He recovered fully. The CI believed the attack occurred because 'He [the Sgt.] had incurred hostility of the local Sinn Feiners'.[59] Sullivan reported 'no disturbances during the election' and while there were some accounts of impersonation, these had no effect on the outcome.[60] The election was held on 14 December and though the results were not announced for some time, the outcome was never in doubt. The *Sligo Nationalist* stated: 'In South Sligo Mr O'Dowd is in all probability defeated and in North Sligo, Mr Scanlan although confident himself, is scarcely likely to be elected'. The returns for North Sligo were Clancy 9,030 votes to 4,241 for Scanlan, and in South Sligo McCabe secured 9,103 votes to just 1,988 for O'Dowd. McCabe's share of the valid poll was 82%, Clancy's 68%. The turnout in North Sligo was 72% and in South Sligo just under 62%. The lower turnout in the south was apparently because the result there was regarded as not in doubt.[61] 'The young people have triumphed over their elders', CI Sullivan observed, 'Moderate politicians and those with any stake in the country await with anxiety the future action of the Sinn Fein party.'[62]

Sligo Corporation's financial troubles were so bad that at one stage the sheriff was called in by a debtor and town hall furniture put up for sale. Cleaning, lighting and other services were curtailed. A government inquiry blamed irregularities and 'a lack of prudent business-like management'. Due to the Sligo Borough Improvement Act (1869), the Corporation was unable to raise sufficient funds to cover costs so the government agreed to amend the act. The Ratepayers' Association declined to support this unless their demand for fair representation on the Corporation be met. Tadhg Kilgannon led a successful campaign for proportional representation (PR) and a bill including the amendment to the 1869 Act and the use of PR was drafted. The Corporation and the Ratepayers' Association approved, the bill received the royal assent in July and the Corporation election under PR was fixed for 15 January 1919.[63] This was the first time PR was used in elections in Britain and Ireland and Sligo was the only place where people went to the polls on that day. Forty-eight candidates – eighteen Ratepayers, thirteen SF, thirteen labour and four independents – vied for the twenty-four seats. There were no UIL candidates but John Jinks went forward as an independent. The *Sligo Independent* exhorted its readers to vote for the Ratepayers' Association candidates.[64] The Sligo electorate used the system well and there were less than two per cent of spoiled votes. The Ratepayers' candidate, Harper Campbell Perry, headed the poll in the West Ward, independent John Jinks in the North Ward and SF mayor, Hanley, in the East Ward. Other notables elected included Michael Nevin and John Lynch for labour, T.H. Fitzpatrick for SF and Hal Wood-Martin for the Ratepayers' Association. SF received a total of 674 first preference votes and seven seats, Ratepayers 823 first preference votes and eight seats, labour 432 first preference votes and five seats and independents 279 first preference votes and four seats. The labour councillors were either SF members or supporters as was one independent, so the Corporation was SF-controlled with a strong opposition.[65]

In the mayoral election, outgoing mayor Hanley defeated a Ratepayers' candidate on a vote of twelve to eight. Labour and SF councillors and two independents voted for Hanley. His election was celebrated by bonfires and the hoisting of a republican flag on the town hall but the *Sligo Independent* was displeased: 'He [Hanley] is largely responsible for basing municipal affairs on "Ireland a Republic" and creating a political atmosphere in the town'.[66] Sligo Corporation became the first Irish public body to be SF-controlled and have a SF mayor.

The 1918 election was a triumph for SF nationally and saw the demise of the IPP as a potent political force. The collapse of its constituency organization, the UIL, allied with the fact that the party had not been seriously challenged at the polls for years meant that it had little to offer the greatly enlarged electorate. SF, on the other hand, had a vibrant constituency organization. Moreover, its members were able to stress their success in leading the recent fight against conscription, denounce oppressive British government actions against the party, and trumpet their policy of abstention from Westminster. SF carried both Sligo constituencies but support for SF was weaker in North Sligo, which included Sligo town and which had a higher percentage of non-Catholic voters. The town also had a strong anti-SF minority on the Corporation as a result of the PR election. As elsewhere SF membership in Sligo was a broad coalition, from former UIL and AOH members to members of the Irish Volunteers and the IRB. Some Sligo members saw themselves as politicians first and foremost but others had continually flouted law and order during the conacre and anti-conscription campaigns and were anxious for a more openly aggressive campaign. Volunteers and Cumann na mBan had also increased their activity in Sligo but generally in a supportive role. SF now found itself in the same position as the IPP had previously, having no significant political opposition, and the party quickly lost its leading position as the focus shifted to the establishment of Dáil Éireann, the reactions of the British government and the activities of the Volunteers. The SF-controlled Sligo local government bodies soon declared allegiance to the Dáil but Sligo Volunteers took some time to escalate their campaign.

6 'Disloyalty and contempt for the law'[1]

Activity by the Volunteers, or IRA as they were styled from 1919, increased generally in Ireland during the latter part of 1919 after the suppression of Dáil Éireann and SF and the rejection of Irish demands to be heard at the Paris Peace Conference.[2] While the development of SF in County Sligo matched the rest of the country, IRA operations notably did not. There were a number of contributing factors. No significant Sligo Volunteers were interned after the Rising, so none returned full of enthusiasm for an armed struggle, as happened elsewhere. Second, few of the Sligo IRA leadership possessed any proper military experience. Joost Augusteijn's analysis of a number of Irish counties suggests that while Sligo's Volunteer membership was at a comparable level to others in 1916, it developed more slowly and by early 1919 lagged significantly behind counties such as Mayo, Tipperary and Cork.[3] The implementation of a brigade and battalion structure in Sligo was still not completed by the end of 1919 (see map 5). This weak organizational development was compounded by a scarcity of arms and hence attacks on policemen or barracks in Sligo did not take place until mid-1920. However, during 1919 there were instances of low level Volunteer operations in Sligo such as drilling, arms raids, raids on the mail and activities in connection with the Dáil Loan, resulting in what the CI called 'a widespread spirit of disloyalty and contempt for the law'.[4] There was also the distraction of agrarian campaigns in 1919 and 1920 and some friction between IRB and Volunteers as regards leadership roles. The arrest and imprisonment of some of the most prominent Sligo IRA leaders – Pilkington, O'Connell, Carty and Hunt – was also detrimental to the development of guerrilla activities. When the RIC closed most of its smaller barracks in the county in late 1919 and early 1920 it was as a result of national policy, not pressure from Sligo IRA. Finding itself in nominal control of large areas of the county by default, the Sligo IRA still had difficulty in carrying out simple operations such as the destruction of the evacuated barracks at Easter 1920.

Volunteer activities in Sligo in 1919 were, according to Gurteen Volunteer leader Jim Hunt, 'confined to drilling and training'.[5] Michael Nevin of Sligo town recalled 'no special Volunteer activity in the area in 1919 beyond routine training and organisation'.[6] There were a small number of raids involving little danger of confrontation with police. Sligo IRA raided a gelignite store and the railway station stores in May. In November they raided a number of what they called loyalists premises, including the Masonic Lodge and the Grammar School, looking for Sligo UVF rifles but got only cartridges.[7] There were local echoes of the violence elsewhere in the country. A large number of Volunteers took part in the funeral of Ballisodare man, Martin Savage, shot dead during the unsuccessful ambush of Lord French at Ashtown in Dublin at the end of December.[8] When DI Michael Hunt, a native of the Killaville area, was shot dead in Thurles at the end of June, prayers were said for him in Gurteen and Canon James O'Connor PP criticized the shooting as 'diabolical in the extreme'. Such popular revulsion at the shooting of policemen was common in 1919.[9]

It was the end of 1919 before the organization of the IRA in County Sligo was regularized, and even then it was not complete. A Sligo Brigade IRA convention at that time appointed commandants to the six or so battalions in existence, and returned incomplete lists of brigade, battalion and company officers to IRA GHQ.[10] Billy Pilkington, who succeeded J.J. O'Connell as brigade O/C when the latter became GHQ director of training in late 1919, complained about the difficulty of 'getting suitable men'.[11] The organization of the Sligo IRA was still not complete by May 1920 but Pilkington assured GHQ that the work was 'being pushed forward'. Pilkington's imprisonment in early 1920 was detri-mental to the development of the brigade.[12]

GHQ sent an organizer to help form battalions and companies in south Sligo during the second half of 1919.[13] The IRB originally took control of battalion and company staffs there and this may have complicated centralized brigade control.[14] When Alec McCabe was jailed in late 1919 Michael J. Marren, not an IRB member, succeeded him as O/C Ballymote Battalion and did not relinquish control on McCabe's release.[15] In March 1920 Pilkington complained to Michael Collins that a south Sligo mail car raid had been carried out without the brigade's knowledge or sanction and, referring to the IRB, wrote 'The Battalion Commandant [Marren] … believes there are forces at work that are not working for the greater efficiency of the Volunteers'. Collins, then president of the IRB Supreme Council, replied that there were no differences in the aims and methods of the Volunteers and the IRB. He instructed Pilkington to place the men responsible under arrest, recover as much of the stolen money as possible and hold a court of enquiry. Nothing more was heard of the matter or of further tensions in the area due to the IRB.[16] Owen Tansey, South Sligo SF executive chairman and O/C Gurteen Battalion, died of influenza in November 1918 and was succeeded as O/C by Jim Hunt. He had joined the RIC in 1911 and was stationed in Laois during the 1916 Rising but deserted in May 1916 and returned to join the Gurteen Volunteers.[17]

Instead of armed confrontation in Sligo during late 1918 and 1919 there was growing defiance of British authority. Tansey's funeral saw a display of strength by the IRA preventing the RIC from entering the cemetery. Two IRA members involved were arrested in early 1919 and sentenced for unlawful assembly.[18] In early 1919 the most important IRA commandants, none of whom appears to have been on the run, were arrested. Public meetings in Sligo, Tubbercurry and Ballymote, which involved drilling by IRA, demanded the release of these prisoners.[19] On 2 March a SF lecture in Sligo town hall was proclaimed and fifty soldiers of the Essex Regiment took possession of the building, fixed machine guns at upper windows and turned people away. As the soldiers left at midnight an IRA group, led by Pilkington, marched into the hall and the meeting was legally held at 00:15 a.m. A week later Sligo republicans cut off the gas supply to the same building while an Essex Regiment dance was in progress.[20] The three prominent Sligo prisoners, Clancy, O'Connell and McCabe, were greeted by large crowds on their release in March.[21] At a meeting in Sligo to protest about the death in prison of Pierce McCann, SF MP for Tipperary East, Clancy proclaimed: 'We stand for the right of Ireland to be mistress of her own destinies and for the flag of a free and independent Irish Republic'.[22] Later in March Pilkington was arrested and charged with unlawful assembly on the night of the town hall lecture. While in custody he was charged with two other drilling offences and was jailed for six months.[23] J.J. Clancy was also charged with unlawful assembly and was sentenced to three months.[24] In March, when Jim Hunt was charged with collecting money without a permit, he told the magistrate, 'We don't recognise the jurisdiction of this court at all'.[25] At the end of May a large force of police and military were booed by a crowd in Templeboy after a fruitless search for fugitive James Hayes.[26] Alderman John Lynch was welcomed by a large crowd including members of the Transport Union and Volunteers after his release in early April.[27] In June military from Sligo cordoned off the road where a proclaimed Skreen & Dromard SF aeraíocht was to take place but it was held at an alternate venue without any interference. Subsequent aeraíochtaí went ahead without police intervention at Collooney, Ballymote, Drumcliff, Ballisodare and Sligo.[28]

Activity increased after Dáil Éireann issued republican bonds for sale to the public.[29] It was illegal to solicit contributions to this 'Dáil loan' and the *Sligo Nationalist* was shut down in early October for almost a month because of its full front page advertisement for the bonds.[30] 'Buy Dáil Éireann Bonds' was painted on walls and advertisements were posted around Sligo. The police obliterated the slogans and tore down the posters. Alec McCabe was arrested once again in early October on an unlawful assembly charge and while on remand was convicted of soliciting contributions to the Dáil loan.[31] Sligo SF organizer Patrick Hegarty, a native of Mayo, promoted the loan in south Sligo. His exploits during October and November were sensationally reported in the local press. One Sunday morning Hegarty was cornered by the police outside the home of the Hannons, well-known Ballymote republican activists. Family members, including Susan Hannon, attacked the RIC, allowing Hegarty to escape and fulfil his after-Mass speaking engagements in south Sligo. Two of the Hannons were later arrested and charged. At Riverstown the crowd prevented police from arresting Hegarty and at Geevagh he used a revolver to escape the RIC. Two weeks later Hegarty addressed meetings at Cloonloo and Killaraght with local Commandant Jim Hunt. On the return journey to Gurteen they encountered about a dozen policemen blocking the road. They drove through the police barrier and fire was exchanged. The *Sligo Champion* reported, 'Bullets were whistling overhead and smashing through the car, still it went on and took the corner to safety at a pace of 50 mph'. Hunt was arrested and jailed in December. As a result of these dramatic events, relations between the people and police became very strained in the Gurteen area. An IRA notice warned: 'Any person found talking to or in any way helping the police will in future be severely dealt with'.[32] In December the CI recorded that prosecutions had had a good effect and that no reference was being made to the loan in speech or newspaper. He noted a great improvement especially in the Ballymote area because 'the prominent and dangerous Sinn Feiners of that area are now in jail'.[33] Although the figures may be incomplete, they suggest substantial contributions to the Dáil loan. North Sligo constituency contributed £2,345 up to May 1920 and South £3,743 up to 18 September 1920.[34]

These actions were part of a noticeable increase in IRA and police activity towards the end of 1919 and early 1920. In September there were police raids in south Sligo areas at Ballinacarrow, Collooney, Cloonacool and Tubbercurry but no arrests. In Collooney the SF clubrooms were raided and documents and the SF newspaper, *Nationality*, seized.[35] A new management team, including R.G. Bradshaw and Seamus MacGowan, took over the *Sligo Nationalist*, which took a strong pro-Sinn Féin stance. Its office was raided at the beginning of September as was Sligo Municipal Technical School and the houses of some Sligo town activists. The police took documents but made no arrests.[36] In November the CI unsurprisingly reported 'considerable political unrest. There is a growing feeling of hostility to the police'.[37] In January motor cars owners in Sligo town and Ballymote, who had complied with the motor permit order, had their vehicles damaged by the IRA and a short hunger strike to seek political status took place in Sligo jail.[38]

IRA raids on private houses in Sligo in early 1920 captured some serviceable weapons.[39] Cliffoney Company, then part of the Donegal Brigade, assisted in the capture of a building in Belleek, County Fermanagh believed to contain UVF arms but only a few guns were obtained.[40] At the end of January Frank Carty led a raid on the south Sligo residence of Charles Graham, a Protestant shopkeeper, and seized two rifles, three revolvers, three shotguns and ammunition.[41] The following month he led a larger party, which included Marren and Hunt, to raid the residence of Colonel Alexander Perceval at Templehouse. They carried off a number of small arms, including an old duelling pistol, one old six-barrel pistol, two shotguns, assorted ammunition, swords and even military texts. Carty was arrested three days later during searches by military and police and jailed for his part in the raid.[42] Occasionally the IRA met opposition. In one house the owner barricaded the door and wounded one of the raiders; in another a woman used a knife to defend the house.[43] The local press reported that the RIC had been very busy collecting weapons lest they fall into IRA hands.[44] In response to IRA activity, the police, assisted by troops, carried out searches including what the *Sligo Champion* called the 100th search for the notorious Hayes.[45]

Mail cars were also raided by the IRA. At the end of January 1920 the Sligo–Ballyshannon and the Ballymote–Aclare services ceased temporarily owing to the number of raids. At the end of April the Ballymote to Aclare mail car was held up by armed and masked men and letters for Tubbercurry RIC, registered items and a sum of money taken. Some of these raids were the work of ordinary thieves and in May the IRA arrested and punished those responsible for some south Sligo mail raids.[46] The jailing of Carty and Hunt at this time meant that the impetus started by Carty's arms raids waned and IRA activity tailed off. By the time Carty was active again, the smaller rural and isolated RIC barracks had been evacuated. Hunt recalled that his area was quiet until July 1920.[47]

The authorities adopted a policy of abandoning small rural police stations and consolidating the RIC in more substantial and better defended barracks in late 1919.[48] In County Sligo, Strandhill and Rosses Point were evacuated in September and Grange, Ross, Clogher, Templehouse and Keash followed suit in November.[49] The CI explained that the purpose of these closures was 'to augment the remaining stations with a view to resisting any sudden attack' in light of the considerable political unrest and growing feeling of hostility to the police (see map 4 and plate 9).[50] There was a general IRA order to destroy all evacuated RIC barracks and tax office records on Easter Saturday night, 3 April 1920. Pilkington led a raid on Sligo Custom House/Income Tax office as well as the houses of three tax collectors and destroyed records. Only five of the eleven unoccupied RIC stations in the county were burned on that night, four in south Sligo and one in the Mayo Brigade area of west Sligo. Those still occupied by policemen's families were not destroyed and Pilkington asked GHQ what to do about those.[51] In early May the three abandoned north Sligo barracks – Rosses Point, Drumcliff and Strandhill – were demolished, the occupants having first been removed and made comfortable.[52] From then on police stations were burned or demolished by the IRA soon after they were vacated. Seven were burned in Sligo in July as was the coastguard station at Skreen. Cloonacool barracks was 'dismantled' rather than destroyed because the owner was a local IRA member, and when Ballintogher was evacuated the owner occupied the building.[53]

The agrarian question was never far from the surface in Sligo. Unrest during 1919 centred on the purchase of a number of farms that SF considered should have been divided among local smallholders. These included Oldrock farm near Bunninadden, bought by Ballymote businessman and hotelier, Matthew Hannon. In early June four IRA members opened shotgun fire on the windows of Hannon's Hotel in Ballymote where Judge Wakely was staying on the eve of the trial of six men due to be charged with unlawful assembly in connection with this agitation. Hannon accused Sinn Féiners of adopting 'blackguardly methods' because their boycotting campaign had failed. This dispute was settled in July after the intervention of Fr Thomas Quinn, PP Bunninadden, McCabe and P.J. McDermott, a Bunninadden businessman and IPP supporter. Hannon relinquished the farm for the cost price plus interest.[54] In the Easkey district there was a campaign to have a farm owned by Robert Hillas Williams divided. A large meeting there on Sunday 29 May resulted in five men being jailed for unlawful assembly.[55] Agrarian agitation reached its peak in County Sligo during the summer. In July there were fourteen agrarian indictable offences, including three cases of firing into dwelling houses, two of cattle maiming, seven of masked and armed men breaking into dwelling houses and two of malicious injury. Sligo DI Alexander Dobbyn, writing the monthly report in the absence of the CI, believed that SF was behind the campaign. However, in fact SF was striving to control such agitation, which it viewed as an unwelcome distraction. In August Dobbyn reported that the unrest was settling down but 'the settlements in prospect are in reality surrender to the pressure exerted by the Sinn Féin clubs'.[56]

A wave of agrarian agitation swept the south and west of Ireland in early 1920 with parts of Galway, Roscommon and Mayo especially affected.[57] South Sligo was also disturbed; there were reports of cattle drives and intimidation of herdsmen by armed and masked men in May and June. The aim was the typical one of intimidating landowners into selling lands for division among locals.[58] In Sligo SF appears to have taken control of the agitation. Local committees were formed and landowners or agents approached with purchase offers. If the landowner agreed a price, then he was allowed to work the lands until the buyers could finalize the acquisition. If the landowner refused, stock were driven off the lands and workmen intimidated. Thomas O'Donnell, South Sligo SF president, was a leading figure in these negotiations and he represented south Sligo land committees in meetings with land agent Hal Wood-Martin on a number of occasions.[59] In May 1920 Wood-Martin successfully plotted with livestock dealers to take sheep off the south Sligo lands of absentee landlord Sir Douglas Newton, later an English MP, and sell them without the knowledge of the locals. Wood-Martin had advised the landlord: 'It is utterly impossible to work lands in hands, especially when the owner does not live in the country, and owing to intimidation the herds having ceased to work'.[60] Wood-Martin's customary advice to clients was to negotiate and agree a price, even if it was low, on the basis that the sale might not go through. No sales to local committees had taken place by July 1920 and in at least some cases, negotiations were still going on in early 1921.[61] In December 1920 some rents for south Sligo lands were being paid, though reductions were also being demanded.[62] The new Sligo CI, Thomas Neylon, reported no agrarian incidents in July or August. Two south Sligo landowners who had been the subject of agitation decided to sell farms, one to the agitators and the other to the Irish Republic.[63] Some loyalists had agrarian disputes settled by SF courts; at Mullaghroe, a court ordered republican police to protect those suffering violent land agitation.[64] Only five agrarian incidents were reported for Sligo for the rest of 1920.[65] Dáil Éireann appointed Kevin O'Shiel as a special judicial commissioner for agrarian disputes in May 1920 and in September he was appointed judicial commissioner of the newly established Dáil Land Commission.[66] His only sitting in Sligo was in January 1921 when he adjudicated in favour of the landlord in a north Sligo case.[67]

In the absence of local government elections, the dominance of SF was still not reflected in Sligo county public bodies and in June the party lost the chairmanships of Tubbercurry RDC and Board of Guardians which it had gained in 1919. In Dromore West, by contrast, M.J. Hanley, who had declared for SF, became chairman. John O'Dowd was re-elected chairman of Sligo County Council.[68] The uncertain hold of SF on Sligo town politics was reflected in the co-option of the nominee of Alderman Jinks, over Seamus MacGowan of SF, to a vacancy on Sligo Board of Guardians.[69]

By the beginning of 1920 the IRA in some Irish counties had intensified their activity, moving beyond low level operations such as raids for arms to attacks on defended RIC barracks. This increase, a 'sudden lurch from low to high gear' according to Peter Hart, did not happen in Sligo.[70] There was a reluctance to move from the intensive public activity that had characterized the county during 1918. IRA and SF leaders continued to be involved in defiant open drilling and parading, which resulted in their being imprisoned for short periods. Crucially this removed key IRA men when their services were most needed, disrupted the development of the organization and retarded a move to more coordinated activity. Normal agrarian agitation, especially in south Sligo, also proved a distraction. Some raids did yield arms but Sligo IRA did not have the leadership, the experience, or the numerical support to engage in more intensive operations. By mid-1920 the abandonment of smaller rural barracks left the Sligo IRA in nominal control of large areas of the county. The example of more advanced counties, severe criticism by headquarters and changes in British government policy resulted in a sudden change of approach by Sligo IRA in the second half of 1920 resulting in a series of attacks, ambushes and killings. These, though not comparable to those in more active counties, allowed Sligo IRA to claim to have played a significant part in the War of Independence.

7 The drift to violence in County Sligo

In mid-1920 the newly appointed Sligo CI, Thomas Neylon, was alarmed by the fact that the IRA 'have now got possession of large areas of the county which cannot be patrolled owing to the lack of police and military transport'. Having obtained information that IRA GHQ considered Sligo insufficiently active, he feared that 'the campaign of murder against police is about to be put into active operation in this county'.[1] Sligo IRA implemented a boycott of the RIC and significantly increased its military activity during the second half of 1920. Small groups under Pilkington, Carty, Hunt and Marren took offensive action that resulted in the first police fatalities. At the same time a hardening of the British government's attitude led to a more aggressive response by the Crown forces. Their increased presence in and near County Sligo resulted in British reprisals after the ambushes at Moneygold and Chaffpool and the killing of RIC Sergeant Fallon in Ballymote. Public revulsion at the IRA killings was immediately overshadowed by reaction to the reprisals, resulting in a general increase in support for the IRA. The arrests of prominent leaders in late 1920 together with seizures of IRA arms successfully reduced the capacity of the Sligo IRA to undertake large-scale operations by the end of the year; these developments also forced the most determined of the Sligo IRA to go 'on the run'.

IRA GHQ sanction for attacks on RIC barracks in January had been followed by assaults in the more active counties such as Cork. None took place in Sligo until early June when a party from Sligo town and north Sligo, led by Pilkington, attacked Fivemilebourne barracks, Leitrim. Although this failed, the station was subsequently abandoned and burned by the IRA.[2] The first sniping at barracks in Sligo took place in August at Castlebaldwin and Tubbercurry barracks.[3] Closures and consolidation meant that by the time IRA activity increased, the number of targets in Sligo had greatly diminished. By September only eight barracks remained occupied in the county: Cliffoney, Collooney, Ballymote, Tubbercurry, Easkey, Dromore West and two stations in Sligo town (see map 4).[4]

In mid-1920 GHQ extended the boycott of RIC to all those associated with the force. As this intensified, Sligo emerged as one of the most active counties.[5] In August CI Neylon reported 'a rigid boycott' of the RIC, which appears to have been especially enforced in Tubbercurry, Ballymote and Cliffoney.[6] Peter Gallagher RIC, stationed in Tubbercurry, believed 'People were friendly until the troubles. Then you wouldn't have one to talk to you'. This particularly applied to Protestants, he said, 'because they were afraid to be accused of giving us news'.[7] Notices and letters threatened those who worked for or supplied goods to the RIC. A hackney car and a donkey cart used by Ballymote RIC were burned and houses occupied by policemen were damaged in Sligo and

Ballymote. In the Tubbercurry area a policeman on leave was kidnapped, held for two days and released on promising to resign, and a girl who had associated with police was tarred and had her hair cropped.[8] That the boycott was never completely observed is clear from continued threats such as a notice in Tubbercurry at the end of September warning that 'certain ill-disposed persons in this town have been found in communication with and supplying goods to the members of the enemy army of occupation'.[9] The evacuation of Bunninadden barracks was regretted by some business people 'who were loyal to the police by leaving goods in their back yards to suit their requirements while at the same time trying to keep the fair side of the Volunteers'. In September Collooney police visited the person they considered to be behind the boycott there, which ended within three weeks.[10]

There were few overtly sectarian incidents at the time but the Protestant graveyard in Tubbercurry was vandalized in mid-January 1920 and an attempt was made to burn Tubbercurry Church of Ireland church at the end of August. The damage was slight and the local IRA arrested three men who were released after pleading guilty and paying compensation.[11]

The most spectacular Sligo operation was the rescue of Frank Carty from Sligo jail on the night of 26 June in a well-planned, well-executed brigade operation led by Pilkington. A friendly warder facilitated communication with Carty. Ten men from south Sligo, as well as IRA from Sligo town and north Sligo, took part. Outlying sections blocked and guarded the approach road. Thirteen men climbed into the jail on wooden ladders and overpowered the night patrolman, the warder and the governor. The cell keys were taken and Carty released. The Volunteers smashed in a door and all got out safely.[12] After this morale-boosting jailbreak there was a significant increase in IRA activity, although a number of ambushes, at least one near Ballymote and two in north Sligo, failed when the RIC did not turn up.[13] The first successful ambush took place on 26 July when eight members of the Riverstown Battalion, armed with two revolvers and six shotguns, held up a four-man RIC cycle patrol at Ballyrush near Castlebaldwin. After a 'lively exchange of shots', in which one policeman was injured, the police surrendered. They were disarmed and released.[14] In September north Sligo IRA took part in a successful arms raid on Tempo barracks in Fermanagh.[15]

In line with the rest of the country, the railways were a particular target for the IRA. The diminished police presence, especially in the Ballymote-Gurteen area where the IRA was very active, led to frequent hold-ups on the railway line there from May 1920. Mail, official correspondence and goods consigned to the RIC were taken.[16] A large sum of money sent from the Ulster Bank, Ballymote to Belfast was kept for IRA expenses with Pilkington's agreement.[17] An IRA scout often travelled on a train to inform waiting IRA of the presence of police or military; Crown forces were then usually disarmed.[18] The railway strike, a refusal by railwaymen to transport British soldiers or munitions, which began in

May, was uneven in its adoption and effect. At the end of June an engine driver refused to take armed soldiers from Sligo to Enniskillen. On the following day the soldiers were transported only when the railway workers were assured that they carried no arms or ammunition.[19] The Collooney to Claremorris line was reported to be closed for a period in July as a result of the strike.[20]

Throughout 1920 the government continued to view the Irish situation as a policing operation and reinforced the RIC with temporary constables, the so-called Black and Tans, and the highly mobile Auxiliary Division, which was deployed in disturbed areas in companies of about one hundred men. This development, together with the Restoration of Order in Ireland Act in August 1920, described as a 'halfway house to martial law', changed the nature of the conflict.[21] From mid-October Auxiliaries were stationed at the residence of The McDermott at Coolavin, south Sligo, recognition no doubt that this area had become disturbed. After a month there, following representations by the house owners, the company moved to Boyle.[22] The British military presence in Sligo was also strengthened. On 20 August the 1st Battalion, Bedfordshire and Hertfordshire Regiment moved from Belfast to Finner Camp at Ballyshannon. C Company, comprising just over 100 men, was sent on detachment to Sligo military barracks. Their motor transport consisted of one 3-ton lorry and two Crossley cars. This contingent and B Company from Finner Camp were active against the IRA. Captain Dunnill of the Bedfordshire and Hertfordshire Regiment recorded that 'Raids and searches were carried out almost every day in every part of the county which was at this time in a very disturbed state'.[23] The 1st Battalion East Yorkshire Regiment, with a detachment of 3 officers and 68 other ranks at Boyle and one officer and 34 men at Drumdoe, in Roscommon, operated in south Sligo.[24] Drumdoe, south of Lough Arrow, was the country residence of Lord French.

Previously safe IRA areas were now threatened. Raids in the Gurteen district on 20 August resulted in three arrests and the narrow escape of Commandants Marren and Hunt after an exchange of fire. One of those arrested, John Finn, captain of Gurteen Company IRA, was charged in September with aiding and abetting two privates of the East Yorkshire detachment at Drumdoe who came to the area as deserters on 2 August. Finn secured work for them at Kelly's Hotel, Gurteen and questioned them about the Drumdoe garrison. A few days later the soldiers gave themselves up at Ballymote barracks. Finn was sentenced to two years' hard labour. Around this time the IRA in the Conway's Cross/Geevagh area were contacted by another British soldier claiming to be a deserter from Drumdoe. They were sceptical and the soldier, named as John Watt, was court martialled, convicted of being a spy, executed and buried in a bog.[25]

Increased activity by Crown forces resulted in a drop in IRA action nationwide during September and October but this was not so in Sligo.[26] The late escalation of IRA operations and Carty's morale boosting rescue resulted in the August to November period being the most disturbed in the county. West Sligo IRA, part of the North Mayo brigade, captured and burned Enniscrone coast-guard station on 26 August. The garrison of ten was disarmed after a short exchange of fire and six rifles, six revolvers, telescopes, binoculars and gelignite were captured. The following Saturday military and police raided Enniscrone and arrested four men, three of whom were later convicted of having taken part in the attack.[27]

The first ambush involving Sligo IRA that resulted in fatalities occurred on 1 September. Hoping to capture arms, Marren and Hunt with a group of twenty-five men from Gurteen and Ballymote Battalions ambushed a five-man RIC cycle patrol, on its way from Ballaghaderreen to Frenchpark petty sessions, at Ratra Crossroads just across the county boundary in Roscommon. The ambushers were armed with four or five rifles, shotguns and revolvers. The extended police formation was unexpected and upset the IRA's plans. When the leading cyclist reached the ambush position, fire was opened. Constable Martin McCarthy was mortally wounded and two others surrendered. At the rear of the main ambush position, out of range of the main party, Captain Thomas McDonagh of the Gurteen Battalion and Constable Edward Murphy died in an exchange of fire. The IRA withdrew, taking the captured arms but leaving McDonagh's body behind: the corpse was said to have been dragged through the streets of Ballaghaderreen by Crown forces. A number of buildings were burned in the town as a reprisal that night.[28]

After his rescue Carty intensified IRA activity in the Tubbercurry area. His group had only four or five rifles but GHQ informed them that if they carried out an ambush they would be entitled to buy arms. He and a group of about twenty men from Tubbercurry, Ballymote and Gurteen ambushed and disarmed a cycling party of four RIC near Chaffpool on 10 August. Carty duly went to Dublin with £360 collected from merchants and purchased six Lee Enfield rifles, 1,000 rounds of .303 ammunition, some hand grenades and gelignite.[29] Tubbercurry IRA sniped the local barracks on several nights in August, injuring two policemen on one occasion. The police returned fire but did not pursue their attackers.[30]

The upsurge of IRA activity led to more intense activity by Crown forces. On 30 September Carty, with about twelve riflemen, set an ambush at Chaffpool on the usual police route from Sligo via Ballymote targeting the new DI, 21-year-old Dublinman James Joseph Brady, who had just transferred to Sligo from Monaghan. When the RIC's Crossley tender reached the ambush position, fire was opened. Brady was mortally wounded and two constables less seriously so. The police returned fire and the tender continued to Tubbercurry barracks where Brady died. Carty maintained that he had plans to protect Tubbercurry town and local creameries from reprisals but these proved totally ineffective. DI

Russell arrived with RIC and soldiers from Sligo and later that night police and military carried out reprisals. Press reports state that Russell did his best to restrain the police and military but they burned at least fourteen shops and business premises believed to be owned by republican sympathizers. Rathscanlon and Achonry creameries were also burned. Of the IRA's futile attempts to protect Tubbercurry, Jack Brennan commented: 'This wasn't good for our reputation'.[31] Dunnill's account mentions no burnings or reprisals, merely stating that a party from C Company, Sligo carried out extensive searches in Tubbercurry and it appears that both military and RIC took part in the burnings.[32]

The Tubbercurry reprisals made headlines. A Dublin Castle statement stressed the effect that the killing of Brady had on Crown forces: 'When the men [RIC and military] saw DI Brady lying dead on the floor ... they broke out of hand and rushed out into the streets calling on the Sinn Feiners to come out and fight them like men. Reprisals continued until early in the morning despite the efforts of the officers'.[33] Sir Hamar Greenwood, the Chief Secretary, claimed that everyone who suffered in the reprisals connived at or condoned the murder.[34] Brady's father wrote to the Tubbercurry parish priest: 'We forgive from our hearts whoever was responsible for this deed. My wife and I were deeply grieved to learn of the reprisals which have taken place in your parish' and the parish priest asked for prayers for the dead policeman.[35] A statement from Bishop Morrisroe, read at Masses in Tubbercurry, expressed his sympathy with the people. He said that he held 'bad government' primarily responsible but he also blamed the IRA, criticizing 'the fostering during the latter years of ideals clearly impossible of attainment'.[36] The *Sligo Independent* appealed to the RIC to maintain their self-control and 'to the people of Sligo to see that this will be the first and last murder committed in our midst'.[37] The surprisingly unsympathetic official IRA reaction surely coloured Sligo Brigade's subsequent dealings with GHQ. *An t-Óglach* commented:

> In the West the guerrilla warfare was not so energetic to greatly relax the grips of the old RIC on the countryside and they are now striving desperately to regain their role with the aid of foreign reinforcements by wholesale terrorism. The volunteers of those parts of the West where this reign of terrorism is being carried on have only themselves to thank for it.[38]

Large-scale searches followed in the Tubbercurry area but there were no arrests. A Tubbercurry RIC constable who resigned in protest at the reprisals was warned to leave the town and did so after his house was fired on.[39] This pattern of unofficial reprisals in 'almost instantaneous response to ambushes or shootings' by Crown forces had become commonplace throughout the country during the second half of 1920.[40]

It appears that whether central co-ordination was involved or not, north Sligo IRA now believed that it was their turn to mount a serious operation to emulate those of Ballymote/Gurteen, west Sligo, and Tubbercurry IRA. Between thirty and forty north Sligo IRA under the command of Pilkington and Seamus Devins ambushed a nine-man RIC cycle patrol from Cliffoney, led by Sergeant Patrick Perry, just before noon on 25 October at Moneygold, three miles from their barracks. The RIC had been lured out to investigate a report of malicious damage. Five or six of the ambushers had rifles, some borrowed from Sligo, others had shotguns. Perry was killed outright (see plate 16) as were Constables Keown and Laffey. Constable Lynch died that evening. The others surrendered. Linda Kearns, a nurse, was present and attended to some of the wounded. Some ambushers stayed close by to defend the area in the event of reprisals but when no Crown forces arrived that night, they moved to Glenade in Leitrim. Auxiliaries from Coolavin travelled to north Sligo some days later and carried out searches and reprisals. Constable Thomas Kelly, Sligo RIC, pointed out houses belonging to IRA activists and at least ten were burned as well as the SF hall, a public house and shop, Grange hall and Ballintrillick creamery. Eugene Gilbride had been a member of the ambushing party but his parents' house was spared by a Sligo officer on learning that Gilbride's father had just died.[41]

The jubilation at this IRA action and arms seizure did not last long. The arms were recovered one month later when a car driven by Linda Kearns and containing three prominent north Sligo IRA men, Devins, Gilbride and Andrew Conway, ran into a convoy of RIC and military on the outskirts of Sligo. It appears that the men and arms were being driven to the south of the county for an ambush. Pilkington was said to have been advised by headquarters to take pressure off north Sligo in this manner. The men were badly beaten and, with Kearns, were sent to Belfast for trial but no witness could be found to identify them as participants in the Moneygold ambush. Gilbride claimed that Constable Joyce, who survived the ambush, refused to identify him.[42] Tensions were high in the days following the arrests and triumphant Auxiliaries visited north Sligo and Sligo town, searched civilians and painted slogans, 'Shinners Beware', 'Remember Balbriggan', 'Up Lloyd George'. The *Sligo Independent* asserted that 'The law was certainly not one-sided, Roman Catholics, Protestants, Sinn Féiners, Nationalists, Unionists, Loyalists all got the same sauce'. The same group painted similar slogans in Enniscrone and burned a hall. Houses occupied by Kearns' relations were searched, windows broken, slogans painted on walls and a haggard burned.[43] The arrest of such senior IRA from the same area together with the capture of arms was a serious blow. As Daniel Waters of Cliffoney IRA put it, 'These events paralysed the IRA in North Sligo for a time'.[44] Further setbacks followed. When Ballintrillick creamery was being rebuilt, the manager employed non-union workers, small farmers generally, something resented by union members. Although both groups belonged to the IRA, a split resulted, with the O/C taking the union side and the vice O/C the other.[45]

November, the most disturbed month of the war elsewhere in the country, saw a reduction in IRA activity in Sligo following debilitating arms seizures and arrests. Pilkington broke his ankle in a fall in Sligo Abbey ruins while evading a search party and was out of action for a time. In his absence, Carty organized thirty members of north and south Sligo IRA for an ambush close to the scene of the 1798 battle of Carrignagat near Collooney. When four military lorries came along instead of the expected police patrol, he let them pass unwilling to engage such a large force.[46] Carty himself became ill with pleurisy and was recaptured on 25 November by military and Auxiliaries who surrounded the house near Tubbercurry in which he was recuperating. He was taken to Sligo barracks and transferred to Derry jail.[47] Charles Gildea, who became O/C Tubbercurry Battalion on Carty's arrest, reported low IRA morale due to the arrests and increased enemy activity. He tried to counteract this by concentrating on the Belfast boycott, court martials of supposed enemies and opponents, and organizing an active service unit (ASU) and an intelligence unit.[48]

The Belfast boycott began in August 1920 when the Dáil passed a motion imposing an embargo on goods from Belfast in retaliation for attacks on Catholics there.[49] At the end of August public meetings in Tubbercurry, Ballymote and Sligo asked traders to stop dealing with Belfast firms.[50] The IRA regularly searched trains and removed Belfast products with railway officials and workers passing on information about such items.[51] Shops selling Belfast goods were also raided: 'The goods collected were usually destroyed, but in some cases they were sold and the monies put into our funds. We of course made good use of cigarettes when we found them'.[52]

The pressure from increased police and military activity in late 1920 forced active IRA men to go on the run in Sligo as elsewhere, particularly after the Ratra, Moneygold and Chaffpool ambushes. As enemy activity and searches intensified, these small groups merged into active service units or flying columns.[53] In the Sligo town area, Tom Scanlon went on the run at the end of 1919 with three or four others from Sligo Battalion. These, including Pilkington, operated with men from north Sligo until the arrests and arms capture in November 1920. They then formed a small ASU of fourteen men with some IRA from south-east Sligo.[54] The south Sligo ASU comprised members of the Ballymote and Gurteen Battalions, led by Hunt and Marren, with a base in the Falleens area close to Lough Gara.[55] These columns were loosely organized and took advantage of mountainous terrain along the Ox Mountains and in the south and east of the county but also used safe houses in and near towns and villages.[56] Each group operated independently, though prominent activists sometimes took part in operations outside their own areas. Arms were occasionally shared, but Linda Kearns' statement that 'It seemed as if a couple of flying columns were using the same material. I would bring them to Chaffpool one day and perhaps the next day back to Grange' does appear to be an exaggeration.[57] An attempt was made in January 1921 to form a Sligo Brigade ASU comprising men from Tubbercurry, Collooney, Ballymote and Gurteen Battalions with a base in a hunting lodge near Coolaney. This body had to be disbanded after a week because of sickness and the men went back to their own areas and operated as before.[58] The CI's reference in March 1921 to the formation of a murder gang of twenty-four of the most prominent IRA officers and men may pertain to this flying column.[59]

The progress of Terence MacSwiney's hunger strike in Brixton prison was followed carefully in Sligo. All business premises in Sligo town closed on 23 October for one hour to enable citizens to attend a Mass in the cathedral for MacSwiney and other hunger strikers.[60] Following MacSwiney's death on 25 October, a day of mourning in Sligo was observed on 29 October with practically all businesses closed and a special Mass celebrated in the cathedral. In Ballymote mourning flags were widely displayed and in Collooney police arrived about eleven o'clock and ordered the shops which had remained closed to open. They complied.[61] The only other killing of a policeman in Sligo in 1920 was that of Sergeant Patrick Fallon in Ballymote on 3 November a few days after MacSwiney's death when tensions remained high. He was shot by two local members of the IRA; however, it appears that the killing was not sanctioned by battalion officers. There was widespread fear that reprisals on the scale of Tubbercurry or north Sligo would ensue and consequently shops were closed and many people fled the town. Auxiliaries from Ballaghaderreen and a party of the Bedfordshire Regiment from Sligo arrived and burned a number of local business premises and houses. Local newspapers reported that were it not for the exertions of local RIC, including DI Russell, many more premises would have been destroyed. Two IRA men from the Ballymote area, neither of whom were involved, were arrested in connection with the killing.[62] Ballymote December fair was subsequently proclaimed and SF halls at Geevagh, Gleann, Riverstown and Skreen were burned.[63]

The changed circumstances of 1920 meant that the activities of Cumann na mBan took on a much more military role in Sligo.[64] The organization was proscribed in mid-1920 and an early 1921 reorganization saw branches closely attached to IRA companies.[65] Margaret Kennedy, an organizer from headquarters, worked in Sligo in 1920 and 1921 and cooperated in setting up links between the IRA and Cumann na mBan.[66] As the conflict developed, it appears that the branch structure ceased to exist in Sligo but Cumann na mBan members, as individuals and in small groups, performed a range of key functions. Traditionally women provided safe houses for the fighting men, fed them,

washed their clothes and tended their wounds. While some Sligo members did
carry out this sort of work, their statements stress more dangerous assignments
such as carrying dispatches, passing on intelligence about enemy strengths and
movements and moving IRA arms and ammunition.[67] Male soldiers did not
search females and few female searchers were employed by Crown forces at this
stage in the conflict.[68] Typically female Sligo activists were unmarried and many
were members of prominent IRA families. For example, the Molloy, Coleman
and Hannon families in the Ballymote area had both male and female activists.[69]
The best-known Sligo woman activist at this time, Linda Kearns, was not a
Cumann na mBan member. She carried dispatches between Dublin and Sligo by
train until she acquired a car in 1920 which she then also used for carrying arms
and ammunition. In autumn 1920 she operated extensively in the Sligo area,
assisting Pilkington and Carty in particular.[70]

At the end of 1920 the Sligo CI boasted about the number of prominent IRA
members arrested and claimed that 'The police are slowly but surely becoming
masters of the situation … they are absolutely confident that the battle will end
in the complete rout of the revolutionary forces'.[71] He also reported that 'secret
information' led to two arrests at Ballisodare and the uncovering of a cache of
ten revolvers, ammunition and gelignite in the O'Connor tomb in Sligo
cemetery.[72] Military searches in Sligo town led to a number of arrests in
November and December and some revolvers were found in a search of the
Wanderers Gaelic club.[73] Members of Sligo's unionist community organized a
Christmas concert for the military in Sligo town who also played football and
rugby matches and attended a New Year's Eve ball in Finner Camp.[74]

The intensification in the offensive operations of Sligo IRA during the second
half of 1920 resulted in three ambushes of RIC and ten deaths; all but one of
these were members of the Crown forces. Forty-nine Crown forces had been
killed in all of Connacht during 1920. The increase in Sligo was significant but
the county remained far behind the most active counties such as Cork,
Tipperary, Limerick and Kerry.[75] Increased action did, however, confer on the
Sligo IRA a level of local credibility and reprisals by the Crown forces increased
their popular support. Arrests and arms seizures caused a lull in activity towards
the end of 1920 but as elsewhere in the country an unexpected result of greater
pressure by the Crown forces was the emergence of IRA active service units
(ASUs). In Sligo such small determined and mobile groups were able to elude
capture and continue to engage in small-scale offensive actions until the truce in
mid-1921 due to their local knowledge and support. While the more aggressive
policy and stronger presence of the Crown forces certainly curtailed the effectiveness of the IRA, a comprehensive victory was never achieved.

8 Stalemate

The first six months of 1921 saw the Crown forces improve their position throughout the country by using more flexible operational methods that limited the effectiveness of IRA ASUs and increased pressure on the most active IRA areas. The ability of the IRA to carry out major operations such as attacks on police barracks was curtailed. Recognizing this, IRA GHQ encouraged regular, smaller operations to harass the enemy. Road-trenching, tree felling and destruction of bridges restricted the mobility of the Crown forces and limited their ability to dominate the countryside, thus enabling the IRA columns to survive. At the same time full-scale martial law was not imposed due to political considerations. County Sligo during this period witnessed a continuation of generally small-scale IRA activities especially in the south of the county. A few more ambitious operations were also carried out, such as the Culleens ambush, the Sligo jail break and the killing of two policemen at Ballisodare. Nevertheless, IRA headquarters was consistently dissatisfied with the level of performance of the Sligo IRA. An attempt to respond to this criticism in the form of a major attack on a police barracks proved an embarrassing failure. During this period there were various changes in the deployment of Crown forces, army and Auxiliaries in Sligo and neighbouring counties in an apparent effort to contain IRA activity in south Sligo. The British response was hampered by trenched and blocked roads never designed for heavy vehicles, by the IRA's local knowledge and by the availability of replacement officers when arrests were made. Efforts at large-scale round-ups by the Crown forces did not yield many arrests and by mid-1921 a stalemate had developed.

In January IRA activities included frequent raids on the mail services, sniping at Sligo prison, the wounding of two RIC constables during sniping in Tubbercurry and an attack on a police patrol on the Bunninadden to Ballymote road.[1] In February the IRA bombed Ballymote courthouse in an attempt to draw police into an ambush. When this failed, shots were fired at the barracks. That same month south Sligo IRA cooperated with East Mayo Brigade in what was to be a major attack on Ballaghaderreen barracks. A home-made mine was brought from Keash to Ballaghaderreen, concealed in a hay cart, but when Volunteers trying to position the cart at the barracks wall were challenged by an RIC patrol, the attack was abandoned.[2] The Auxiliaries stationed in Boyle workhouse had made little progress in south Sligo and Jim Hunt taunted their commander in February, writing: 'Your men have invested our area again and again ... You have failed in fulfilling your objects ... The men "on the run" are still at liberty ... You have failed to get any information to bring about their capture'. He challenged the Auxiliaries to meet his men in an open fight on equal terms.[3]

In an apparent response to the continued activity in south Sligo, the just over 200 men of the 1st Battalion, Bedfordshire Regiment moved headquarters at the end of February from Finner Camp to Boyle and took responsibility for Sligo, Leitrim and north Roscommon. Dunnill recorded that this area was in a 'considerably more disturbed state than our previous stations'. C Company remained at Sligo.[4] The main weapon used against the IRA in Ireland in early 1921 was the large-scale search. It was, according to Dunnill, the only 'effective way to locate these men'. The first of these drives in Sligo was carried out east of Cliffoney at the beginning of January with troops from Sligo and Finner Camp, Auxiliaries from Boyle and RIC from various stations surrounding the area and meeting eight hours later at the centre. All houses were searched and men were sent to collection points for identification by local police. The drive proved ineffective; only five men were detained, four of whom were subsequently released.[5] Such searches and drives were common during the next six months and were similarly unsuccessful (see plate 12).[6] In March Dunnill and a sergeant of the Bedfordshires attended a three-day course in guerrilla warfare at the Curragh in County Kildare; the commencement in April of what Dunnill called 'circus patrols' may have been a result. These were motorized patrols of twenty to forty troops that visited a number of villages and sometimes stayed overnight. The advantages, according to Dunnill, were 'it enables an area to be searched much more thoroughly' and the element of surprise. In fact the trenching of roads and destruction of bridges by the IRA disrupted travel and nullified much of the surprise.[7]

The Sligo Brigade report for April listed 'extensive road cutting and blockading'. Deep trenches cut in the railway bridge at Mullaghroe made it impassable for vehicular traffic. In April the military forced locals to repair trenched roads at Cloonloo so that their lorries could pass but then to reopen the trenches to prevent local farmers attending Boyle market the following day. In May bridges were demolished near Ballymote and Gurteen and at Drumcliff and Grange.[8] Jim Hunt recounted that by the truce people were beginning to resent the inconvenience caused by road blocking and trenching.[9] The state of the road network in south Sligo was a major issue for the military, judging by Dunnill's comments and the number of photographs of damaged roads his account includes (see plate 14). He does not mention any steps taken to deal with this apart from compelling locals, who may have also been involved in digging the trenches, to repair them.[10] In June a circus patrol encountered one road in south Sligo trenched in thirty-six places and blocked by two fallen trees! While admitting that few arrests resulted from such patrols, Dunnill claimed that their importance lay in their 'moral effect ... it is found that after a visit by a patrol of this kind there is a very pronounced falling off in the number of outrages committed'.[11] In fact, this was just wishful thinking.

There was considerable activity by Crown forces in Sligo town in February.

Three platoons were sent from headquarters to reinforce the company there. Extensive searches were conducted including all patrons at the Picture Theatre and the Harp and Shamrock Hotel and the grounds, interior and vaults of the Catholic cathedral. The *Connachtman* claimed that seven civilians were taken as hostages on military lorries during these searches. On 8 February a patrol in Sligo town was said to have searched over 200 people between 9.45 p.m. and midnight without any significant arrest. Curfews imposed throughout the 5th Division area and month-long curfews in Sligo and Tubbercurry in mid-February had little effect. The *Sligo Independent* thought the curfew unnecessary but reported no difficulty in its enforcement.[12] The CI's boast that 243 IRA members had been arrested in raids during February seems grossly inflated and may include those released almost immediately. The only prominent IRA leader arrested at this time was Charles Gildea, O/C Tubbercurry Battalion, described by CI Neylon as one of the most dangerous men in Sligo.[13] Michael Nevin, Sligo Battalion I/O, was arrested in March but was released in May as a result, he believed, of representations made by Bishop Patrick O'Donnell of Raphoe who was a friend of his employers and 'had some influence with the British authorities'.[14]

During the first half of 1921 CI Neylon continually described Sligo as being in a very disturbed state, particularly the Ballymote-Gurteen area, where Hunt and Marren were active. Their small-scale activities continued to net weapons and ammunition. The railway line between Ballymote and Kilfree Junction and the branch line from Kilfree to Ballaghaderreen proved easy targets.[15] Trains were regularly stopped, RIC and soldiers on board were disarmed and Belfast goods taken. There were also break-ins at Sligo, Carrowmore, Ballymote and Curry stations for Belfast products.[16] In January an IRA party under Hunt overpowered and disarmed a DI and two constables at Kilfree station and later the same day opened fire on train carriages occupied by a group of the Bedfordshire Regiment as the train left the station.[17] On 6 May Marren led a party of between thirty and forty IRA armed with ten to fifteen rifles and various other firearms, which held up the Dublin to Sligo train. Two soldiers and five Auxiliaries were disarmed and dispatches taken.[18]

The ease with which south Sligo IRA raided trains led to Hunt's capture in mid-May when, in a bizarre escapade, he and two other IRA men hijacked a train near Kilfree. They took it as far as the railway bridge at Ballaghaderreen from where they opened rifle fire on the RIC barracks. Fire was returned and one attacker injured. Unable to reverse the locomotive, they abandoned it and retreated under fire but Hunt was captured. Dunnill called him 'one of their most capable and clever leaders'. He was court-martialled but an attempt to have him identified as a participant in the Ratra ambush failed when a policeman, whose life Hunt had spared, refused to identify him.[19] Joe Finnegan replaced Hunt as O/C Gurteen Battalion and the raiding of trains continued with hold-ups recorded on 19 and 26 May, 10, 14, 23 and 29 June, and 6 July.[20]

At the end of May Marren held up a train on which Major E.S.C. Grune, commander of the Sligo contingent of the Bedfordshire Regiment, was travelling to a dance in Boyle, off duty and unarmed. The major was identified by a visiting card in his wallet. Grune was impressed with the organization and armament of the IRA. Signallers were equipped with flags and field glasses and the IRA were armed not with shotguns but with Winchester and service rifles and 'a selection of revolvers'. Marren identified himself to Grune and they chatted and smoked while the train was being searched. The fifty or so IRA then travelled on the train as far as Kilfree. Discussing history with Grune, Marren told him 'We are fighting for freedom, political freedom, that's all' and asked him to do whatever he could for Jim Hunt, then a prisoner in Boyle. Grune duly contacted Hunt whose requests for a pane of glass to be taken out of his cell window for ventilation and whitewash to brighten up the cell were granted.[21]

There was no indication of increased brutality in Sligo such as that noted in Longford.[22] Crown forces were disarmed and released unharmed by the IRA. There was only one fatality in the south Sligo area during this period. Just after midnight on St Patrick's Day, a police patrol in plain clothes ran into an IRA party in Ballymote and in an exchange of fire Constable James O'Brien was fatally wounded. An IRA man, Jim Molloy, was captured at the scene and beaten up at the barracks. He was imprisoned in Boyle barracks.[23]

Other parts of the county were much less active. North Sligo IRA never recovered from the arrests and arms seizures by Crown forces in 1920. The battalion O/C could only instance four cases of firing on enemy forces during 1921. One was an attempted ambush hurriedly organized in which the Crown forces were unaware of the IRA gunfire because, one of the attackers surmised, their lorry was backfiring badly.[24] Given the concentration of Crown forces in Sligo town, unsurprisingly, little activity took place there in 1921. However, prominent Sligo town IRA leaders, including Pilkington and Scanlon, remained at large and there were Belfast boycott raids on the railway station, a jailbreak in June and the burning of a BP oil depot in early July.[25]

Sligo Brigade never functioned to the satisfaction of IRA GHQ which repeatedly complained during early 1921 of unacknowledged dispatches, queries unanswered and reports being generally unsatisfactory.[26] Michael Collins berated Pilkington in March for lack of activity and in response a major brigade assault on Collooney barracks was planned. Men from Sligo, Ballymote, Gurteen and Collooney battalions assembled on the night of 20 March and a bomb made by Marren in Keash was used to blow in the barracks door. There was confusion as the attacking party, led by Pilkington, tried to get through the smoke and debris. The defenders opened fire immediately, forcing the IRA to withdraw. 'Everyone started to ask everyone else what the so and so happened', recalled Harold McBrien, O/C Riverstown Battalion, 'Pilkington, after saying a few angry words to us made off in the direction of Sligo'.[27] Pilkington's March report enumerated only seven actions, including the failed Collooney attack. The IRA AG informed Richard Mulcahy, chief of staff, that he considered 'this from Sligo is very poor indeed.'[28] The reports for April and May were no better – brief and lacking detail.[29] Pilkington depended on battalion commandants to supply him with details for his reports but there was little evidence of a proper chain of command or reporting system in the Sligo Brigade at this time. Many of the south Sligo IRA activities were never reported to GHQ. When Pilkington told GHQ that he could not take responsibility for increasing activity in his area unless he received more resources, Mulcahy criticized his 'tendency to poor mouth and complain' and warned that if he was unable to increase activity in his area, he could resign. Sligo Brigade battalion officers subsequently wrote to Mulcahy asserting their confidence in Pilkington: 'Taking into consideration the small amount of war material at our disposal and the extraordinary enemy force in the area very few men would accept the responsibility'.[30] In a letter to Mulcahy, Pilkington conceded: 'My faults, my shortcomings, my incapacities you have emphasized and depicted very vividly and admittedly correctly' but asserted that the majority of his communications to GHQ had remained unacknowledged and unanswered.[31] Pilkington's complaints seem to have elicited at least the promise of some supplies from GHQ to be sent direct from Liverpool. But Sligo Brigade had independently sent John Lynch to Liverpool to buy arms in April in contravention of GHQ rules. The brigade was ordered to recall Lynch, yet he was still in Liverpool in June.[32] There were some impressive operations by Pilkington and the Sligo IRA. Constable Thomas Kelly of Sligo barracks had been a marked man since pointing out houses to be burned after the Moneygold ambush. On 19 April a group of nine IRA led by Pilkington, acting on intelligence, took Kelly and Constable James Hetherington from a train at Ballisodare and shot them dead.[33]

The IRA were involved in a range of other activities in the county, enforcing the Belfast boycott, collecting rates, constructing dugouts, cautioning spies and warning off those suspected of assisting the enemy.[34] In May two sisters from the Cliffoney area had their hair cropped because they spoke to policemen and two girls in Sligo had their hair cut for 'keeping company with soldiers'.[35] The IRA collected dog licence money and in some cases, as at Culfadda in May, shot dogs found to have been already licensed. In retaliation the RIC served summonses in about 400 cases of non-payment of dog licences and many dog owners had to pay twice.[36]

Only one person was shot as an alleged spy by Sligo IRA, contrasting sharply with other parts of the country.[37] On the night of 14 April Thomas Walker, a 72-year-old civil bill officer of the county court living north of Sligo, was shot and his body left on the roadside with a notice 'Spies and Informers beware. IRA' attached. The IRA I/O for the area opposed the action but was over-ruled.[38] Other suspected spies were exiled. In the Gurteen area, for example, an ex-

British naval officer, believed to have given information about the IRA to Ballaghaderreen RIC, was banished. In the Easkey area two or three were exiled and another in south Sligo was sentenced to death but fled to Canada.[39] Harold McBrien said 'We had suspicions about certain individuals in the area but we were not able to trace it down to them' and Tom Scanlon claimed that they did not meet anyone in the Sligo area acting for the enemy.[40] Two Sligo Protestant businessmen, Joseph Graham and George R. Williams, later claimed to have given important information to the RIC including some which led to IRA arrests.[41]

That the execution of alleged spies in the county was rare may have been because intelligence gathering by the Sligo IRA was poorly developed. Michael Nevin, I/O Sligo Battalion, never succeeded in making contact with any member of the RIC or British forces in the town. The IRA's principal source of information in Sligo town was believed to be Fr J.J. Hanly of Summerhill College, a friend of DI John Russell, who, according to Nevin, 'was inclined to be friendly'.[42] R.G. Bradshaw, I/O Sligo Brigade, told Michael Collins in February that they had reliable men in Sligo post office but Collins was displeased with the irregularity and illegibility of Bradshaw's communications: 'The slovenly character of this despatch is a disgrace'. In July Bradshaw said that although he had not yet established direct contact with the military he was 'in definite touch with police in DI's office through a third party' who may have been Fr Hanly.[43] J.J. Dockery, I/O Ballymote Battalion, made contact with Constable Patrick Madden, who supplied details of armaments, strengths and some information on raids from mid-1920 until the truce.[44]

The stationing of P Company, Auxiliary Division in Tubbercurry during April seems to have been a response by the authorities to IRA activity in south Sligo. According to Martin Brennan, 'they were a damn decent crowd'.[45] On 15 May the O/C Tubbercurry Auxiliaries was fired on as he drove from Easkey to Tubbercurry but escaped injury.[46] More seriously, on 23 May two constables were wounded near Keash when an IRA party under Tom Brehony, O/C Keash, fired on three Crossley tenders and a Ford car carrying thirteen Auxiliaries and thirteen RIC.[47] In June IRA attacks were reported between Tubbercurry and Charlestown and near Collooney, and a consignment of huts for P Company, Auxiliary Division was burned outside Tubbercurry.[48] Towards the end of the month, two Crossley tenders containing military and police from Ballymote were ambushed near Collooney but drove off their attackers when reinforced by police from Collooney.[49] These ambushes appear to have been sniping attacks rather than serious attempts to engage and destroy the patrols.

In response, the Crown forces continued swift reprisals and search operations. In mid-April they destroyed SF halls at Kilmacowen and Knocknarea as a reprisal for the killing of Thomas Walker. Keash parish hall was burned at the end of May, following an ambush in the vicinity, and early in June Curry creamery was destroyed after an attack on a police patrol in the area.[50] Ballymote April fair and markets and fairs within three miles of Riverstown were prohibited because of the murders of policemen at Ballymote and Ballisodare.[51] May fairs at Riverstown, Ballymote, Collooney, Coolaney and Grange were banned and all fairs in the county proclaimed in June.[52] Male members of the congregation at Culfadda Catholic church were searched in February and Dunnill recorded: 'One man who is wearing a pair of stockings in the Sinn Féin colours is made to take them off'.[53] In a similar search at Keash in April, men were forced to kneel on the road and repeat invocations such as 'To Hell with de Valera', 'God Bless the Black and Tans', 'Down with the Republic'; those who refused were beaten up.[54] Early in May the congregation at a Mass in Gurteen was searched.[55] In late May Frank O'Beirne, O/C Collooney Battalion, was captured.[56] In early June troops of the Bedfordshire Regiment, Auxiliaries from Boyle, Longford and Tubbercurry, two regiments of cavalry with RIC from Sligo, Boyle and Ballymote carried out a day-long drive of the countryside between the Bricklieve Mountains, Keash and Gurteen. They encountered major transport disruptions because of road cutting and the poor state of the roads, which caused an armoured car to sink. Three thousand men were rounded up and taken to three identification points where they were checked by local RIC and some military who had been held up on trains, including Major Grune. Only seven men were detained and sent to Sligo for further questioning. Tom Deignan, O/C Riverstown Battalion, was the only notable arrested.[57] The CI's claim in June that practically all prominent IRA leaders were in jail was inaccurate. Some such as Carty, Hunt and Devins were; however, Pilkington, Scanlon and Marren were not. In any case, they were replaceable. In the Tubbercurry area, for instance, Frank Carty was succeeded by M.J. O'Hara, who in turn was succeeded by Charles Gildea, who was succeeded by Jack Brennan – all active, capable leaders.[58]

While the supply of arms and ammunition was never adequate, active IRA areas increased their arsenals, allowing more operations. A *6d.* in the pound IRA levy or rate had been imposed and collected in Ballymote, Tubbercurry and Collooney areas and the funds used to buy arms where possible. When unionist landowner Bryan Cooper refused to pay the levy, Frank O'Beirne, O/C Collooney Battalion, took two of his bullocks.[59] The six revolvers that the south Sligo IRA obtained from GHQ in April 1921 may have been a reward for their activity. By contrast, north Sligo had little or no arms. When Cliffoney IRA mounted an ambush in June they had to borrow arms – shotguns for the most part – from an adjoining area.[60]

As 1921 progressed there was no reduction in IRA activity in Sligo and there were significant successes. Jim Molloy, arrested for the shooting of O'Brien in Ballymote, escaped from Boyle military barracks on 21 May with the help of a soldier.[61] In an operation very similar to the rescue of Carty, a group under

Pilkington's command broke into Sligo gaol on 29 June and freed Charles Gildea, Tom Deignan and Frank O'Beirne with help from a prison warder. CI Neylon complained 'there was a military guard on the prison at the time but the guards were asleep'.[62]

Corporal Williams, a marine stationed at Rosses Point, was shot dead on 17 May by three members of the local IRA and his body dumped on a byroad. The IRA deemed him a dangerous spy and Neylon claimed that he had been killed because 'some local murderers were afraid he would get information regarding them'.[63] In an ambush near Cliffoney police barracks on 26 June Constable Patrick Clarke was shot dead. There are contradictory accounts of the ambush but it appears that Clarke, an older well-liked Mayoman, was shot dead without orders. Local IRA member Daniel Waters recalled that 'It was a sad day for the community'. Auxiliaries from Tubbercurry arrived on the scene and the house from which the shooting was carried out was burned in an unauthorized reprisal. Dunnill reported that it was 'burned down by unknown men'.[64]

The Mayo IRA were increasingly active during 1921. Sligo Volunteers from Easkey and Enniscrone areas were members of a North Mayo Brigade ASU of twenty-five to thirty men, armed with twelve to fifteen rifles, operating in the Ox Mountains during early summer 1921.[65] This unit attacked Easkey and Dromore West barracks and burned Easkey courthouse in April.[66] Thomas Howley of Enniscrone was wounded in an attack on Ballina RIC and died in military custody in Athlone on 28 May. His funeral, attended by 200 Volunteers and two lorry loads of Crown forces, passed off without incident.[67] The Ox Mountains ASU ambushed a seven-man RIC cycle patrol on 1 June at Culleens. Three south Sligo IRA men, Martin Brennan, Jack Brennan and John Durcan, joined the ASU for this operation. As in Ratra the previous year, the extended police formation caused problems. One policeman was wounded, others returned fire and Constables Thomas Higgins and John King, both Galway natives, were taken prisoner. A motor car which came on the scene was commandeered by some of the police and driven towards Easkey barracks. Fearing the arrival of reinforcements, the ambushers took the two prisoners and retreated to the mountains but not before a strong exchange of fire with additional police from Ballina and Tubbercurry. At a hurried council of war there was disagreement among the IRA about the fate of the captives. In the event, 'We gave them a short few seconds in which to say their prayers' one IRA man recalled, and they were executed. The *Irish Bulletin* claimed that the policemen had been killed in the running fight.[68]

The local Catholic bishops continually coupled disapproval of violence and condemnation of the reprisals of the Crown forces with support for the 'legitimate aspirations' of the people 'in their desperate attempt to recover their political rights as a nation'.[69] Some Sligo priests were especially favourable to the IRA. Dr Michael Louis Henry, a former World War I chaplain and curate at

Curry, supported the IRA in the Tubbercurry area not only spiritually but with advice on military matters; he is believed to have taken part in at least one ambush.[70]

In May 1921 a general election was held under the Government of Ireland Act (1920). Changes in electoral boundaries saw the establishment of a five-seat Sligo-East Mayo constituency. In Sligo there was no mention of SF involvement and Sligo Brigade IRA nominated candidates who were unopposed. Pilkington was initially nominated but was unwilling to run and was replaced by Carty. The other nominations were McCabe, outgoing, Seamus Devins, Dr Frank Ferran from Mayo and Thomas O'Donnell from Gurteen who was put forward by Jim Hunt.[71] One surprising omission was J.J. Clancy, the sitting TD for North Sligo. CI Neylon suggested that Clancy's 'views were not extreme enough – he did not approve of police murders etc.'. SF headquarters queried Clancy's being dropped but received no response from Sligo. The election aroused little interest and there were no election meetings. The SF candidates, dubbed 'prominent members of the murder gang' by the CI, were returned unopposed.[72]

In response to the continued IRA activity in the area, a company of the Bedfordshire Regiment moved from Carrick-on-Shannon to Ballymote towards the end of June.[73] Military communications was generally by wireless but pigeons were used between Ballymote and Boyle. A military pigeon-carrying car en route from Boyle to Ballymote was held up by the IRA on the Curlew Mountains at the end of June, driver and helper disarmed and sent on foot to Boyle and the car set on fire (see plate 15). The military claimed to know who the leader was, presumably Marren, and a party left Boyle the following night to raid his house. They muffled their boots to increase the element of surprise but complained that dogs barking at every cabin gave them away. When they arrived at their destination, the wanted man, unsurprisingly, was not at home.[74]

At Sligo assizes on 8 July Judge Wylie deplored the 'crime and outrage committed in your county since last assizes'. Only 48 of the 180 or more jurors on the list attended, many having been kidnapped to prevent attendance. Some were anxious not to attend. Michael Walsh of Curry recalled his brother-in-law asking the IRA to arrest him to avoid jury service.[75] The truce came into effect on 11 July. A few days beforehand Pilkington had sent instructions to battalion commanders not to engage in any further activity. The *Sligo Independent* reported that on the Sunday (10 July) 'Crown Forces seem to have practically left down their arms and roamed about with the civil population and took advantage of a day at Rosses Point or Strandhill' and that a large number of men on the run turned up in jubilant spirits.[76]

By the time of the truce, County Sligo fitted into the general provincial picture in Connacht where counties showed a moderate level of activity and violence in the latter part of the struggle. It lagged far behind the most active counties, especially in terms of fatalities. If we include the deaths at the Ratra ambush, just across the county boundary in Roscommon, the number of fatalities in County Sligo for the period 1920–1 was 18: one civilian shot as a spy, 16 Crown forces (14 RIC, one British soldier and one marine) and one IRA volunteer were killed. No civilian was killed by the Crown forces. These figures contrast sharply with those from Tipperary where 114 Crown forces were killed and 51 IRA, and also Cork where 190 Crown forces, 135 IRA and 167 civilians were killed during 1920–1.[77] Except for Leitrim, which had 16 fatalities, other Connacht counties had much higher fatalities, Galway 57, Roscommon 56 and Mayo 42.[78] There was disagreement about the IRA's capacity to continue the fight at the time of the truce.[79] Unlike Longford, there was no sense of desperation in Sligo. Harold McBrien maintained: 'There was no doubt that we could have carried on the fight as we were well 'blooded' now and our morale was high. We had gained an enormous amount of experience and had learned how the enemy operated and how to outwit them but the whole bogey was arms and ammunition'.[80] Tom Deignan agreed: 'We in this battalion were in a good position to carry on the fight. There was plenty of good fighting material amongst the members of the battalion and we now had six service rifles with a small supply of ammunition ... and a vast amount of experience which we were lacking at the start'.[81] There was no indication that Sligo IRA was on its last legs by July 1921. IRA columns were surviving on the run in a number of areas and were engaged in regular harassment of the Crown forces, fulfilling Mulcahy's injunction: 'What we want at the moment is to harass the enemy as much as possible, while providing our own forces with just sufficient activity to get them used to active service and to let them gain confidence in themselves'.[82] The moderate amount of military activity that the county had seen, including a few significant actions and many small-scale operations, was enough to allow Sligo IRA to convince themselves at least that they had played a significant part in what they regarded as a national victory. It also encouraged them to demand general respect and obedience especially from those who, in their estimation, had played no part in that victory.

9 The republican counter-state in County Sligo

The establishment of Dáil Éireann in January 1919 was designed to indicate to Ireland and to the world that a republican state had been set up to replace British rule in Ireland and to provide a mandate for an international propaganda campaign aimed at having Ireland's claim heard at the Paris peace conference. In fact, the Dáil had difficulty in functioning at all; it met only twenty-one times between January 1919 and the truce in July 1921. Many of its departments never operated to any great degree but in two areas – local government and justice – it had a significant impact. No county council elections had been held in Ireland since the outbreak of war in 1914 and it was only after the local government elections of 1920 that SF took control of the majority of the county councils. These SF-controlled councils then declared their allegiance to the Dáil, which found itself having to formulate policies to deal with the new situation. In Sligo, and throughout the country, the withdrawal of British local government grants and difficulties in collecting rates caused severe financial problems for local government bodies. After major curtailments in services and expenditure and the use of the IRA to collect rates, the system survived and by the time of the truce conditions were improving.

Sligo Corporation was in a unique position, having had an election in January 1919, but the slender SF/labour majority there was continually threatened by the enforced absences of republican members. The SF mayor of Sligo for 1920, T.H. Fitzpatrick, made it clear that he would not take an oath of allegiance to the British Crown or sit as a magistrate.[1] However, it was not until 30 June that Sligo Corporation acknowledged the authority of Dáil Éireann. The clerk was directed to send copies of the minutes to the Dáil's department of local government but complaints from the latter in January 1921 suggest that he had not complied.[2] Ratepayers' Councillor Harper Campbell Perry took advantage of poorly attended Corporation meetings in December 1920 to have a proposal carried that British LGB correspondence be answered, in effect recognizing that body.[3] This decision was rescinded at the better-attended January meeting to which Perry welcomed members whose faces, he said, had almost been forgotten. The clerk warned members that by severing their connection with the British LGB they would be acting illegally.[4] In January 1921 the independent John Jinks proved himself the consummate local politician. With the help of the Ratepayers' councillors and the support of Peter Heraghty, elected on the SF/labour ticket, Jinks defeated Michael Nevin of SF by a single vote to become mayor. The *Connachtman* suggested that Jinks's election proved that the Ratepayers' Association was 'purely a political party bitterly opposed to the Republic'. According to the CI, Sinn Féin and IRA recognized this as 'a crushing

74

defeat'.[5] Subsequently, the Dáil minister for local government instanced two cases in March where Sligo Corporation did not comply with strict allegiance to the Dáil. On one occasion they gave instructions to have claims for malicious injuries defended and on another they applied to the British LGB for a loan.[6] Their experiences with Sligo Corporation appear to have prejudiced Sligo IRA leaders, especially those based in Sligo town, against all elected representatives even those elected under the banner of SF.

After the May 1920 local elections SF controlled the majority of public bodies in the country.[7] Events in Sligo were similar to those elsewhere with contests avoided by SF clubs choosing candidates who had to sign pledges recognizing 'the Republic established by the will and vote of the Irish People as the legitimate Government of Ireland'.[8] Most outgoing members did not stand and election duties were carried out by IRA instead of the RIC. Intimidation was used against those who attempted to oppose SF. In Ballymote and Tubbercurry areas independent candidates withdrew after being visited by armed and masked men. SF won all the Sligo County Council seats. In the Sligo area John Hennigan, outgoing, an early supporter of SF, headed the poll and labour leader John Lynch was elected for SF. The *Sligo Independent* reported 'wholesale person-ation'. There was little need for personation in the country areas but the fact that three Ratepayers' candidates and outgoing independent Jinks did not between them poll a quota in the Sligo area suggests irregularities there, especially since Jinks was elected to Sligo Board of Guardians a week later.

No IRA leader was directly elected to Sligo County Council but Carty, Hunt and Frank O'Beirne were elected to Rural District Councils, became chairmen of those bodies and thus *ex-officio* members of Sligo County Council.[9] The IRA was also represented on the council by two co-opted members, Seamus Devins, O/C Grange Battalion and Michael J. Marren, O/C Ballymote Battalion (plate 7).[10] J.J. Clancy TD was appointed chairman and resolutions acknowledging the authority of Dáil Éireann, supporting the revival of Irish, congratulating Carty on his escape, calling on able-bodied men to join the IRA and asking JPs to resign were passed in June and July.[11]

The Dáil, fearing the loss of British financial benefits, which accounted for nineteen per cent of the annual revenue of local authorities, was happy for councils that pledged allegiance to Dáil Éireann to continue to receive British LGB grants. The British government issued an ultimatum on 29 July: no grants or loans would be made without assurances that accounts would be submitted for audit.[12] In early August the Dáil recommended that councils break with the LGB and replace banks as treasurers by trustees to conduct councils' financial affairs.[13] At the August meeting Clancy explained that the Council had followed the Dáil's instructions and estimated that the loans and grants lost amounted to £26,000. A motion was passed that the Council undertake no new work for at least twelve months.[14]

The break with the LGB had a detrimental effect on local authority finances nationwide. Dismissal of the banks meant the loss of overdraft facilities. Rate collection, already difficult because of the disturbed state of the country, became even more problematic as collectors were unsure where to lodge monies. By December 1920 the system nationally was in 'a virtual state of collapse'.[15] Local authorities responded by implementing a range of economies. In October Sligo County Council dispensed with the services of some officials and reduced the salaries of others.[16] A finance committee recommended that all able-bodied persons be discharged from the workhouse, that fees be charged to those in a position to pay and that some dispensaries be closed.[17] A Sligo–Leitrim asylum committee meeting heard that salaries had been reduced, some staff pensioned off, cows sold and tillage increased. Labour protests at such treatment of Sligo workers had no effect.[18] At a Sligo Board of Guardians' meeting Alderman John Lynch responded to a refusal to grant an increase to ambulance drivers with: 'God help us if this is what we are to get under an Irish Republic'.[19] The Sligo workhouse master told the guardians in January that some inmates were without sufficient food and the meat and milk contractors threatened to stop supplies. Deputations met the County Council and contractors who were owed in the region of £4,000. Suppliers promised to continue to deliver milk having been assured that they would be paid. The *Connachtman* praised such traders but the *Sligo Independent* carried the headline: 'Sick on Brink of Starvation'.[20] Dromore West guardians reported a general reduction in food and fuel in their workhouse; outdoor relief cases received nothing after 15 January and none of the officers had received salary since the previous October. Prolonged negotiations with the bank for an overdraft fell through when the signatures of twenty guardians could not be obtained for a guarantee.[21]

Early in February 1921 Sligo County Council considered the estimates. The total demand for the year was £143,878; the large increase on the previous year's £82,800 was accounted for by the lack of government grants. This resulted in an increase of 6*d.* in the pound in the rates.[22] A large portion of the rate was still outstanding and, as in other areas, the IRA was asked to help.[23] They raided rate collectors and tendered money already collected to the County Council. Dunnill recorded that the rate collecting campaign started on 7 May and that a total of £10,722 was collected on 9 May in the Ballymote, Tubbercurry and Easkey areas. The IRA then demanded £1,000 from the Council as poundage but this was refused on the basis that they had not actually collected the rates. J.J. Clancy, County Council chairman, on his own responsibility offered them £500. They refused and ordered him to have £1,000 ready 'or take the consequences'. The Dáil LG inspector in Sligo saw no reason why the IRA should not be paid and, in the presence of a council official, Clancy handed over the money, apparently to R.G. Bradshaw acting for the IRA.[24] Richard Mulcahy asked Pilkington in mid-June about the demand for £1,000 from the County Council, which he said, if true, was 'entirely irregular'.[25] After an investigation by the Dáil department of local government, Sligo IRA was ordered to refund the money but apparently never did. The IRA action had a positive effect on rate collection in the county and it was claimed that a total of £30,000 was eventually collected.[26] This eased the local government crisis in Sligo and there were fewer accounts of financial hardship in mid-1921. Tubbercurry guardians expected that the bank would be accommodating when they spent more than the £1,000 forwarded by the County Council to pay salaries and contractors. In January 1921 the Hibernian Bank allowed Sligo Asylum an overdraft. Such references suggest that many of these bodies had either never dismissed banks as treasurers or had reinstated them in late 1920 or early 1921. This also occurred in other counties with the reluctant approval of the Dáil.[27] Clancy resigned his seat on the county committee of agriculture in April 1921 'owing to circumstances over which he had no control' and the Dáil inspector described him as being under a cloud 'from which he is unable to clear himself'.[28] In 1921 Clancy was replaced as chairman of Sligo County Council by James Gilligan, a SF councillor from the Tubbercurry area first elected in 1920.[29] Clancy's initial refusal of the IRA's demand for payment for collecting the rates was not forgiven by that body. This may also explain why he, the sitting TD for North Sligo, was not selected for the 1921 election.[30]

This was one example of tension between the IRA and local bodies. Councillors who were active IRA members, unable to attend meetings and influence decisions, sometimes tried to exercise control by other means. In January 1921 they forced SF Alderman Luke Gilligan, manager of a public house in Sligo in which a revolver had been found in a military search, to resign from Sligo Corporation because he had pleaded not guilty at a court in Belfast.[31] A special meeting of Sligo County Council was held in March in the Coolaney Mountains to allow men on the run, including Hunt, Marren, McCabe and O'Beirne, attend. Co-options were made at this meeting including Michael Nevin, later referred to as 'the IRA spokesman' on the Council.[32] The Dáil minister for local government had suggested that republican members unable to attend meetings regularly should resign and be replaced by people who could attend. A number of Sligo councillors, including Jack Brennan, John Lynch, Marren, Hunt and Carty, did so in early July and replacements were agreed.[33]

The RIC's withdrawal from smaller barracks left a void in policing that Dáil Éireann attempted to fill in 1919 by recognizing and developing the arbitration courts that had been operating in some parts of Ireland since 1917.[34] SF courts were first reported in Sligo in November 1919 when they were said to be operating in the Grange and Collooney areas but it was not until the Dáil introduced a formal scheme of organization in May 1920 that they became more widespread, variously described as arbitration, SF, republican or Dáil courts. The Dáil scheme sanctioned courts based on Catholic parishes with three arbitrators, one of whom could be a clergyman, and district courts with five members, two of whom could be clergymen.[35] The establishment of Gurteen SF court was announced on 9 May and Mullaghroe court sat on 13 May.[36] On 23 May the setting up of Cloonacool SF court was announced and a sitting reported in June. Sooey court sat on 3 July.[37] When Tubbercurry courthouse was burned at the end of May it was said that many of the cases which were to have been heard there had been before SF courts at Aclare and Curry. Mullaghroe petty sessions in mid-July heard only two cases while the local Dáil court was said to have 'dealt with an extensive list of cases'.[38]

By mid-1920 Dáil courts were being formally organized in many parts of the country.[39] A conference in Sligo town in early July appointed SF court arbitrators for each parish in north Sligo. The list of courts and justices published as a result of this meeting included a note that Grange court was already in existence, implying that none of the others were. North Sligo district court was also established and its justices included Fr Browne, Dromore West, veteran Sinn Féiners D.A. Mulcahy and John Hennigan and R.G. Bradshaw, I/O Sligo Brigade. Of the thirteen parish courts set up at this meeting, only five included clergymen as justices. Sligo Borough court arbitrators were representatives of the three wings of the movement: D.M. Hanley (the older SF element), John Lynch (labour) and Michael Nevin (the IRA).[40] The first arbitration court in Sligo town sat in the courthouse on 10 July with local solicitors attending. One case had been referred from Sooey court suggesting that this was the North Sligo district court. It convened again in Sligo town hall on 16 September.[41] An arbitration court in Knocknarea in early September heard cases involving publicans not obeying closing time orders issued by the IRA, assault cases and property disputes. Local Protestant clergyman, Revd Dr F.E. Wagner, who had indicated that he would adjudicate at this court, resigned his membership because representations had been made to him that serving on the court might lead to dissention among his parishioners and 'probably no little trouble for me not only in my parochial work but also with my bishop'.[42] Arbitration courts were reported in Coolera, Skreen & Dromard, Riverstown and Tubbercurry in September and October.[43] The *Irish Bulletin* claimed in July that in Sligo 'no cases are now brought to any but the Republican courts'. CI Neylon noted the existence of SF courts and the boycott of petty sessions courts and revealed that many loyalists had had agrarian disputes settled in SF courts. Bryan Cooper wrote of the favourable impression made on the unionist mind by the discovery 'that on the whole Sinn Féin is trying to prevent anarchy and maintain order'.[44]

As the Dáil courts flourished, the Crown court system declined.[45] The petty sessions in the county were boycotted and courthouses, including Tubbercurry, Collooney, Coolaney, Riverstown and Enniscrone, were burned or damaged during 1920.[46] Very few cases were heard before Sligo Borough court at the end of August 1920 and its September sitting was said to have lasted only two minutes.[47] Similarly, in Ballymote the quarter sessions business for September –

mostly undefended malicious injury cases – was completed in four hours; it would normally have taken three days.[48] Petty sessions courts at Tubbercurry, Dromore West, Easkey and Enniscrone were held irregularly during 1920. There were no cases for Ballinafad petty sessions in February or July, Grange court was not held in July, and there were no cases for Riverstown in November. There was nothing for the magistrates to do at Mullaghroe petty sessions in mid-October except sign publicans' licenses.[49]

On 15 May *An tÓglach* declared that the IRA had been entrusted with the duty of enforcing the decrees of the Dáil courts and the AG announced on 19 June that Republican police would serve Dáil courts. In July battalion commandants in Sligo were instructed to organize a system of police in their areas. There is little evidence that such a scheme operated in Sligo and it appears that IRA volunteers were called on for policing purposes as the need arose. This is borne out by Sligo statements to the Bureau of Military History.[50] In mid-1920 the local press reported crimes being investigated, wrong-doers punished and stolen property recovered by what were variously described as IRA, Volunteers or Republican police in Sligo and Ballymote. These also kept order at Tubbercurry and Grange fairs and were said to patrol Strandhill on Sundays.[51] As in other counties, poteen-making was a particular target and Sligo Brigade issued a circular against it in July. Later, in 1920, treacle, believed to be for poteen making, was destroyed at Tubbercurry and confiscated poteen stills were displayed outside Tubbercurry and Castleconnor churches.[52] On the first Sunday in July 1921 republican police chained three young men to the railings near Sligo cathedral in full view of Mass-goers with a notice: 'Tried by the IRA and convicted. All thieves and robbers beware'. The RIC later released them. The CI recorded the general belief that 'they broke into a house in Sligo and carried away goods', though Dunnill said their crime was that they were ex-soldiers.[53]

The Dáil courts were tolerated by the British until the Restoration of Order in Ireland Act in mid-1920 from which time raids on such 'illegal assemblies' were common. No such raid was reported in Sligo, though a SF court was held in Sligo workhouse instead of the town hall in early October because of the likelihood of its being broken up in the latter venue.[54] By the time the south Sligo district court was established in September 1920, the British crackdown was already in force and only one sitting took place in 1920, on the same day as the Chaffpool ambush near Tubbercurry. The adjudicators were Tom O'Donnell, chairman of South Sligo SF, Councillor James Gilligan and two local medical doctors with no previous political involvement.[55] By the end of 1920 there were few reports of republican courts in Sligo and it seems they were curtailed by the increased activity of the Crown forces. The CI claimed that no arbitration courts were held in December 1920, in February or April 1921. The *Sligo Independent* reported in April that British courts were regaining their position, describing the Sligo Borough court the previous week as being like 'an old time sitting before Sinn Fein's onslaught'.[56] Alec McCabe later told the Dáil that in his area 'They found they could never summon a district court during the war without attracting the attention of the enemy. They had to go back to the old system of getting parish courts together'.[57] This supports the explanation of the south Sligo registrar that some parish courts in his area ceased to function but that he with two justices of the district court (O'Donnell and Marren) travelled around the area holding courts with a local justice where cases were pending. South Sligo district court did sit on 13 June 1921 with O'Donnell and Marren presiding.[58] There was no sitting of the Dáil circuit court in Sligo before the truce and only one sitting of a land court appears to have been held. Kevin O'Shiel, the Dáil land judge, held a secret land court in Sligo town hall in January 1921 at which he gave judgment in favour of a Protestant landowner, John A. Barry, in a long-running land dispute in north Sligo.[59]

The operation of local government and the Dáil courts in Sligo, in the main, followed the national pattern. These underlined the Dáil's intent to operate as an alternative government. By the time of the truce, local government had survived a period of hardship and turmoil, and local administration had been maintained. Dáil courts, while they flourished, were a clear manifestation of the commitment to the rule of law of the alternative administration. The British attempt at suppression severely curtailed their operation at the end of 1920 and during the first half of 1921, but they survived to emerge again during the truce period. In Sligo, however, both these areas proved divisive and were used by Sligo IRA as proof that 'mere politicians' were not to be trusted with power and that the IRA alone were the guardians of the republic. In the fields of local government and justice, Sligo IRA claimed to have played a vital role in areas originally outside their remit. They had indeed contributed to the survival of republican local government by their rate collecting activity but the day-to-day burden of maintaining local services had been shouldered by those who operated primarily as politicians. When the republican court system came under enemy pressure, the IRA took on the role of dispenser of justice. The truce period saw this tension become a bitter conflict in the county, something reflected in the subsequent disagreement over the Treaty and in the Civil War divisions.

1 Keash United Irish League banner by Samuel A. Watson, Dublin.

2 Tom Scanlan, MP, speaking at a home rule meeting outside Sligo town hall on Sunday 7 Sept. 1913.

3 Early pioneers of Sinn Féin in Co. Sligo, Owen Tansy, Gurteen (*left*), and Patrick Dyar, Tubbercurry (*right*).

4 Fr Felix Burke.

5 Henry Monson, Sligo AOH and Sinn Féin.

6 Reception at Sligo courthouse on 14 June 1919 for Sligo native Private Martin Moffatt, Leinster Regiment, who had just been awarded a VC.

7 The first meeting of the newly elected Sligo County Council on 22 June 1920.

8 South Sligo IRA. Jim Hunt is second from left, front row. Joe Finnegan, who succeeded Hunt on his arrest, is to his left and Thady McGowan is to Finnegan's left. Third from left in the back row is Tom Brehony.

9 Keash RIC Barracks, evacuated in late 1919 and burned by the IRA on Easter Sunday night 1920.

10 Cliffoney RIC Barracks with reinforced protection.

11 A group of the Bedfordshire and Hertfordshire Regiment with a Lewis gun at Sligo military barracks *c*.1920.

12 A round-up during a large-scale military search somewhere in Sligo.

13 Soldiers searching a load of peat for arms on a country road.

14 A trenched road near Ballymote.

15 Members of the Bedfordshire and Hertfordshire Regiment inspect the burned out pigeon car between Ballymote and Boyle on 30 June 1921.

16 Sgt. Patrick Perry, RIC, killed at the Moneygold ambush on 25 Oct. 1920.

17 Bernard Brady (*left*), and Pat Hunt (*right*), Ballymote Battalion, IRA, during the Truce, 1921.

18 Group of Cumann na mBan probably during the Truce period, autumn 1921.

19 Frank O'Beirne and Brian MacNeill.

20 Billy Pilkington (*seated*), with Harry Doherty.

21 A group of anti-Treaty IRA including Seamus Devins, with hat, on left, Harry Benson top left and Harry Doherty in the centre.

22 Griffith's Sligo meeting, Easter Sunday 1922. An injured anti-Treaty soldier, probably Michael Mullen of Bunninadden, is taken into an ambulance.

23 Griffith's meeting in progress at the corner of O'Connell Street and Grattan Street.

24 Griffith's meeting. Anti-Treaty soldiers outside their post at the Imperial Hotel where bullet holes are visible in the windows as a result of an earlier exchange of fire.

25 Griffith's Sligo meeting. A group outside the residence of Dudley M. Hanley, Old Market Street, Sligo.

26 Bishop Bernard Coyne of Elphin in negotiation with Tom Scanlon, O/C, 1st Battalion, 3rd Western Brigade, IRA outside the Harp and Shamrock Hotel, Stephen Street, Sligo, prior to the bishop's entering the Provisional Government post at Sligo Courthouse on 14 July 1922.

27 Lieut. P.J. McDermott of the Free State army, a native of Riverstown, the first fatality of the Civil War in Sligo, killed at Markree Castle in June 1922.

28 Frank Carty, on right with rifle, and Martin Brennan in the hat with the Rolls Royce armoured car *Ballinalee* in Tubbercurry when the anti-Treaty forces unsuccessfully attacked the Free State post there on 9 Sept. 1922.

29 Two of the six anti-Treaty IRA killed on Benbulben in Sept. 1922. *Left*: Captain Harry Benson; *Right*: Lieut. Paddy Carroll.

30 A hearse bearing one of the anti-Treaty IRA killed on Benbulben moving off from Sligo Cathedral on 22 Sept. 1922 flanked by a Cumann na mBan escort.

31 Charles Phibbs inspecting the grave dug in front of his residence, Doobeg House, in May 1922.

10 Martial law for Sligo?

The truce, which came into effect on Monday 11 July, occasioned little immediate public celebration in Sligo, even though the CI noted public relief and the hope that a settlement would be reached.[1] Those IRA who had been on the run were able to come into the open and others who had been reticent in their support were now able to proclaim it safely. Sligo IRA claimed full credit for what they regarded as a victory. CI Neylon captured this: 'The IRA leaders believe there will be peace and take to themselves the entire credit of same'. Devins claimed 'It was the Irish army that brought the Irish question to what it was today and it was the army that would carry them to success in the end'.[2] Sligo IRA leaders who were also TDs displayed a notable ambivalence towards the democratic mandate, disparaging politicians, even those on the same side, and continually clashing with the County Council in particular. Carty regarded himself 'not a man of words but ... a man of action'. Devins believed that he was elected because he 'represented what was now popularly known as "the gunmen"'.[3] These IRA leaders attempted to concentrate local political and military power in their hands during the second half of 1921. The summer and early autumn saw exceptionally fine weather and large numbers of IRA, many of them new recruits, took part in training camps all over the county. IRA GHQ seems not to have interfered until it inspected the area in November with a view to extending the divisional structure to include County Sligo. The RIC could only look on and its frequent claims that much of the IRA activity, training camps and public parades in particular, breached the terms of the truce got little hearing. The Sligo IRA's assertion of power in the county ensured that they were in a strong position by the end of the year but it also created numerous enemies who, when the opportunity came, were more than willing to oppose them.

The most prominent Sligo IRA leaders, including Brigadier Pilkington, were free at the time of the truce, while Carty and Devins were released with other SF TDs in early August. As elsewhere, they were honoured guests at public events, recipients of laudatory addresses and the subjects of poems in local newspapers comparing them to patriots of old and they posed for the cameras (plates 17–21). Special events at sports meetings, football matches, tugs-of-war and relay races were confined to IRA members.[4]

Michael J. Marren, O/C Ballymote, was drowned accidentally at Strandhill the day after the truce and his funeral presented Sligo IRA with an opportunity to display its strength publicly at a crucial time. Ballymote on the day of the funeral was 'a seething mass of people' and over 2,000 IRA men marched after the coffin.[5]

Immediately Sligo IRA became embroiled in a public squabble with Sligo

County Council. One of the key figures was R.G. Bradshaw, I/O Sligo Brigade, editor of the *Connachtman*, and truce liaison officer for the Sligo area.[6] In a report in early 1922 the Dáil LG inspector mentioned 'the sinister influence of a man [Bradshaw] who has ever been causing trouble to the inspectors in this county'.[7] John Jinks's son, Frank, in what the local government inspector described as 'downright jobbery', had been appointed temporary clerk to the County Council in 1916 and was made permanent three years later.[8] In October 1920, as part of a cost-cutting exercise, Jinks was made redundant but was kept on in place of a clerk who had been arrested.[9] On the latter's release in May 1921 the services of Frank Jinks were dispensed with. On 9 July Michael Nevin proposed Jinks's reinstatement but James Gilligan ruled this out of order. The *Connachtman* claimed that Gilligan was 'incapable of carrying out the duties of chairman with impartiality or efficiency'.[10] The Dáil department of local government said that although not competent when first appointed, Jinks had become so in the meantime and was now needed in the office. It suggested that he be given three months' probation but the Council refused to sanction this.[11] The IRA's support of Frank Jinks appears not to have been motivated by any shared feeling or pact with his father, who had defeated the SF candidate for the 1921 mayoralty. Rather, the IRA saw the issue as an opportunity to assert its control.

Another protracted disagreement concerned union amalgamation. The Dáil department of local government proposed the amalgamation and streamlining of poor law unions. In County Sligo the scheme would result in the creation of one union with one workhouse at Sligo. Facing abolition, Tubbercurry and Dromore West guardians protested strongly; a Sligo conference on the issue in April 1920 came to no decision.[12] Initially the *Connachtman* enthusiastically supported amalgamation but by July 1921 spearheaded the opposition.[13] This volte-face coincided with the paper's attacks on Gilligan and positions on the matter mirrored almost exactly divisions on Jinks's reinstatement. The amalgamation scheme was adopted at the end of August by Sligo County Council, which was instructed by the department to put it into effect 'with all speed'.[14] While Tubbercurry and Sligo Boards of Guardians adopted the scheme in principle, they continued to delay it. The transfer of inmates and patients from outlying institutions to the county home was only completed in November 1921.[15] Dromore West guardians were particularly upset with the failure of their clerk, a prominent IRA member, to obtain the position of secretary of the county home.[16] Sligo guardians refused to conform until well into 1922 and made strenuous but unsuccessful efforts to have their clerk appointed secretary to the new county committee.[17]

There were other instances of Sligo IRA dictating to the County Council. At the meeting after Marren's death an adjournment was proposed as a mark of respect. Councillor Patrick Connolly from Tubbercurry, attending his first meeting, queried the value of an adjournment and suggested that they continue.

In the absence of any support, he did not pursue the matter and the meeting was adjourned.[18] Tubbercurry IRA demanded that Tubbercurry RDC, which had nominated Connolly, rescind the appointment and he was duly replaced. The Dáil inspector commented: 'Sligo Brigade appears to have declared martial law for Sligo' but no action was taken.[19] In September the IRA demanded by letter that Elizabeth McGettrick from Portinch, Ballymote, a niece of John O'Dowd, be co-opted to fill a County Council vacancy. Councillor Jack Brennan, Tubbercurry O/C, who had signed the letter, told the meeting 'You have got your orders and it is for the council to obey'. The co-option was carried unanimously; she served on the County Council until 1925.[20] Alarmed, the AG wrote to the minister for local government asking for further information: 'The question of principle must be faced and the Tubbercurry IRA must confine their activities to selections and operations of a different nature'.[21] There is no record of the minister's reply and no action appears to have been taken.

The issue of IRA dictation to the Council came to a head at the meeting on 8 October 1921. Tenders for the Council's advertising contract had been received from three Sligo newspapers as well as from Ballina and Boyle publications. Gilligan claimed that Bradshaw had organized a price-fixing 'ring'. Bradshaw, present as a journalist, admitted that the three Sligo newspaper proprietors had met, but maintained they were justified in taking steps to safeguard their business interests. Carty then proposed the former master of Tubbercurry workhouse who, he said, had the support of Tubbercurry Battalion, as rate collector for Tubbercurry electoral division. Gilligan, the chairman, said he would refuse to 'allow the IRA to interfere with the civil affairs of the county' claiming that a meeting had been held in Bradshaw's office that morning to select the rate collector. Bradshaw denied this but admitted that the selection of rates collector had been handed over to him by the Tubbercurry O/C. Devins and Carty both claimed that the civil administration had fallen into the hands of the IRA during the war when otherwise it would not have functioned. Gilligan protested strongly: 'I was here on every occasion to help carry it on' and others protested that they had also regularly attended. Despite more 'hot and excited remarks' the IRA nominee was selected.[22]

On foot of this meeting Gilligan complained to W.T. Cosgrave, minister for local government: 'From what has taken place at some recent meetings of this County Council in Sligo, it would seem that the civil powers are not masters of their own actions and have to obey the orders of the IRA'. A local government inspector reported in October that Sligo County Council affairs were

> to put it mildly, somewhat perturbed ... Mr Bradshaw and the IRA are out to run the business of the council according to their own ideas and there is a good deal of underhand work going on ... the IRA seem to think that they can interfere when and where they like in public affairs.

He also claimed that he had been watched while in Sligo and had been advised not to report from there in writing. Despite Gilligan's protests and the report, the department of local government took no action.[23] Sligo was not the only county with such difficulties and the department was unable to influence the business of councils to any great extent.[24] Nonetheless, Sligo County Council functioned well during the truce period and came to terms with the problem of rate defaulters. It replaced a number of unsatisfactory collectors and by December Gilligan could report that the amount outstanding totalled no more than £5,000.[25]

The IRA engaged in a programme of training and reorganization during the summer of 1921.[26] The British army's 5th Division reported more of these 'rebel camps' in Sligo than in any other part of the divisional area.[27] Captain T. Burke from IRA GHQ singled out Sligo Brigade for praise: 'practically all the rank and file in addition to the officers and NCOs have been put through a course of camp training'.[28] At least sixteen training camps, distributed throughout the county, catered for numbers ranging from 25 at the smallest to 120 at the large divisional camp at Cloonamahon sanatorium near Collooney. Officers and men attended in relays. The RIC repeatedly complained about the military training, public parading and drilling which accompanied these camps. DI Russell wrote: 'If much of this thing occurs it will be hard to answer for the police who resent this drilling and carrying of arms by rebels in open display of sedition and antagonism'. The IRA response was that such activities were no more a breach of the truce than the training of the RIC or the British army.[29]

No IRA divisional organization had been set up in Sligo before the truce; the same was true throughout Connacht. As a preliminary to such an undertaking, two GHQ officers, T. Burke and Brian MacNeill, son of Eoin MacNeill, the former chief of staff of the Irish Volunteers and government minister, inspected Sligo Brigade in November. Burke reported that in spite of the training camps the district was 'very poorly armed and prepared for war' and that it resented the failure of GHQ to supply material during the war. His comments on individual officers were perceptive. Pilkington was deemed a 'promising type' and a 'good militarist'; Devins 'means business' though 'he might possibly need a little steadying influence'; and Carty interested himself 'too much in petty local politics' but would be a suitable O/C for the proposed South Sligo Brigade. Burke reported that the other officers were very promising, 'intelligent and willing to work'.[30] The new 3rd Western Division comprised five brigades: South Sligo, North Sligo, North Roscommon, East Mayo and North Leitrim. Burke recommended that the divisional staff be drawn almost exclusively from Sligo Brigade. Pilkington was appointed divisional O/C and Devins and Carty commandants of North and South Sligo Brigades respectively. Brian MacNeill was the only outsider appointed to the staff, presumably to provide a steadying influence.[31]

A scheme for republican police does not appear to have been implemented fully in County Sligo and reports suggest that while a rudimentary republican police system operated there, it was indistinguishable from the IRA proper.[32] Alec McCabe's assessment was harsh: 'Organisation of police force in this and all areas I have come in contact with leaves a lot to be desired … The common expression I hear is that if the Republican law is to be anything like this give us back the old system again as soon as possible'. He blamed this on the 'the mix up of volunteers and police' with the police being under IRA control.[33]

Austin Stack, minister for home affairs, decided that there would be no return to the British court system and circulated details of a new Dáil court scheme in August.[34] North Sligo district court sat for the first time after the truce on 15 August. Stack expressed his approval of the operation of the north Sligo courts and asked only that they be regularly constituted at a convention that was held on 5 November. The court functioned regularly until the outbreak of the Civil War.[35] A convention to organize south Sligo courts was held on 14 November.[36] Stack repeatedly complained about south Sligo courts in spite of the district court registrar assuring him that 'the Parish and District Courts are now in full working order in south Sligo and are functioning in accordance with your instructions'.[37] Tubbercurry SF district court appears to have been held monthly from September 1921.[38] The *Connachtman* held up Tourlestrane parish court, sitting regularly during August and September, as an example to neighbouring districts.[39] The Sligo CI's office complained about eleven such court sittings, five in September and three each in October and November.[40] The relatively few reports of SF parish courts in Sligo during the truce reflect official policy, Stack's advice being that 'the work should go on quietly and unostentatiously'.[41] Newspaper reports did not indicate an increase in crime in County Sligo in the second half of 1921. In the rural parts of Sligo, petty sessions had not functioned fully since mid-1920 and this situation continued during the truce. At Collooney, the only petty sessions court functioning outside Sligo town during this period, over one hundred cases were heard in September 1921 most of which involved signing publicans' certificates from the whole south Sligo area. Indeed the court may have been held specifically for this purpose.[42] Sligo Borough court continued to sit regularly with Mayor Jinks in the chair.[43]

The position of the courts became even more confused in early 1922. In January the Provisional Government directed that all law courts that had acted under the authority of the British government were to continue to operate until the establishment of the Free State and that Dáil courts were also to remain in operation.[44] North and South Sligo SF district courts functioned until the outbreak of civil war and Sligo parish court sat regularly.[45] The former British courts continued to operate as they had during the truce period although there was a falling off in the volume of business especially of Sligo Borough court after the departure of the RIC.[46]

During the truce friction between Crown forces and IRA led to incidents throughout the country.[47] The few reported in Sligo were minor and did not lead to serious injury or death. On 10 August IRA officer Edward J. Bofin, acting as a policeman, attempted to clear a public house in Rosses Point of customers, including some marines stationed nearby. Shots were fired by Bofin when the marines attempted to disarm him. The IRA liaison officer reported that the marines believed that Bofin was responsible for the killing of a marine near Rosses Point in 1921.[48] A shot was fired at policemen by a party of IRA drilling at Mullaghmore in September.[49] On 19 September hay belonging to a family friendly with the RIC was burned at Cliffoney. Two female members of the same family had previously had their hair cropped.[50] In November 1921 the IRA stole three cars belonging to south Sligo policemen.[51] When the Bedfordshire Regiment took over the Loftus Hall in Ballymote, the IRA complained that it had been their headquarters and shots were fired at the building during the night.[52]

IRA collections also caused complaints: at the end of August the Dáil government ment decided that all non-voluntary IRA levies should cease and in mid-October the *Sligo Champion* carried a notice from the minister for defence ruling that all such collections must be voluntary.[53] IRA collections, rates or levies, were reported from many parts of Sligo during the truce. The RIC complained that in the Easkey area subscriptions of between 5s. and 50s. were being 'extorted under threats of boycott or illegal arrest' from traders. In the Dromore West area, £1 per house was demanded and in Banada a farmer who refused to contribute found that a calf was missing the following morning.[54] In October the IRA collected a tax on alcohol from publicans in Easkey and Dromore West.[55] At Ballymote fair in October, the IRA demanded that traders using the Ulster Bank pay fines ranging from £25 to £100. Armed IRA guards were posted on the premises of traders who refused to pay and prevented them from serving customers. After reduced fines were paid, the guards were withdrawn. This was not specifically targeted at Protestants. Of the 27 Ballymote traders who made claims relating to this matter, either to the Irish Grants Committee (IGC) or the Free State department of finance, 16 were Catholic and 11 non-Catholic.[56] There is no evidence of the Belfast boycott being implemented in this manner in other parts of Sligo at this time. Some of the money collected was presumably used to purchase weapons. According to Dunnill arms for the IRA were landed at Sligo in October and some were distributed in the Ballymote district.[57]

In Sligo town Protestants were pressured to contribute to the White Cross hardship fund set up in February 1921 to assist republicans and their families. Dunnill stated that Sligo loyalists were threatened with boycott if they did not pay.[58] In August the *Connachtman* expressed dissatisfaction with contributions to the fund made by those of more substantial means in Sligo and warned that such people would be revisited. When a Sligo Protestant complained to the national

White Cross that the Sligo committee was using 'compulsory measures' to secure contributions, the Sligo committee, chaired by Michael Nevin, denied this and promised to refund monies to anyone who had contributed under duress.[59] Sligo Protestant businessmen, prominent in the published list of White Cross contributors, included Henry Lyons, who donated £20, and Arthur Jackson, Harper Campbell and the Pollexfens who gave £25 each.[60] There were some claims from loyalists for compensation from the British government relating to this period including five referring to shops being looted by masked and armed men presumably to supply IRA training camps.[61] There is little evidence of new agrarian outrages during this period but where such agitation was already in progress, it generally continued. William Fenton, clerk of the Crown and Peace, had some of his cattle maimed in early November but IRA responsibility was strongly denied in the local press.[62]

The attitude and actions of the IRA led to some public confrontations with Catholic clerics. In October a party from Gurteen IRA training camp found members of the ladies' sodality occupying the front six pews in Gurteen Catholic Church that the IRA had normally occupied. The IRA officer insisted that the sodality members vacate the seats despite protests by the lady in charge. An IRA battalion meeting decided to fine the woman £5 for obstructing the IRA. Fr James O'Connor, PP Gurteen, complained to the minister for defence, who passed the complaint to the AG. He demanded an apology for the lady and the dismissal of the IRA officer responsible.[63] Pilkington alleged that the whole affair had been engineered by Fr O'Connor who, he claimed, had been a long-standing enemy of SF and the IRA, and cited six examples dating back to 1916.[64] In November Fr Michael Durcan, CC Collooney, was accused of being motivated by 'imperial sympathies' and 'prejudice against the national language' when he preached that some parishioners were 'putting the language movement before the cause of their spiritual salvation', apparently objecting to mixed Irish classes for teachers. When the Irish teacher involved defended himself in the *Connachtman*, all but one of the teachers who had been attending the classes absented themselves. The IRA supported the teacher and imposed a boycott on two schools where the teachers taught.[65]

By December 1921 the IRA had achieved a position of dominance and control in County Sligo. Though forty-six SF cumainn (branches) were affiliated in 1921 there was no indication that these were active.[66] Most of the Sligo IRA leaders had been free for the whole truce period and there had been little interference from IRA headquarters until November when Sligo IRA officers were appointed officers of the newly organized 3rd Western Division. The position of the Sligo IRA was stronger than ever: its officers and men had received at least a rudimentary training, it had levied funds and bought new arms, it was able to ignore complaints by Crown forces and its discipline showed no sign of disintegrating. Its distance from Dublin and the absence of a pre-existing divisional structure meant it enjoyed a greater degree of independence. This may have contributed to the IRA's continual interference in local government affairs in Sligo which was not replicated in other counties. There is no mention of such a degree of interference in Longford, Westmeath or Cork, where the IRA had been more active during the previous period. This appears to have been a Sligo manifestation of the tendency of the IRA 'to domineer over civilians and to despise "politicians"', identified by Dorothy Macardle. Sligo IRA's anti-democratic distrust of elected representatives and their assumption of the role of only authentic agents of the republic was a clear example of what Tom Garvin calls the 'Public Band' mentality.[67] With this attitude, the Sligo IRA could not but be profoundly shocked when the Treaty was signed, the terms of which did not include recognition of their republic. It therefore came as no surprise when most of the Sligo IRA leadership and significant numbers of volunteers took the anti-Treaty side and subsequently took up arms against the elected government.

11 'Let it be war'[1]

The Anglo-Irish Treaty was signed on 6 December 1921 and the 'slow and confused' national reaction on the part of those who eventually opposed it was also evident in Sligo.[2] The *Sligo Champion* immediately declared its support. It stressed that Ireland would have full control over her trade, finance and commerce, acknowledged difficulties with the office of governor general and accepted that the north of Ireland would most likely opt out.[3] The *Connachtman* did not make up its mind until 17 December when it declared for 'the Republic founded by Pearse at Eastertide 1916'. At a Sligo Corporation meeting on 7 December Michael Nevin successfully objected to a proposal to congratulate de Valera, Griffith and Collins on the Treaty, saying that such a resolution was premature.[4] No particularly local issues were considered in the debate in Sligo and the arguments there reflected those voiced during the Dáil debate and in national newspapers. In spite of Sligo's proximity to and connections with Ulster, the issue of partition was hardly mentioned apart from an acknowledgment that the six counties would probably remain outside the Free State.[5]

On the anti-Treaty side, the main issue was the ideological attachment to the Republic, the chief element in the *Connachtman*'s December editorials. The oath of fidelity and the office of the governor general were signs, it claimed, that the Free State was 'simply the British government masquerading in a new guise'.[6] The anti-Treaty side in Sligo accepted that it was in the minority but insisted that the majority in favour of the Treaty was being 'stampeded by a consistently hostile and bitter press, coerced and intimidated by threats of war'.[7] After the ratification of the Treaty in January 1922 the anti-Treaty forces and their supporters refused to recognize the decision of the Dáil and asserted their autonomy. The conflicts and confrontations during the following six months resulted in great uncertainty and confusion in Sligo with bank raids, military confrontations, tense election meetings and a general increase in crime. Both sides were reluctant to spark a military conflict and there were many unsuccessful attempts at compromise. Sligo IRA leaders, through their positions in the 3rd Western Division, were deeply involved in much of this activity and their resolve was strengthened. Yet there was little unity of purpose among the anti-Treaty side with the result that they were unprepared for civil war.

All of the 3rd Western Division officers, including Brian MacNeill, opposed the Treaty though, according to Martin Brennan, Carty wavered initially and 'was going to vote for the Treaty but we told him what to do about it'. Pilkington, as O/C 3rd Western Division, was a vocal anti-Treaty presence at the meetings held by the anti-Treaty IRA and between them and GHQ in early 1922. At a joint meeting on 18 January he told the pro-Treaty officers, 'All you want [is] to build up a Free State army so that you can march in step into the British Empire ... We stand by the Republic'.[8] A special Sligo Corporation meeting on 29 December supported the Treaty on a vote of fourteen to five. The SF/labour coalition divided, two former SF mayors (Hanley and Fitzpatrick) voted in favour while Nevin led the opposition. 'Let it be war', he said, 'We may go down in the fight but there is one thing that will live and that is the spirit of uncon-quered Ireland'. Ratepayers' councillors supported ratification, Councillor Harper Campbell Perry welcoming 'this opportunity ... of joining with the majority for the ratification which I hope will bring lasting peace'. The *Connachtman* complained that councillors were 'in pursuit of peace ... at any price'.[9]

In the period leading up to the ratification of the Treaty by the Dáil on 7 January 1922 there was a wave of declarations of support in Sligo. Alec McCabe TD, strongly pro-Treaty, was responsible for a large body of south Sligo IRA taking that side. He argued that no republican could refuse to accept a treaty which had practically given them complete control of the army and natural resources.[10] Sligo Trades and Labour Council chairman, William Reilly, called for ratification 'in the interests of the workers of Ireland, although we are convinced we will have to fight no matter who rules'.[11] Sligo Farmers' Association unanimously supported 'this great measure which offered them complete control of their own house'.[12] Parish meetings to discuss the Treaty had been encouraged especially in the diocese of Killala and Elphin and Bishops Naughton, Coyne and Morrisroe were clearly pro-Treaty.[13] Meetings of SF clubs at Tubbercurry, Killaville, Gurteen and Cloonloo voted for ratification and delegates from twenty-four south Sligo clubs overwhelmingly supported ratifi-cation.[14] By 5 January a total of 328 statutory public bodies nationwide had declared in favour of the Treaty with only five against.[15] Sligo County Council never voted on ratification. A meeting called at the end of December was adjourned as a mark of respect to 19–year-old Michael McCrann from Sligo town IRA who had been accidentally killed.[16]

Sligo TDs McCabe and O'Donnell voted for ratification; Carty and Devins against. News of ratification was received in Sligo with relief but no public show of rejoicing. In Tubbercurry there was 'calmness mingled with relief' and while Ballymote people were glad peace was in sight 'they refrained from expressing the joy in illuminations or band parades'. The *Sligo Champion* celebrated the approval of the Treaty and the establishment of the Provisional Government as 'the most fateful days in Irish history' and asked all Irishmen to support the task of establishing 'order out of chaos'.[17]

The next crucial event after ratification should have been the February SF Ard-Fheis. The *Connachtman* speculated that Treaty supporters 'are likely to receive a severe shock when the result of the ballot [at the Ard-Fheis] is made known'. At South Sligo comhairle ceantair meeting, six cumann voted anti-Treaty while twenty-four voted pro-Treaty. An *Irish Independent* claim that Tubbercurry cumann's anti-Treaty decision was influenced by intimidation was denied by the chairman. There is no record of a North Sligo comhairle ceantair meeting but Sligo SF club appointed R.G. Bradshaw as one of its two anti-Treaty delegates.[18] The Ard-Fheis avoided a vote on the Treaty and delayed the election for three months. The *Sligo Champion* opined: 'Those who desired a split ... have been sadly disappointed. We hope the postponement of the General Election for three months will ... prove a breathing space for the Irish electorate'.[19]

'A big loss to Sligo' was how the *Sligo Independent* described the departure of the British military and it was clear that a substantial number of Sligo people were not afraid to demonstrate their regret at the withdrawal. A special church parade was held on Sunday 29 January and on the following day a tea, social and dance was given by the Calry Church of Ireland parishioners for the military. The officers and men of the 1st Battalion, Bedfordshire and Hertfordshire Regiment gave a grand farewell dance for friends in Sligo town hall on the Tuesday. All events were well patronized and fully reported in the *Sligo Independent*. When the troops evacuated Sligo military barracks on 1 and 2 February the local anti-Treaty IRA took possession.[20] On 9 March they took over both police stations in Sligo town on their evacuation by the RIC. Ballymote barracks was evacuated in mid-February and was handed over to the local pro-Treaty IRA.[21] With the departure of the British military, loyalist nervousness increased. The *Sligo Independent* started to publish leading articles hailing the country's 'new era' but warned that its readers might 'have no opportunity of voicing their opinions through any other source except the medium of this newspaper'.[22] The publicity given to the sectarian outrages in Northern Ireland added to Protestant unease and a meeting of Sligo Protestants at the end of March condemned such violence. The chairman, Arthur Jackson, stressed that 'they could not be living in a community which had shown itself to be more liberal to the many and various opinions which they held'.[23] Other events increased Protestant anxiety. In January members of the Monaghan GAA team, including IRA men, were arrested in Tyrone. With the approval of Mulcahy and Collins, prominent loyalists were kidnapped in cross-border raids and held as hostages for the footballers and for three prisoners in Derry. As part of this action, the 3rd Western Division kidnapped a number of prominent Sligo Protestants. They were released almost immediately, the Derry prisoners having been reprieved on the day of the kidnapping. The *Sligo Independent* called it 'a poor response to the willingness with which the minority in the South and West of Ireland agree to work with their fellow-countrymen in the interests of peace and progress and prosperity'.[24] The election of Michael Nevin as Sligo mayor in January was a boost for the anti-Treaty side, though some pro-Treaty councillors had voted for him. In his acceptance speech, Nevin stressed 'The only authority we recognise is the Republican government of Ireland'.[25]

In Ireland generally the months following the approval of the Treaty were marked by confusion and a drift towards chaos which exasperated and frightened those who had hoped that ratification would end the troubles. During this period the *Sligo Champion* continually warned about the dangers of 'acts which can only result in ultimate chaos and disaster'; 'Until stable government backed strongly by public opinion is established the country will continue to drift into a state that will compare unfavourably with Mexico at its worst'.[26] No proper police force operated in the county and in February the 3rd Western Division IRA claimed: 'evilly disposed persons are taking advantage of the unsettled conditions and it is our duty to trace and bring to justice such individuals'. Anti-Treaty republican police were reported to be restoring law and order in the Ballymote district, mounting patrols, meeting trains and guarding local banks.[27] A number of armed robberies were reported in January and February. In early February over £10,000 was taken in raids on the Bank of Ireland and the Provincial Bank in Sligo town by young men with country accents. The local IRA, who denied involvement, chased the raiders in the direction of Northern Ireland but no one was ever prosecuted.[28] Until June 1922 the local press continued to report criminal activities from all parts of the county including raids on houses, businesses and mail cars and it was impossible to distinguish between the actions of the anti-Treaty IRA securing funds and transport and the work of common criminals.[29]

Protestants were especially vulnerable during this lawless period and suffered in many parts of the country.[30] Although there is no evidence of a systemic anti-Protestant campaign, many incidents were reported in Sligo especially in the south. Protestant houses were raided, shops looted, land taken, vehicles commandeered and fines imposed.[31] In May Gurteen SF condemned raids on private houses of Protestants for 'mere loot'.[32] The *Roscommon Herald* reported in June that several Protestants in the Riverstown area had been warned to clear out but it suggested that this had no effect since 'notices and warnings are of such common occurrences nowadays'.[33]

Disbanded members of the RIC, who returned to or settled in Sligo, were also liable to intimidation. Most left the county, though some fled to Sligo town. In mid–May ex-RIC men were said to have left the Castlebaldwin district after their houses had been fired into. A notice was posted at Gurteen warning ex-RIC to leave and shots were fired into some of their houses.[34] On 17 June the brother of an ex-RIC man was shot dead near Ballymote by masked anti-Treaty IRA who wanted to question the ex-RIC man and apparently panicked when recognized by his brother.[35]

The Killala and Elphin pastoral letters in early 1922 expressed delight at the achievement of freedom, appealed for 'loyalty and allegiance to the government constitutionally established and controlled by Irishmen' but warned that 'any threats or intimidation on the part of one political party to enforce their ideas on

their opponents would be against the moral law and gravely unjust'. Bishop
Morrisroe gave his flock no counsel on the political situation, perhaps finally
realizing the futility of such advice.[36]

As the nationwide split in the IRA continued to harden, 'minor clashes
occurred between pro-Treaty and Republican units'.[37] There were very few such
incidents in Sligo because of the strength of the anti-Treaty IRA. Boyle barracks
had been handed over by the British to Martin Fallon, O/C North Roscommon
Brigade, who took the anti-Treaty side and attended the banned Army
Convention in Dublin on 26 March. The following Wednesday, after meeting
pro-Treaty officers, he and his staff changed sides. Sligo anti-Treaty divisional
officers, who happened to be visiting Boyle barracks at the time, took over the
post after an exchange of fire and 3rd Western Division anti-Treaty reinforcements arrived to garrison the barracks.[38] Ballymote RIC barracks was taken by
anti-Treaty forces on the night of 2 April when most of the pro-Treaty garrison
were attending an election meeting at Castlebar. The pro-Treaty forces then
occupied Ballymote courthouse. They also commanded a post at Gurteen.[39]

At the anti-Treaty Army Convention on 26 March Pilkington was elected to
the temporary executive. This convention represented a clear break by the anti-
Treaty IRA from GHQ. The cabinet decided they should get no further
financial assistance. Local fund raising efforts included the re-imposition of the
Belfast boycott, the collection of dog licence money, bank raids and comman-
deering of goods.[40] Raids for Belfast goods led to an upsurge in attacks on
railways and the Midland Great Western Railway reported that the Kilfree
Junction area was the single most raided place on their network. The 3rd
Western Division ordered that all dog licences were to be paid at the nearest IRA
barracks and the IRA raided post offices for dog licence money.[41] The anti-
Treaty IRA executive organized nation-wide raids on branches of the National
Bank on 1 May. Charles Gildea, QM 3rd Western Division, organized a raid on
the Sligo branch, in which almost £2,000 was taken, and a raid on the Boyle
branch.[42]

In March 'a state of guerrilla warfare' was said to exist along the border and
a 3rd Western Division ASU operated there, had several engagements with B
Specials and destroyed some outposts.[43] Part of a national plan for a northern
offensive involved IRA units exchanging their British-supplied weapons for guns
imported from Germany. This was to avoid the embarrassment of British forces
finding that their attackers were using British-supplied weapons. Members of
the 3rd Western Division went to Birr where they got about 150 Mausers.[44] In
early March troops from the Division were among those rushed to Limerick
where a crisis developed when rival units contested the right to occupy evacuated barracks.[45]

A general election was fixed for 16 June and by early April the campaign was
said to be 'in full swing in Sligo' with directors of elections appointed, candi-

dates selected and meetings being held.[46] Labour was split on the question of participation with Lynch's anti-Treaty faction strongly against it. A Sligo Trades and Labour Council delegation attended the special Labour congress in Dublin in February which decided to contest the election. A Sligo branch of the Labour party was subsequently formed with William Reilly as president, apparently without any support from Sligo TGWU. The Sligo Labour branch postponed selection of a candidate pending a series of regional meetings and a conference. There is no record of such meetings being held and no candidate was selected for Sligo.[47]

Election meetings increased military tension during the campaign and the Easter Sunday pro-Treaty Sligo meeting was 'the tensest of all these public gatherings'.[48] It proved a significant victory for the Provisional Government in terms of publicity and establishing a military presence in Sligo town. A 'monster pro-Treaty meeting' to be addressed by Arthur Griffith was announced for Sligo for Easter Sunday 16 April. Pilkington then published a prohibition of 'the holding of public meetings and demonstrations of a political nature' in his divisional area.[49] When Mayor Nevin telegraphed Griffith asking for clarification Griffith replied: 'Dáil Éireann has not authorised and will not authorise interference with right of public meeting or free speech. I, as President of Dáil Éireann, will go to Sligo on Sunday next'.[50] Government troops led by McCabe entered Sligo under cover of darkness on Thursday night and occupied the jail. Large numbers of anti-Treaty troops were drafted into Sligo from the 3rd and parts of the 4th Western Divisions and occupied strategic public buildings. The bishop of Elphin made unsuccessful efforts to mediate. On Easter Saturday anti-Treaty GHQ instructed Pilkington not to prevent the meeting. During that night Griffith reached Sligo with an armed escort under Seán Mac Eoin and on Sunday morning a patrol of forty pro-Treaty troops in three lorries, under the command of J.J. O'Connell, arrived from Dublin. The patrol stopped outside one of the hotels, unaware that it was occupied by the IRA; a ten-minute exchange of fire resulted in some injuries. Pro-Treaty IRA from the Ballymote and Gurteen posts also were in Sligo at this time. Pilkington remained in his office during the day communicating with his officers through Bradshaw. He refused to allow any of his men patrol the town and as Tom Scanlon later recalled: 'It ruined us. We were powerless. We could not do a thing to stop the Free Staters from walking up and down'. Martin Brennan said that as a result 'Good lads of ours ... joined up [with] the Free State'. Rory O'Connor and Seán Moylan came down soon afterwards to try to heal the breach.[51] Carty, who was in Sligo on the day, was severely critical of 'the way the divisional staff had mishandled the situation ... and the disastrous effect which this had on the morale of our troops'.[52] A large crowd attended the meeting which was chaired by D.M. Hanley and passed off without incident. Local speakers included Sligo TDs O'Donnell and McCabe, County Council chairman James Gilligan and

Labour leader William Reilly (plates 22–5).[53] The *Sligo Champion* offices were raided early the following week to prevent it publishing reports of the meeting and the paper later hinted at the involvement of someone from the *Connachtman* office.[54]

Griffith's meeting had allowed the pro-Treaty forces gain a foothold in Sligo and two weeks later they occupied three more posts in the town. The rival forces engaged in a considerable amount of sniping. By mid-May it was said that 'not a night has passed but rifle and revolver shots have been heard in Sligo'.[55] Attempts in early June by pro-Treaty forces from Sligo town to establish posts at Dromore West and Charlestown were foiled by the prompt action of anti-Treaty forces but they did occupy Markree Castle near Collooney and the market house in Collooney.[56]

The election campaign continued. Pro-Treaty election meetings were reported at the end of April and early May, including four in north Sligo, the first of the campaign there. This, together with the lack of reports of anti-Treaty election activities, may indicate pro-Treaty confidence and low morale on the opposing side following Griffith's meeting in Sligo.[57] At the end of April and early May, anti-Treaty troops twice opened fire on pro-Treaty soldiers and election workers in the Curry district.[58]

The Collins-de Valera pact in mid-May agreed a national SF coalition panel in an effort to avoid a divisive election. SF was to nominate only the outgoing TDs; however, alternative candidates could be nominated by other interests.[59] The anti-Treaty side in Sligo welcomed the pact more enthusiastically than the pro-Treaty side. The *Connachtman* proclaimed: 'We as a people are at all times ready to ... stand together when the common cause of the nation so demands'. The *Sligo Champion* was disappointed: 'It means to an extent the muzzling of the Irish electorate'.[60] The pact caused no difficulty for the anti-Treaty side as only three outgoing TDs – Carty, Devins and Ferran – had been selected and they were allowed go forward under the terms of the pact. Five pro-Treaty candidates had been selected but only the two outgoing TDs, McCabe and O'Donnell, could go forward as official SF candidates. John Hennigan and Seamus MacGowan, who had to be dropped, immediately announced that they were standing as independents.[61] A joint manifesto from the panel candidates criticized their 'acting against the best interests of Ireland'.[62] At a Sligo Corporation meeting that unanimously endorsed the national panel, there were attacks on the independents from anti-Treaty councillors, including Lynch and Nevin. Lynch did, however, credit McGowan as being 'one of the earliest Sinn Féiners in Sligo, with himself'.[63] Sligo-Mayo East and Galway were the only contested Connacht constituencies. Pressure was successfully exerted by pact candidates in Mayo South-Roscommon South, Mayo North and West and in Leitrim-Roscommon North, where farmers' candidates withdrew at the last moment.[64] The claim by the *Connachtman* that organized labour and the majority of farmers repudiated both independents was not true. McGowan stood as an independent Labour candidate proposed by William Reilly, chairman of Sligo Trades Council, who was also election agent for both independents. Sligo Labour Party supported both independents. Hennigan, chairman of both Grange branch and Sligo executive of the Farmers' Association, stood as an independent farmers' candidate and the Sligo Farmers' Association executive undertook to have collections to defray the independents' expenses and to provide personating agents.[65]

The election pact seemed to dampen public enthusiasm in Sligo as elsewhere and most of the electioneering was done by the anti-Treaty side.[66] There was little evidence of panel cooperation during the campaign. What was announced as a panel meeting in Sligo on 11 June was attended by anti-Treaty speakers only, although Tom O'Donnell sent a telegram of apology and Devins told the voters to 'give their first and second preference to any one of the panel candidates'. Eamon de Valera toured the constituency with Devins and O'Donnell and held meetings at Ballymote, Tubbercurry and Sligo, which seem to have been the only instances of pro- and anti-Treaty candidates appearing on the same platform in Sligo.[67] The independents did hold meetings but the *Connachtman* claimed that these had to be abandoned in north Sligo because of hostility.[68] A number of Protestants in the Drumcliff district received threatening letters ordering them not to vote and the *Sligo Independent* claimed that some of these were impersonated on election day.[69]

The *Connachtman* published a special edition on Wednesday 14 June, two days before the election, urging people to vote pro-panel. The *Sligo Champion* was unenthusiastic: 'If the national panel were returned in its entirety it is morally certain that the bear garden proceedings would be resumed exactly where they were left off and the country's drift towards disaster would be accelerated'. The *Sligo Independent* supported the independents.[70] Their election agents were kidnapped on the morning of the election and held in Sligo military barracks. The independents withdrew from the count as a protest against this and 'the gross impersonation and intimidation which was practised on and before the day of the poll'. There were complaints of widespread impersonation in the constituency and McCabe hinted at irregularities after the count: 'Certain circumstances were not what they might have been'.[71]

The Sligo-Mayo East turnout was 55 per cent, significantly higher than the national figure of 45 per cent. McCabe topped the poll; the five seats went to the five outgoing members and this constituency was the only one in which the anti-Treaty candidates secured an overall majority. Anti-Treaty SF won 56.4 per cent, pro-Treaty 29.5 per cent. An explanation for the exceptionally high anti-Treaty vote, apart from personation, may be geographic. Carty came from south Sligo, Devins from north Sligo and Ferran from east Mayo while the two pro-Treaty candidates lived within ten miles of one another in south Sligo. Transfer patterns in the constituency reflected the national pattern; anti-Treaty voters were more inclined to give preferences to remaining pro–Treaty candidates while pro–Treaty voters were more likely to favour independents.[72]

Sligo County Council had remained bitterly divided all through this period but on the day before the election, the statutory Council meeting had seen agreement on the selection of chairman. Carty proposed pro–Treaty councillor Martin Roddy, describing him as an 'honest, straight man', McCabe seconded this and Roddy was unanimously elected.[73] By the time the election results were finalized, signs of cooperation had faded. On the declaration of the results Devins said that the fight was only starting. The election outcome in Sligo greatly heartened the anti–Treaty side. The *Connachtman* coupled satisfaction with the results with criticism of Collins' apparent last-minute repudiation of the pact and of the new Free State constitution, which it called 'an unqualified surrender and abandonment of the nation's rights'. Less than two weeks later the Civil War began and the newly elected TDs were in full armed opposition.[74]

By June 1922 Sligo anti–Treaty IRA had established a strong position in the county having taken over almost all the positions vacated by the British army and RIC. They had increased their strength and armaments during this period and had been involved in action on the border and in the stand-off in Limerick. They had found common cause with the large numbers of like-minded IRA men throughout the country. However, internal disagreements and a failure to develop a common strategy or formulate a coherent plan to deal with an outbreak of hostilities meant that the anti–Treaty side were ill-prepared for the Civil War that their stance and actions made almost inevitable. In addition, their flouting of the popular will, the increased disturbances and criminality crucially increased the desire of the majority for acceptance of stable government and peaceful conditions under the Free State. As one might expect, this further reduced support for the anti–Treaty position and thus armed opposition to the government was unlikely to win public sympathy or popular support. The attempt to prevent Griffith's meeting proved an embarrassing failure for Sligo anti–Treaty IRA. It should have provided some indication of the probable outcome of a wider struggle. But the warning went unheeded and the people of Sligo would have to endure another nine months of fratricidal conflict and widespread disruption.

12 'Pressing back the forces of disorder'[1]

After months of dissention and failed attempts at compromise, the Civil War began on 28 June 1922 with the Provisional Government's bombardment of the Four Courts held by anti-Treaty forces. Fighting spread throughout the country with attacks on the many urban positions held by the anti-Treaty side. By August the republicans had either been driven out of, or had abandoned, their fixed positions and the war entered a guerrilla phase. Over the next ten months the government forces gradually extended their control. Both sides were badly prepared for war. The anti-Treaty side had the advantage in numbers outside Dublin at the start and were better armed than before but as the weeks went by the size, arms and resources of the National army improved. The absence of any coherent national direction or preparation for war prevented the anti-Treaty IRA from taking advantage of their initial superiority. Given that a majority of the people favoured the Treaty, the longer the war dragged on the more unpopular it naturally became.[2] This same malaise prevented Sligo IRA from flourishing from the outset. As soon as significant pro-Treaty forces reached Sligo town the anti-Treaty forces abandoned their positions and reverted to guerrilla tactics. By the end of July, the National army was in possession of all town posts in the county. The war in Sligo, after some spectacular confrontations in the early weeks, settled down into an attempted re-run of the War of Independence. However, with a war-weary populace and a native enemy there was little likelihood of anti-Treaty success. The pacification of Sligo, in what was regarded as the isolated north-west, was never a government priority. It took a long time before the National army was strong enough to attend to the Sligo anti-Treaty IRA who had still not been completely defeated when the conflict ended in May 1923.

On hearing of the attack on the Four Courts the 3rd Western Division staff met in Sligo but there was no agreement on coordinated action. Carty was in favour of attacking government posts in the area; Tom Carney, East Mayo, wanted to advance towards Athlone but Pilkington advocated attacking British forces on the border. In the absence of any communication from the executive in Dublin, Pilkington left to confer with Michael Kilroy, O/C 4th Western Division. Carty and Carney decided to operate independently and on 2 July they captured Collooney market house. Operating unimpeded in the area for the next ten days, they demolished bridges, blocked roads and, in sniping attacks on Markree Castle, killed a soldier, Riverstown native P.J. McDermott (plate 27). There was no coordinated action with anti-Treaty forces in Sligo, Ballymote or Boyle and they waited to be confronted by the better equipped and manned National army. The North Sligo Brigade captured a government position on the Leitrim-Fermanagh border.[3]

Government forces seized the initiative in Sligo town. On 28 June the courthouse garrison occupied an adjoining garage directly facing the anti-Treaty IRA
post in No. 1 RIC barracks. A clash seemed imminent but early on Saturday, 1
July the republicans withdrew, burned the barracks and joined their comrades at
the military barracks. The following morning they evacuated and burned Sligo
military barracks and established a new headquarters at Rahelly House near
Lissadell. Brian MacNeill, adjutant 3rd Western Division, wrote:

> The tactics in this area will have to be altered to the guerrilla form as
> attacks on enemy posts on a large scale are impossible for the following
> reasons (a) too expensive on ammunition, (b) strength of enemy posts,
> (c) more effect can be gained by ambushing them when passing between
> posts.[4]

However, the government's grip on Sligo town was far from secure and shooting
incidents during the following days and nights resulted in the death of one
National army soldier. Sligo post office was attacked and telephone and
telegraph equipment wrecked. Government reinforcements, including the
Ballinalee armoured car, arrived in Sligo on 5 July and on the following day the
Wine Street republican police post was taken and a civilian killed. The *Ballinalee*
was then used to maintain communications by a circuitous route between Sligo
town and Markree Castle. On 13 July the armoured car with a convoy of lorries
was ambushed by Carty at Rockwood on the shores of Lough Gill. After a two-
hour fight in which four of their soldiers were killed, the National army party
surrendered. The *Ballinalee* drove towards Sligo but was captured when it ran
into a republican road block operated by north Sligo republicans.[5] The following
day Devins triumphantly entered Sligo town with the *Ballinalee* and delivered an
ultimatum to Martin Fallon, O/C National army courthouse garrison, who
refused to surrender. After intervention by clergy was rejected, Bishop Coyne of
Elphin left his sick bed and when his efforts at mediation failed, he entered the
courthouse and refused to move until the danger of violence was averted. Tom
Scanlon, who negotiated with the bishop (plate 26), recalled: 'Realising the
propaganda the enemy would make of it if the bishop was either killed or
wounded by our attack we left the town with all our men'.[6]

On the night of 14 July Seán Mac Eoin, O/C Western Command, National
army, took a troop train of 300 to 400 men from Athlone and surrounded
Collooney. Local clergy were allowed to evacuate townspeople before the battle
which lasted five hours. The town was taken and forty republicans captured,
including Frank O'Beirne, O/C Collooney Battalion.[7] Carty later stated that he
was unable to come to the aid of Collooney because he had not been informed of
the attack but Martin Brennan claimed 'We heard the shooting but Frank Carty
wouldn't let us go in so O'Beirne had to surrender. That was jealousy'.[8] After the

fall of Collooney, Carty decided to abandon all town positions and operate in columns only. In this way Tubbercurry was occupied by government forces on 28 July.[9]

This marked the end of the first phase of the Civil War in Sligo. The National army controlled the main towns and the republicans reverted to familiar guerrilla tactics, as they did throughout Ireland. A key aim of the National army had been 'to prevent enemy troops evacuating barracks in possession of rifles and ammunition and reverting to guerrilla warfare'.[10] The failure of this policy in Sligo ensured that a quick victory over the anti-Treaty side would be difficult to achieve. The position was similar in large areas of Connacht, where republican strength still posed major challenges. A National army report in August described the situation in the 3rd Western Division as the next most serious military problem after Waterford, Cork and Limerick. Government forces rarely ventured out of their town positions, which were often sniped at, though such activity decreased in Sligo town when reinforcements arrived at the end of July. The captured *Ballinalee*, liable to turn up anywhere in the county as it was passed among the republicans, caused terror in Sligo on 5 August when it was used to attack and capture a small government post, which was held for only a short time.[11]

In early August there were three strong republican groupings in County Sligo. An estimated 100 men with 90 rifles, 70 revolvers and 4 machine guns, based at Rahelly with the divisional staff, controlled most of north Sligo but were constricted by the National army's 1st Northern Division, which held Finner Camp and Bundoran. Carty's group of forty to sixty men was based in the Ox Mountains between Coolaney and Curry. In the Geevagh/Arigna area, Harold McBrien and Edward Bofin led a party estimated at 150 with a plentiful supply of rifles and revolvers. In south Sligo, where large numbers of IRA had taken the pro-Treaty side, a small anti-Treaty group estimated at about thirteen men armed with rifles and revolvers operated near Ballymote.[12]

Neither side took decisive action during August or September 1922. The National army lacked numbers, transport, intelligence and the confidence to undertake large-scale attacks. An intelligence officer in Sligo claimed that although National troops were aware of many ambushes set by republicans, nothing could be done 'as the garrison in each place is too small to admit of raiding parties being sent out'. Warnings of probable republican attacks were frequent. In early August the I/O 3rd Western predicted anti-Treaty attacks on Sligo, Ballymote and Tubbercurry. On 22 August he warned 'the irregulars are rapidly completing preparations for an attack on National forces in Sligo town'.[13] These attacks did not materialize. The government forces in the Ballymote/Gurteen area were the most active at this time. Carty supposedly complained about the condition of his feet 'on account of Alec McCabe's Lancia cars being on all the roads'.[14] During this time the anti-Treaty side in Sligo lost a chance to inflict severe setbacks on the National army before it could build up its strength. There was little significant collaboration between republican groups within the county or with republicans in adjacent counties, apart from the limited joint actions in the early days of the war and the sharing of the *Ballinalee*. Lack of arms and ammunition was not a problem. Between the outbreak of the Civil War and the beginning of August, the 3rd Western Division anti-Treaty IRA had captured 160 rifles, one Lewis gun and an armoured car equipped with a Vickers gun. 'From the point of view of armament we are much stronger than when we started', MacNeill reported.[15] There had been some effort to create a republican Western Command in the early months of the war but this never functioned satisfactorily. A Western Command meeting in November, attended by four 3rd Western Division officers, 'principally concerned with bringing about unification of action and complete co-operation within the Command', was disrupted by a National army round-up and abandoned. In mid-January 1923 the command adjutant reported communications had not been acknowledged by any of the divisions which comprised the command.[16]

The extent of the republicans' ambitions seemed to be the occasional successful ambush or temporary seizure of an enemy post. The August 1922 diary of activities of the north Sligo 1st Brigade lists only four actions: the successful attack on the National army post in Sligo town and three attacks on Bundoran army posts. This was despite the availability of the *Ballinalee* and the inaction of the government forces.[17] The diary of Carty's 4th Brigade for the same period reveals that for all his early emphasis on action, his forces were just as lacking in offensive ideas. Carty himself admitted that there was 'a lull as far as large scale operations were concerned until near the end of August', when he lured a party of 45 National army troops from Tubbercurry into an ambush in which one soldier was killed and forty rifles and a Lewis gun captured. 'From this date', Carty wrote, 'we were pretty well supplied with arms and ammunition'.[18] Communications, especially railways, were an easy target. The Collooney to Claremorris line, which ran through Carty's territory, was damaged in a number of places and no trains operated on this line during the remainder of 1922. The Sligo, Leitrim & Northern Counties line was subject to constant attacks during July and August. By contrast, the main Sligo–Dublin line, running through an area more-or-less controlled by government troops, operated normally with only one attack reported during August.[19]

There were difficulties for the National army in terms of organization, morale and supplies. In August headquarters attempted to reorganize the large and unwieldy Western Command that stretched from Westmeath to Sligo and Galway. Total strength was to be reduced to 2,100 men with a new emphasis on consolidating positions and training troops. This involved evacuating about thirty of the smaller posts, including Gurteen in Sligo, and sending men to the Curragh for training. Mac Eoin reported difficulties, especially opposition from traders in towns, which were to lose posts, and asked for two weeks' grace. This was granted but with a rebuke from Mulcahy: 'We are simply going to break up what we have of an army if we leave it any longer in small posts and do not give it proper military training.'[20] On 4 September Mac Eoin reported that the scheme was ready to be put into operation but that he was waiting for promised supplies. Notably, he complained of 'serious trouble with some of the men – in fact mutiny in some places for want of pay', although Mulcahy's reply pointed out that 3,000 men were being paid regularly in the Western Command.[21] Later that month Mac Eoin reported that grave dissatisfaction relating to army appointments, pay and supply of uniforms had existed in the command area for a considerable time.[22]

Early in September Carty borrowed the *Ballinalee* and used it in unsuccessful attacks on government posts at Tubbercurry, where one soldier was killed (see plate 28) and Ballymote where one republican was killed. The *Ballinalee* was passed to the 4th Western Division, which captured Ballina, but then retreated before the advance of a National army convoy under Adjutant Tony Lawlor, Mac Eoin's second-in-command. This was part of the army's drive to subdue the west, beginning with the landing of National army forces at Westport on 24 July. After securing Ballina, Lawlor's convoy with its own armoured car, the *Big Fella*, moved across the Ox Mountains towards Tubbercurry. Carty's men harried the advancing troops and killed two, including Brigadier Joseph Ring from Westport. Eventually Lawlor's men reached Tubbercurry and were joined by another party under Mac Eoin. This joint force swept the Ox Mountains from Tubbercurry to Coolaney on the night of 14 September. Carty demobilized his men, returned the *Ballinalee* to north Sligo and had only one man captured in the sweep.[23]

Mac Eoin and Lawlor then turned their attention to republicans in north Sligo. A coordinated encircling attack commenced on 19 September involving troops from the 1st Northern Division in Finner Camp, 1st Midland Division in Manorhamilton and 3rd Western Division in Sligo and Boyle. Most of the republicans slipped through the National army cordon to the safety of the mountains on the Sligo–Leitrim border. The *Ballinalee* was put out of action rather than be allowed fall into government hands, though it was still mobile enough to be triumphantly towed through the streets of Sligo.[24] During the north Sligo operation, six republicans – Brigadier Séamus Devins, Adjutant Brian MacNeill, Lieutenant Paddy Carroll, Captain Harry Benson and Volunteers Joseph Banks and Tommy Langan – were killed on Benbulben Mountain. MacNeill, son of the Provisional Government minister Eoin MacNeill, had a brother in the National army.[25] Republicans claimed that the six had been shot after surrender, citing evidence from unnamed government troops. Conclusive evidence is lacking but it appears most likely that the republican version of the killings is true. MacNeill was buried in Dublin. The funeral of the others in Sligo was a large demonstration 'attended by all creeds and classes and political opinions' (plates 29, 30).[26]

This operation failed to capture significant numbers of the estimated 120 republican troops in the area but it succeeded in opening up north Sligo to government troops. The deaths were a serious setback for the republicans: 'The loss of Brigadier Devins and his companions was a very severe blow to the Brigade which had practically to be reorganized again'. To make matters worse, Pilkington was incapacitated with a broken limb at this time leaving the quarter-master as the only member of staff still working. The divisional staff vacancies were filled by the end of November.[27]

Following the September operations in Sligo, National army reports were optimistic. A Western Command report claimed: 'Everywhere our troops have gone they have gained the sympathy of the people. The people are coming out, building bridges and repairing roads'. Thirty-six republicans were said to have been captured in another north Sligo round-up and there were also arrests in Tubbercurry and Strandhill.[28] Reports in November claimed that most of Sligo was clear apart from some small groups: 'Carty's column is dwindling. It is reported most of his men have gone home'.[29] Evidence from the other side confirms that this was a low point in their fortunes. Martin Brennan recalled increased popular hostility: 'It looked by their conduct that the people there thought we were beaten'.[30] He said 'During this time we found it impossible to lie in ambush for any length of time especially on the Tubbercurry-Ballymote road owing to the activity of enemy spies', and their activities were confined to destroying communications and sniping enemy posts.[31]

However, government forces were unable to take full advantage of this lull in republican activity because of continuing problems with morale, organization, supplies and equipment. Western Command officers criticized headquarters for not sending requested armaments. They claimed that the garrison of fifty men at Ballymote had only twenty-six rifles and that there were also ammunition shortages at Tubbercurry, Markree, Collooney, Ballisodare and Sligo.[32] Headquarters blamed local administration. Mulcahy complained to Mac Eoin in October that only sixty of an expected one thousand men had been sent from his command for training in the Curragh: 'Personally I cannot sense that there is any solid administration or organisation over the area pressing back the forces of disorder there'.[33]

These difficulties allowed republicans columns to survive and continue their activity. Government posts in Sligo town were sniped in mid-October and ten republican prisoners escaped from Sligo jail. Attempts to repair communications were thwarted. When the Collooney to Claremorris railway line was repaired in late November republicans tore up the rails and destroyed signal boxes. Likewise, road bridges, which had been repaired at Curry and Drumcliff, were demolished again in October. Drumcliff bridge had been repaired in September, damaged on 14 October, repaired by locals assembled by the parish priest on 23 October but demolished again on 28 October.[34] The arrest of eight of Carty's men on 1 November near Tubbercurry appears to have led him to take action to stop increased civilian cooperation with the National army. He had two men shot dead as spies near the town on the night of 5 November and their bodies dumped on the roadside with warning notices. These killings caused a sensation locally.[35] McCabe reported: 'there are crowds of refugees coming in from the terrorized areas to Ballymote and Tubbercurry barracks'. During increased National army activity in the area immediately after these killings, troops accidentally shot dead a civilian and killed a suspected republican.[36] The publicity the killings received nationally was so adverse that Liam Lynch, IRA chief of staff, pointed out to Pilkington that general order no. 6 had not been complied with. Issued on 4 September 1922, the order stated that persons charged with espionage must be tried by military courts set up by the brigade commandant and that death sentences should be passed only where information given to the enemy resulted in a Volunteer's death. All death sentences had to be confirmed by GHQ before being carried out.[37] Carty's adjutant claimed that they had not received the general order and that the divisional command had approved the executions. In the event no action was taken. Carty's column increased its activity during the remainder of 1922. Two National army soldiers were killed in an ambush outside Tubbercurry on 30 November. In December Carty's men were reported to be sniping posts at Tubbercurry, Collooney and Markree, disrupting communications, raiding mail cars and commandeering transport.[38]

Republicans in the vicinity of Sligo town carried out two spectacular operations at this time, which earned national publicity to the embarrassment of the National army. In December they captured the army position in the town hall, killed a soldier and escaped with 21 rifles, 4 revolvers and 1,300 rounds of ammunition.[39] On the night of 10 January 1923 they almost completely destroyed Sligo railway station in one of the largest such acts of destruction in the country during the Civil War. It was alleged that the troops in the town had been slow to respond but it was pointed out in their defence that the effective strength of the Sligo garrison on the night was only seventy.[40]

By the end of 1922 the republican columns continued to operate as they had since the outbreak of the war, although their numbers had dwindled and they were forced on to mountain areas. Twenty to thirty of the north Sligo column operated in the Ballintrillick area while another group of about twenty led by Pilkington stayed in the Calry area nearer Sligo town. Bofin's column of about twenty men was based in the mountains to the south-east. Carty and his column of upwards of thirty men was still active along the Ox Mountains. In November 1922 the National army had six posts in the county: Sligo had 211 men, Collooney 33, Markree Castle 110, Ballisodare 18, Tubbercurry 57 and Ballymote 43.[41]

An army report on north-west Sligo in December was far from optimistic: 'Every day the irregulars are strengthening their position and recruiting more men'. It suggested that if the situation remained as it was, the irregulars might be worn down in two years and criticized the methods adopted by the army, the procedure for paying the troops and the lack of supplies and uniforms.[42] Pilkington also believed that circumstances had improved for his side. New officers had been appointed, valuable intelligence was being obtained and communications were being reorganized. With 300 rifles and three Lewis, one Vickers and one Thompson machine gun, he thought that 'good work can be expected in this area.' Moreover, the attitude of the people was favourable: 'there is no difficulty in finding billets and food for the Active Service Units ... if our fight is maintained it won't be long until we have the people wholeheartedly with us in our struggle for the life of the republic [sic]'.[43]

In early 1923 operations by republican forces nationally became localized and patchy and Sligo was one of the few areas which still witnessed widespread republican activity.[44] From November 1922 the Provisional Government's policy of official executions aimed to discourage republican resistance. Though no Sligoman was executed, the policy was one of a number of developments that combined to undermine the republican position. For instance, following his arrest in January 1923 Cork's Liam Deasy wrote to leading republican officers advocating the cessation of the armed struggle. This damaged morale in Sligo as elsewhere. For Matt Kilcawley, Deasy's letter 'made for a slowing down of interest in further activities'. Frank Carty replied to Deasy. He refused to be 'any party to such a shameful and cowardly surrender of the Republic, whose ultimate victory is assured' and claimed that there was no trace of 'war weariness' in the Sligo area.[45] In a joint pastoral letter in October 1922 the Catholic hierarchy expressed unqualified support for the Provisional Government.[46] Some local priests were antagonistic to republicans, notably Fr P. Butler in Sligo. A few continued to support them and a curate in Dromore West was said to have been 'out' with the irregulars for a time and to have refused to read the pastoral.[47] The hierarchy's pastorals in 1923 were stark and forthright. Coyne of Elphin attacked the 'unscrupulous campaign of murder, robbery and wanton destruction of property ... pursued by the minority' and singled out 'half-crazed hysterical women' who 'assist by carrying dispatches and arms in the slaughter of some of the best and bravest of Ireland's sons'. Morrisroe spoke of the ten innocent people who had been killed in his diocese during the year, some with 'savage cruelty'.[48] There was some interest in Sligo in Florence O'Donoghue's Neutral IRA, founded in December 1922 and consisting of pre-truce IRA. A small number from the county attended a Dublin convention in February 1923 and were said to be organizing a local branch but nothing more was heard of it. The national organization was wound up in March.[49]

The reorganization of the National army command structure arising from the dismantling of the unwieldy Western Command in January appears to have been a turning point in Sligo. The areas north of the Ox Mountains now came under the Donegal Command while the rest of Sligo passed to the Claremorris Command with the exception of a small area in the south-east which remained under Athlone.[50] As Donegal was almost free of republican military activity, that command could concentrate all of its energies on Sligo. A republican report at the end of January admitted as much: 'Since this area has been handed over to the Northern Command under General Sweeney the enemy has been very active. They are raiding the country constantly in large bodies'.[51] The Claremorris and Donegal Commands carried out joint large-scale sweeps which severely limited the republicans' offensive potential and led to their 'constant apprehension of a lightning descent of troops'.[52] February and March saw significant republican losses with the arrest of officers Patrick Coleman, Ballymote, Martin Brennan and Sean Ginty, Tubbercurry and the killing of Harry Brehony in Coolaney and Paul Geoghegan in Beltra. Sweeps of the Arigna area in mid-February and March resulted in important arrests, including that of Edward Bofin. During the first half of February the exertions of the Claremorris Command forced the 4th Brigade to lie low; six of its men were captured and one killed. The establishment of three new army posts by the first week in May at Aclare, Enniscrone and Dromore West consolidated government gains.[53]

Sligo republicans were unable to respond to this increased activity. Only a few incidents of sniping at town posts were reported between February and April, though these included an attack at Tubbercurry in which one soldier was killed. As government troops penetrated republican-held areas, they repaired bridges and cleared roads and these repairs were now generally not undone.[54] House burnings were a common tactic and in Sligo Free State troops burned the houses of two republican activists while the IRA burned at least six houses where a son was in the National army.[55] By the end of April government reports claimed that Sligo irregular columns were reduced in strength and their activities confined to looting, post office raids, road blocking, cutting telegraph wires and some ineffective sniping: 'The inclination to ambush or fight is finished'.[56] A Claremorris report revealed: 'The people are becoming very friendly to the troops and are now feeling more secure as practically every town in the area is now garrisoned'. Carty's column along the Ox Mountains was said to be down to about twenty men and the north Sligo column numbers were estimated at ten to fifteen.[57] Yet, little of the republican arsenal was captured and in mid-March the division still had 300 rifles with 15,000 rounds of ammunition, four Lewis guns, one Vickers and one Thompson machine gun. Much of this material was being dumped as numbers of active volunteers declined. Liam Lynch, angry at the mismatch between arms and activity, complained: 'You should press for more activity ... If all our forces on active service are properly organised into columns and well led they should be able to make things very hot for the enemy'.[58]

On 10 April 1923 Lynch died after being shot in a skirmish in the Knockmealdown Mountains. The end of the Civil War then came quickly. Frank Aiken, Lynch's successor as chief of staff, issued an order to dump arms on 24 May. In Sligo, according to Pilkington, 'although the feelings and opinions of all ranks in the division were against the decision calling off the war and dumping the arms, still the orders enforcing this decision have been faithfully and effectively carried out'.[59] By the end of May Donegal Command found that none of the republican columns in its area showed any sign of activity. Claremorris Command reported on 2 June that all irregular arms seemed to be dumped and reports for the rest of June emphasized the deterioration of the republican columns.[60]

The confusion of early 1922 coincided with a rise in agrarian unrest, intimidation, robbery, petty crime and hooliganism, which became worse during the early months of the Civil War. On the night of 24 July Mrs Nellie McDonagh of Riverstown was shot dead by one of a gang of armed masked youths who broke into her house to 'raid for a gun'.[61] In October gangs of youths were said to be causing wanton damage to property in the Gurteen area. Mullaghroe public houses were raided and tobacco, drink and cigarettes taken. There were reports of similar lawlessness in Sligo town, Ballymote, Bunninadden, Easkey and Collooney.[62] The Bunninadden area had to receive special attention in mid-1923.[63] In early April 1923, 77-year-old Catherine McGuinness of Culleens was shot dead when a row developed after a group of anti-Treaty IRA was entertained in the house late at night and shots were fired.[64] As the Provisional Government forces regained control, they set up an army police force. By the end of July Ballymote had such a force and in October troops were said to be efficiently carrying out police duties.[65] Members of the new Civic Guard (Garda Síochána) began to take up duties in September 1922 and a superintendent was sent to the Sligo-Leitrim division in October. Eighteen members took up duty at Wine Street police barracks in Sligo and seven took up duty in Ballymote at the same time.[66] In January 1923 County Sligo had the lowest number of occupied police stations in the Free State with two, Sligo and Ballymote. Leitrim had three, Mayo four, Roscommon six and Galway fourteen.[67] In April Civic Guards took up duty in Tubbercurry. Sligo then had one sergeant and fifteen guards, Ballymote one sergeant and six guards and Tubbercurry one sergeant and five guards.[68] In July 1923 the Civic Guard reported that 'this county is on the whole in a satisfactory condition and is rapidly recovering from the lawlessness which some time ago prevailed'.[69] Sligo Borough court and Sligo parish court resumed operations in mid-August as the town settled after the early weeks of the war.[70] Superintendent Neary of the Civic Guard attended Sligo quarter sessions in January and in May Judge Wakely presided under an Irish tricolour.[71] The Provisional Government closed down the Dáil courts in October and established a new district court system. No court was held in Sligo from October 1922 until the first sitting of the new district court took place at Sligo courthouse on 8 February, presided over by Donegal-born district judge Charles A. Flattery. Ballymote district court was held on 13 February and continued to be held monthly.[72]

There is little evidence of a systematic 'campaign of loyalist extermination' against non-Catholics in Sligo during the truce and Civil War period. The most serious cases involved loss of earnings, physical hardship and destruction of property including cases of agrarian agitation against landowners and shopkeepers suffering boycotts, raids and looting.[73] Agrarian trouble was frequently a continuation of previous campaigns. Palmer J. McCloughrey, a farmer, veterinary surgeon and a 'strong supporter of British rule in Ireland', claimed that he had been constantly victimized and eventually driven from his 133-acre farm in Riverstown by a campaign that dated from 1920. In 1921 he obtained civil bills for non-payment of rents, but in April 1922 he was beaten and kicked and had to promise at gunpoint not to execute the decrees. He was afraid to sleep at home and he left the area in April 1923 for the safety of Sligo town.[74] John Lougheed, farming about 350 acres also in the Riverstown area, had been the subject of agrarian trouble since 1920. His enquiries about a British soldier shot as a spy in 1920 raised suspicions among local IRA who visited his house and, in his absence, told his wife that he would be shot because 'he was an Orangeman and a spy'. For some time afterwards he was afraid to sleep at home.[75] A long-standing agitation against Charles Phibbs of Doobeg, Bunninadden reached a new level in early 1922 and by May his house had been vandalized, his farm was derelict and stock belonging to neighbours grazed his lands (plate 31). Eventually he sold his Bunninadden land and settled in Wales.[76] Miss Jessie Hunter, a Presbyterian, owned a 175-acre farm near Riverstown which had been the subject of agrarian unrest since 1918. It was taken over by local smallholders in May 1921. She eventually sold the holding, which she claimed was worth around £2,000, for just over £1,000 to the occupiers in March 1923. This farm was only part of her total holdings of 300 acres in the area and she retained possession of the rest, continuing to live and farm there after the Civil War.[77] One loyalist was killed during the period: Edwin Williams, son of Essex Williams of Skreen, was shot dead in April 1923 as a result, it was believed, of a long-running agrarian dispute.[78]

Fourteen non-Catholic shopkeepers and businessmen made claims to the British government's IGC. Those who suffered most appear to have been prominent Crown forces' supporters. These include Jonathan Walpole-Boyers of Rosses Point who was, according to ex-RIC DI Russell, 'of the greatest possible assistance to the RIC in rounding-up parties wanted for serious crime including the murder of crown forces'.[79] Joseph Graham, 'a remarkable loyalist', was an ironmonger and gunsmith in Sligo town who, during the period up to the truce in 1921, 'took a very active part in bringing to justice the perpetrators of crime and assisting the police'. He said that his business was severely boycotted as a result and in 1924 he went out of business but he was unable to produce any accounts for the IGC.[80] George R. Williams, a Sligo flour merchant, told the committee that he had given important information to the police, including some which led to arrests in 1920. Because of this he was boycotted and his business badly damaged. However, the figures he produced for the IGC showed that his income from the flour business was greater in 1922 and 1923 than in previous or subsequent years.[81] Five Sligo Catholic shopkeepers said they had been targeted because they had been friendly with Crown forces. A Tubbercurry shopkeeper who had supplied the Auxiliaries with goods was boycotted after their departure and her premises shot at.[82]

There was no attempt to target the numerous Protestant former landlords such as the Coopers, the O'Haras and the Gore-Booths and none of their 'big houses' in Sligo were burned. All Protestants may have been looked on as enemies but relatively few suffered seriously. Only three non-Catholic claimants said that they had to leave the county permanently and one had to move residence within the county.[83] These claims illustrate a high level of fear and intimidation but not a concerted anti-Protestant or sectarian campaign. Instead, it was an opportunistic continuation of agrarian agitation and the seizing of opportunities for 'inflicting injuries on obnoxious persons, for paying off old scores and for widespread looting'.[84]

Analysis of participants on both side suggests that the Civil War division in County Sligo was not based on social standing or wealth. There is evidence that rather than the poorer sectors providing recruits for the anti-Treaty side they were more likely to join the Free State army. In Sligo farmers' sons provided the majority of both sets of combatants and it is clear that army members came from smaller holdings, while republican internees were more likely to come from substantial holdings. In the urban area there is evidence that National army soldiers were more likely to come from the poorer classes and internees from the better-off sections of the community.[85]

There are no reports of Cumann na mBan branches in Sligo meeting to debate the Treaty and it appears that such branches had more or less ceased to function. As with the IRA, most Sligo Cumann na mBan members took the anti-Treaty side. These activists generally carried out the same kind of activities as during the latter part of the War of Independence, but 'the work was much harder to do during the Civil trouble'. Because these female activists were well known to the other side they were more likely to be arrested during the Civil War. They took prominent parts in the funerals of those killed on the anti-Treaty side. Some recall being arrested and released a number of times due, they thought, to the lack of female prison facilities. At one stage the Bohan sisters were ordered not to leave the town of Ballymote. A number of Sligo anti-Treaty female activists were eventually imprisoned and some joined hunger strikes.[86]

Following the launch of Cumann na Saoirse in March 1922 by pro-Treaty former members of Cumann na mBan, a branch was formed in Sligo town. Its officers included wives of prominent pro-Treaty politicians, D.M. Hanley and J.J. Clancy, and one of its first events was a reception for those attending Griffith's Easter Sunday meeting. Its main activity seems to have been fund raising and it was still in existence in early 1923. One other branch is mentioned in Sligo, Skreen & Dromard founded in late April 1922, but there are no other references to it or other branches in the county.[87]

As far as can be determined, 48 persons lost their lives in Sligo as a result of the Civil War. Of these, 19 were National army soldiers, 18 were members of the anti-Treaty forces and 11 were civilians. Of the army deaths, 6 were accidental, presumably because many of these soldiers were young and inexperienced. One IRA death and almost half of the civilian fatalities were accidental. The greater proportion of the deaths occurred during the first months of the war: 16 in July, 4 in August and 11 in September 1922. There were only 10 war-related deaths during the period January to May 1923.[88]

The end of the Civil War was not greeted with any celebrations in Sligo or elsewhere; relief was the dominant emotion. A desire for a return to normality was manifest. The period since late 1918 had seen the break down of law and order and widespread violence and the threat of violence. The achievements of the War of Independence, the glorious summer of 1921 and the Treaty settlement were overshadowed by the IRA's refusal to accept the Dáil's ratification of the Treaty and the long drawn out nature of the subsequent war. Neither side in the military conflict had much to celebrate. The anti-Treaty forces had tried to replicate the War of Independence guerrilla campaign but found that impossible because the enemy was native and had the support of a sizable proportion of the population. The government forces found it difficult to surmount the problems involved in establishing an efficient National army while simultaneously attempting to overcome an enemy whose main aim was survival. Some of the tactics employed during the conflict including the executions, the murder of politicians, the killing of men who had surrendered, the deaths of alleged spies, reflected no credit on either side. The fact that there was no negotiated settlement, no surrender, no handing over of arms, no large-scale prisoner releases did generate some unease leaving open the possibility that the war might be resumed at a future date. Two of the principal anti-Treaty leaders in Sligo, Pilkington and Carty, had not been captured. Yet, despite these concerns the general feeling in the country and in County Sligo was relief that hostilities had finally ceased.

13 Revolution?

In Sligo the wheel had revolved at least one full circle since 1912. Then Sligo nationalists had been apparently unanimous in their support for the IPP and for home rule, though its details may have been vague and the question of Ulster unresolved. In 1912 the local MPs and the nationalist newspapers stressed the importance of unity, demanding that there be no dissention in the face of unionist challenges, conservative propaganda and British public opinion. County Sligo responded well and in the years before the war was a model of orthodoxy, one of the best organized UIL counties in the country. The Catholic Church, the labour movement, Irish-Ireland movement and agrarian activists all united behind the IPP MPs and the local nationalists bosses. At times there were threats of division, church against unions, rural nationalists against unions, UIL against AOH, but these divisions and the various personal rivalries did not affect support for the IPP and home rule. The agrarian demands in the countryside were also supported though efforts were being made to dampen these down. Local government was under the control of nationalists who could quarrel about patronage and resent and sometimes defy the interference of the LGB but were unanimous in their support for the IPP and its Sligo MPs.

The founding of the Irish Volunteers at an early stage in Sligo town was due to local political rivalries with John Jinks seizing the opportunity to assert his authority and independence in the town. Labour and Gaelic Leaguers joined in, as did the AOH, anxious not to be side-lined. It was only when the movement got the approval of the party leadership that it spread widely in the county.

The outbreak of World War I, the unequal treatment of the two Volunteer groups in the early months of that conflict, the support of the IPP for recruiting and the reaction to the 1916 Rising saw the gradual collapse of nationalist unity in Sligo. In the absence of electoral contests, the county had little opportunity to give political expression of this change. The sitting councillors by and large remained loyal to Redmond. In Sligo town the annual corporation and mayoral elections saw competing cliques strive for advantage. When it became clear that SF would be the dominant power, these groups generally joined that bandwagon. Again there was a demand for unity so that organized labour, clergy and agrarian activists all supported SF without much questioning of policy. SF clubs spread quickly in Sligo and the conacre and anti-conscription campaigns of 1918 ensured that SF would have no difficulty in winning both Sligo seats in the general election. County Sligo once again became one of the best organized counties as regards the prevailing political power. Once again details of the exact nature of what would satisfy various elements in the coalition were unclear.

The emergence of the IRA as a force in Sligo was slow due to a number of factors, including the absence of early radical organizations, few experienced leaders, poor armaments and the slow pace of the escalation of violence. It was led in the county by those who were early Volunteer and IRB activists, McCabe and Carty, for instance. The tradition of clandestine illegal agrarian activity, especially in south Sligo, easily translated into armed activity. The example of other areas in the country and the urgings of headquarters also played a part. The abandonment of large areas of the county by the RIC in 1919–20 allowed great latitude to the IRA, which the Crown forces' counterstroke of 1920–1 only partially reversed. General low-key harassment combined with a small number of spectacular ambushes and prison breaks continued and the campaign showed no sign of collapse by mid-1921. There was little overall direction by Sligo Brigade IRA and the general respect for and admiration of the Brigade O/C, Pilkington, by IRA members may reflect his lack of control. Hectoring of Sligo Brigade officers by IRA GHQ occasioned no marked improvement in efficiency but much resentment.

The unique Sligo Corporation election under PR in 1919 resulted in a small republican majority, which was often overturned due to enforced absences. The new County Council was elected in 1920 when IRA control was stronger but many of those elected were SF politicians rather than military men. All Sligo local bodies pledged allegiance to Dáil Éireann and managed to survive in the face of severe financial problems. Much of this survival depended on local decisions and local initiatives and the assistance of the IRA was vital in collecting rates.

The truce period, with the RIC more or less powerless, gave Sligo IRA the opportunity to train its members and establish itself as the dominant force in the county. Unity was again to be enforced. Vested local interests in local government were used by Sligo IRA to control those authorities and to oppose reforming central control. There was, however, determined local opposition, which refused to acknowledge the supremacy of the 'men of action' over the 'men of words' in spite of the inability of the Dáil government to assist to any great degree. This split at local government level mirrored to a large degree the Treaty division. At the outbreak of the Civil War, the active anti-Treaty IRA members once again found themselves unable to attend council meetings. Pro-Treaty councillors were given ample time to develop local government under the amalgamation scheme and by the time anti-Treaty members were again able to attend in numbers the new order of local democracy had been well established.

The power that Sligo IRA had established during the truce period and its belief that it had won the war for the republic were challenged by the Treaty. It appeared inevitable that a majority of the IRA would oppose it. The leading Sligo newspaper, the *Sligo Champion*, immediately claimed that the popular verdict in Sligo was in favour of the Treaty and the failure of the anti-Treaty side to formulate a coherent immediate response ceded the initiative to their opponents. The confused events of the following six months added to the bitterness of the division in the county. The involvement of Sligo IRA in the Limerick crisis and in skirmishes along the border, and the débâcle, as they saw it, of Griffith's meeting, as well a number of smaller incidents within the county, helped reinforce Sligo IRA's opposition to the new regime and the probability of their taking up arms against the provisional government. The pact election saw little real cooperation between the parties and the apparent victory of the anti-Treaty side gave them added encouragement.

In spite of all this, when the Civil War broke out Sligo anti-Treaty IRA were ill-prepared to make their numerical advantage count. The lack of any realistic offensive planning or coordinated action and personal rivalries led to the abandonment of their urban posts in the early days of the war and a return to the more familiar guerrilla campaign. The fact that the opposing forces included old comrades familiar with the terrain and personnel and that civilian support was less certain meant that this struggle was unlikely to be victorious. However, poor organization and morale, difficulties with troop numbers, armaments, supplies and transport meant that the government forces found it difficult to defeat the Sligo anti-Treaty forces decisively. While the republican side was spent as a serious threat, complete victory had still not been achieved by the time hostilities ceased in May 1923.

The Civil War in Sligo saw much more activity than the War of Independence and resulted in much more disruption and destruction. In the latter part of 1922, in particular, normal daily life was badly affected with a dramatic fall in numbers of social and sporting functions. The continued deterioration of the transport infrastructure, already suffering from the damage of the 1919–21 period and the lack of maintenance, caused considerable hardship. The country areas, more dependent on road and rail transport, suffered most.

The lack of a functioning system of justice caused considerable hardship and disruption. No fully effective system of law and order had been in operation in the county since late 1919 and while Dáil courts were reorganized during the truce period the confusion of the post-Treaty period and the rise of factional strife led to increased lawlessness in early 1922. This included criminality, hooliganism, agrarian agitation, intimidation of Protestants, attacks on ex-RIC and politically motivated actions. Large areas of Sligo were without effective law for much of the Civil War period but as the threat from anti-Treaty forces dwindled the Civic Guard began to occupy barracks and courts began to function again. The county appears to have settled down remarkably quickly after the end of the conflict.

During the 1911–26 period there was an acceleration in the decline of the non-Catholic population in County Sligo which affected all denominations but especially the small, widely dispersed Presbyterian community in rural areas. There was an amount of violence directed against the non-Catholic population in campaigns such as agrarianism, the Belfast boycott, looting, requisitioning of materials by the IRA, and some settling of old scores though these did not constitute a coordinated campaign of intimidation of Protestants. Most Protestants remained in Sligo and looked for security and comfort in increased membership of fraternal and business organizations. The Protestant businessmen of Sligo town had asserted their importance by their membership and promotion of the Ratepayers' Association and their success in the Sligo Corporation election of 1919 ensured their voices would be heard. The founding of Sligo Chamber of Commerce in early 1923 in which the same Protestant businessmen played a leading role showed that group's confidence and their determination to play their part in the new state. Only two of the new chamber's committee of eleven were Catholic and its first president was Harper Campbell Perry. The contribution of the Sligo Protestants was recognized when Sligo businessman, Arthur Jackson, was nominated to the Irish Free State Senate in 1922.

Sligo Protestants, like most others in the county, were delighted when the Civil War ended. Like the rest of the country, Sligo could begin to come to terms with the tumultuous changes of the previous ten years. Most of Ireland was now under a Free State government whose powers were much greater than those envisaged under home rule, though the principal models for the institutions of the new state were British. The revolutionary period had seen widespread disruption of the economy, disturbance of trade and commerce, destruction of infrastructure and communications and the difficult and costly process of rebuilding had now to begin. The decade which had begun with the anticipation of an age of prosperity under home rule had ended in bitter division, widespread destruction, violence and hardship. The Civil War left a legacy of bitterness and recriminations in Sligo as elsewhere. Among significant numbers, the attraction of republican ideology remained as did the distrust of central authority. Some of those most heavily involved in Sligo continued to be prominent in political life. John Jinks, the great survivor, went on to become a National Party TD in 1927 and achieved notoriety when his absence from the Dáil allowed the government to survive a crucial vote of no confidence. He was mayor of Sligo again when he died in 1934. Both Michael Nevin and John Lynch served terms as mayor in the 1930s and 1940s. Frank Carty was successful at each general election, joined Fianna Fáil on its foundation and entered the Dáil in 1927. He died unexpectedly in 1942. Billy Pilkington was arrested three months after the end of the Civil War and interned. Some time after his release he became a Catholic priest, joining the Redemptorist Order. He served most of his life in South Africa and died in Liverpool in 1977. Alec McCabe resigned from the Cumann na nGaedheal party at the time of the Army Crisis in 1924, joined the National Party but left politics the following year. He returned to teaching and in 1935 was one of the founders of the Educational Building Society. John O'Dowd, the ex-

MP, took no further part in public life but lived long enough to see one of his promises for home rule fulfilled under the Free State with the passage of the River Owenmore Drainage Act, 1926.[1] He died in 1937.

The note of hope struck by Bishop Patrick Morrisroe of Achonry in his 1924 Lenten pastoral celebrating 'the cessation of unnatural strife' seems excessively positive but typically magisterial: 'A season of sorrow has been succeeded by an abundant crop of the choicest fruits of virtue. From the hearts of those that sit by the fireside the ugly spectre of fear has fled, giving way to the Angel of Peace, whose spreading wings enfold the household in a protective embrace'.[2]

Notes

CHAPTER ONE *County Sligo in 1912*

1   *Sligo Champion (SC)*, 23 Nov. 1918. Born in Charlestown, Co. Mayo, Morrisroe was ordained
    in 1893 and was on the staff of the diocesan college and of St Patrick's College, Maynooth,
    until appointed bishop in 1911. He died in 1946. See Liam Swords, *A dominant church: the
    diocese of Achonry, 1818–1960* (Dublin, 2004), pp 46, 528.
2   Census of Ireland, 1911; Preliminary report with abstract of the enumerators' summaries, HC,
    1912–13 [Cd. 5691], Summaries pp 4–5.
3   Census of Ireland 1911, Area, houses, and population: also the ages, civil or conjugal condi-
    tion, occupations, birthplaces, religion, and education of the people; Province of Connaught,
    County of Sligo, HC, 1912–13 [Cd. 6052], table XLI, p. 97.
4   Census of Ireland 1911, County of Sligo, table XIX, p. 46.
5   Census of Ireland 1901 part two, General report, Province of Connaught, HC, 1902 [Cd.
    1190], table 63, p. 352.
6   David Fitzpatrick, 'The geography of Irish nationalism, 1910–1921', *Past and Present*, 78
    (1978), statistical appendix, pp 138–9.
7   Census of Ireland 1911, Province of Connaught, County of Sligo, table XXI, pp 56–62.
8   Mary O'Dowd, 'Sligo' in Anngret Simms & J.H. Andrews (eds), *Irish country towns* (Dublin,
    1994), pp 151–3; John McTiernan, *In Sligo long ago* (Sligo, 1998), pp 514–16; *Sligo Champion
    centenary number* (Sligo, 1936), p. 30.
9   Fiona Gallagher, *The streets of Sligo: urban evolution over the course of seven centuries* (Sligo,
    2008), p. 44.
10 Quoted in Gallagher, *Streets of Sligo*, p. 184.
11 *SC*, 10 Feb., 2 Mar. 1912; *Sligo Times (ST)*, 25 Oct. 1913; *Sligo Independent (SI)*, 20 Jan. 1912,
    20 Sept. 1913.
12 *SC*, 4 May 1912.
13 *SC*, 27 Apr., 4 May, 14 Dec. 1912, 8 Nov. 1913; *SI*, 27 Apr., 11 May 1912, 31 May 1913; *Irish
    Times (IT)*, 2, 10 May 1912; *Hansard (Commons)* 4 Dec. 1912, vol. 44, 2263–2452.
14 Census of Ireland 1911, Preliminary report with abstract of the enumerators' summaries, HC,
    1912–13 [Cd. 5691], religious professions summary, pp 6–7; Padraig Deignan, *The Protestant
    community in Sligo, 1914–49* (Dublin, 2010), pp 9–37; Miriam Moffitt, *The Church of Ireland
    community of Killala and Achonry* (Dublin, 1999), pp 15–31.
15 Deignan, *Protestant community*, pp 223–40.
16 Steven Reid, *Get to the Point at County Sligo Golf Club* (Naas, 1991), pp 64–85; Deignan,
    Protestant community, pp 313–15, 331–40; *SC sesquicentenary*, pp 31 & 33; *SC centenary*, p. 41;
    Tadhg Kilgannon, *Almanac and directory of County Sligo, 1907* (Sligo, 1907), pp 71–4; Sligo
    Constitutional Club register of candidates, 1907–17 (Sligo County Library).
17 V.W. Bro. R.H. Campbell-Perry, 'A glimpse of freemasonry in Sligo, 1767–1951', *The Lodge of
    Research transactions for years 1949–57* (Dublin, 1959), pp 34–43; McTernan, *In Sligo long ago*,
    pp 457–73; *SI*, 13 Jan., 10 Feb., 23 Mar., 9 Nov. 1912; Deignan, *Protestant community*, pp
    315–20; Kilgannon, *Almanac and directory*, pp 71–4; information on Sligo Orange Lodges
    supplied in 1995 & 1997 by Cecil Kilpatrick, archivist, Grand Orange Lodge of Ireland;
    Padraig Deignan, 'The importance of fraternities and social clubs for the Protestant commu-
    nity in Sligo from 1914 to 1949', *Corran Herald*, 44 (2011/12), 9–15.
18 E. Rumpf & A.C. Hepburn, *Nationalism and socialism in twentieth-century Ireland* (New York,
    1977), p. 52.
19 Brian M. Walker (ed.), *Parliamentary election results in Ireland, 1801–1922* (Dublin, 1978), pp

372–3; Íde Ní Liatháin, *The life and career of P.A. McHugh, a north Connacht politician, 1859–1909: a footsoldier of the party* (Dublin, 1999), pp 30–40.

20 Fergus Campbell, *Land and revolution: nationalist politics in the west of Ireland, 1891–1921* (Oxford, 2005), p. 30; John C. McTernan, *Worthies of Sligo* (Sligo, 1994), pp 397–401; Philip Bull, 'The United Irish League and the reunion of the Irish Parliamentary Party, 1898–1900', *IHS*, 26:101 (1988), 51–78; Ní Liatháin, *McHugh*, pp 45–54.

21 Fitzpatrick, 'Geography of Irish nationalism', pp 432–3.

22 McTernan, *Worthies*, pp 397–401 & 405–10; *SC*, 30 Oct. 1937; Walker, *Irish parliamentary election results*, pp 372–3; Thomas Scanlan MP should not be confused with Tom Scanlon Sligo IRA officer.

23 Ní Liatháin, *McHugh*, pp 41–57; *SC centenary*, p. 19.

24 John C. McTernan, *Olde Sligo* (Sligo, 1995), pp 489–99; Campbell, *Land and revolution*, pp 85–123; Michael Wheatley, *Nationalism and the Irish Party: provincial Ireland, 1910–1916* (Oxford, 2005), pp 24–25; Ní Liatháin, *McHugh*, p. 57; Seán Duffy (ed.), *Atlas of Irish history* (2nd ed., Dublin, 2000), p. 109.

25 Wheatley, *Nationalism*, p. 26.

26 John Cunningham, *Labour in the west of Ireland: working life and struggle 1890–1914* (Belfast, 1995), pp 64–71, 152; C. Desmond Greaves, *The Irish Transport and General Workers' Union: the formative years, 1909–1923* (Dublin, 1982), pp 66–7.

27 Ciarán Ó Duibhir, *Sinn Féin: the first election 1908* (Manorhamilton, 1993); *Leitrim Observer*, 29 Feb. 1908; Alec McCabe, 'Cradling a revolution', *An tÓglach* (Christmas 1962); McCabe interview, *IT*, 6, 7 May 1970.

28 *SC*, 23 Feb. 1918; Patrick Maume, 'Parnell and the I.R.B. oath', *IHS*, 29:115 (1995), 363–70; Owen McGee, *The IRB: the Irish Republican Brotherhood, from the Land League to Sinn Féin* (2nd ed., Dublin, 2007), pp 67, 78–82; John C. McTernan, 'The Tubbercurry "conspirators"', *Corran Herald*, 43 (2010/2011), 72–3; Swords, *Achonry*, pp 243–9.

29 McCabe, *Cradling a revolution*; Michael Nevin (BMH WS 1384, p. 2); M.J. Kelly, *The Fenian ideal and Irish nationalism, 1882–1916* (Woodbridge, 2006), p. 143.

30 Séamus Marren & Tom O'Grady to McGarrity, 1911 & 1912 (NLI, Joseph McGarrity papers, MS 17,644); Tom O'Grady (BMH WS 917, p. 1); Leon Ó Broin, *Revolutionary underground: the story of the Irish Republican Brotherhood, 1858–1924* (Dublin, 1976), p. 161; Diarmuid Lynch, *The I.R.B. and the 1916 insurrection*, ed. Florence O'Donoghue (Cork, 1957), p. 28.

31 John C. McTernan (ed.), *Sligo GAA – a centenary history, 1884–1984* (Sligo, 1984), pp 31–41, 332, 336; *SC*, 4 Feb., 11 Mar., 1 Apr., 2 Dec. 1911, 9 Mar. 1912; sixteen-year-old William Pilkington, later O/C 3rd Western Division, IRA sang *The Croppy Boy* at the Gaelic club's St Patrick's Day event 1911; John Rupert Treacy, a native of Cork, taught in Limerick and Dublin before coming to Sligo in 1904 to teach in Summerhill College and the Technical School. He was said to have been involved with Arthur Griffith in Sinn Féin while in Dublin; J.R. Treacy obit. *SC*, 30 Nov. 1929.

32 Diarmuid Breathnach agus Máire Ní Mhurchú, *Beathaisnéis: 1882–1982, vol. I* (Dublin, 1986), p. 101; idem, *Vol. II* (Dublin, 1990), pp 101–102.

33 *Glór Shligigh, Conradh na Gaeilge comóradh caoga bliain, 1893–1943* (Sligo, 1943), pp 30–44; *SC sesquicentenary* (Sligo, 1986), pp 34 & 40; *SC*, 2 Dec. 1911; McTernan, *Worthies*, pp 142–5.

34 *IT*, 3 Feb. 1914; this appears not to have been reported in Sligo newspapers.

35 John D. Brewer, *The Royal Irish Constabulary: an oral history* (Belfast, 1990), p. 7.

36 Cecil A. King, *Memorabilia, musings on sixty-odd years of life as a newspaper man* (Ballyshannon, 1989), pp 12–14; official diary of William Herbert Bodley, RIC (NLI, MS 7945); J. Anthony Gaughan (ed.), *Memoirs of Constable Jeremiah Mee, R.I.C.* (Dublin, 1975), pp 15–41; Brewer, *RIC*, pp 2–9.

37 House of Commons, 1914 [Cd. 7064], Judicial statistics, Ireland, 1912, table E, pp xxxiv–xxxvi.

38 *ST*, 29 Mar. 1913; John C. McTernan, *Historic Sligo* (Sligo, 1965), pp 85–98; Wheatley, *Nationalism*, pp 17–21; Smyllie had edited the *Sligo Independent* for a time during the 1890s. He was the father of famous *Irish Times* editor Robert Marie (Bertie) Smyllie.

39 Capt. A.L. Dunnill, 'A summary of events during the period in which the 1st Battalion Bedfordshire & Hertfordshire Regiment was stationed in Ireland, 1920, 1921, 1922' (Bedfordshire and Luton Archives and Records Service, Bedford, X550/2/6).
40 David Fitzpatrick, *Politics and Irish life* (Cork, 1998), p. xii.

CHAPTER TWO *Home rule at last?*

1 Wheatley, *Nationalism*, pp 162–3.   2 *SC*, 13 Jan., 9 Mar. 1912; *SI*, 17 Feb., 13 Apr. 1912.
3 *SC*, 27 Jan., 6 Mar. 1912.   4 *SC*, 10 Feb. 1912.   5 *SC*, 17 Feb., 2, 30 Mar. 1912.
6 *SC*, 20 Apr. 1912.
7 *ST*, 13 Apr. 1912; *SI*, 20 Apr. 1912; *IT*, 20 Apr. 1912; Andrew Scholes, *The Church of Ireland and the third Home Rule Bill* (Dublin, 2010), pp 32–6; McTernan, *Historic Sligo*, pp 85–98.
8 *SC*, 18 Jan., 26 Apr., 26 July, 4 Oct. 1913.
9 *SC*, 5, 26 July, 9, 16 Aug., 7, 13, 20, 27 Sept. 1913.
10 Quarterly UIL returns (TNA, CO 904/20); Minute book of the UIL National Directory, 1904–1918 (NLI, MS 708).
11 Wheatley, *Nationalism*, pp 139–48.
12 CI Sligo, Dec. 1912 (TNA, CO 904/91).
13 *SC*, 8, 22 June 1912; Wheatley, *Nationalism*, pp 48–52, 137–54; Tom Garvin, *The evolution of Irish nationalist politics* (Dublin, 1981), pp 95–9.
14 McTernan, *Worthies of Sligo*, pp 383–7; S. Hennessy, 'The life and career of John Jinks' (SCL, typescript).
15 Wheatley, *Nationalism*, pp 151–2.   16 *SI*, 21 Oct. 1911, 27 Jan. 1912.   17 *SI*, 25 Jan. 1913.
18 *SI*, 9 Aug., 13 Sept., 6 Dec. 1913, 21, 24 Feb. 1914; *SC*, 31 Jan. 1914.
19 *SC*, 13 Jan. 9, 16 Mar. 1912; Peter Cawley of Coolaney had been involved in Sligo electoral politics since 1889, a faithful lieutenant of P.A. McHugh and his successors. In 1899 he had defeated Charles O'Hara in the first Sligo County Council election.
20 CI Sligo, 1912–13 (TNA, CO 904/86–91); Printed intelligence notes 1912–1913 (TNA, CO 903/17–18); *ST*, *SI*, 12 July 1912; *SI*, 23 Aug. 1913; Wheatley, *Nationalism*, pp 24–31.
21 *SC*, 13 Jan., 16, 30 Mar., 20 Apr. 1912.
22 Patrick Buckland, *Irish unionism 1: The Anglo-Irish and the new Ireland, 1885–1922* (Dublin, 1972), p. 22.
23 *Notes from Ireland*, 1913–14; Lennox Robinson, *Bryan Cooper* (London, 1931), pp 64–73; John C. McTernan, *Sligo: the light of bygone days, vol. II: Sligo families* (Sligo, 2009), pp 51–2, 73–4.
24 *SI*, 15 Feb., 16 Mar. 1913; *Notes from Ireland*, 1 Apr. 1912; R.B. McDowell, *Crisis and decline: the fate of the southern unionists* (Dublin, 1997), pp 45–6; Buckland, *Irish Unionism 1*, p. 22.
25 *SI*, 16 Mar. 1912; McDowell, *Crisis & decline*, p. 46; Deignan, *Protestant community*, pp 39–41.
26 *SI*, 29 June 1912.
27 *ST*, 16 Mar. 1912; *SI*, 30 Mar., 13, 27 Apr. 1912; *SC*, 16 Mar., 4, 11, 18 May, 1 June 1912.
28 *SI*, 14 June 1913; McDowell, *Crisis & decline*, p. 32; Alvin Jackson, 'Irish unionism, 1870–1922' in George D. Boyce & Alan O'Day (eds), *Defenders of the union: a survey of British and Irish unionism since 1801* (London, 2001), p. 125; NAI, Census 1911 online, www.census.nationalarchives.ie/, accessed 30 Apr. 2011; McTernan, *Sligo families*, pp 100–3.
29 *SC*, *ST*, *SI*, 29 June 1912.
30 *ST*, 27 July, 17 Aug. 1912; *SC*, *SI*, 17 Aug. 1912; *Notes from Ireland*, 1 Jan. 1912; Philip Dudley Perceval was a son of Perceval of Templehouse and had married Muriel Wynne who succeeded to Hazelwood House and the Wynne property; John C. McTernan, *Sligo: the light of bygone days, vol. I: houses of Sligo and associated families* (Sligo, 2009), pp 307–8, 360.
31 *Sligo Nationalist* (*SN*), 13 Jan. 1912; *SI*, 20 Jan., 20 Apr., 4 May 1912; *ST*, 20 Jan. 1912; *SC*, 20 Jan., 4, 11 May, 22 June, 7 Sept. 1912.
32 Scholes, *Third Home Rule Bill*, pp 10, 16, 20, 25, 45; *SC*, *ST*, *SI*, 14 Sept. 1913.

33 *SN*, 16, 23 Aug. 1913; *ST*, 2, 16 Aug. 1913; *IT*, 24 July 1913.

34 *SI*, 3 Feb. 1912.

35 *SC*, 20 Apr., 11 May 1912; *SI*, 13, 20 Apr. 1912.

36 *SC*, 28 Sept., 5 Oct. 1912; *SI*, 21, 28 Sept. 1912; Scholes, *Third Home Rule Bill*, pp 40–8.

37 PRONI, Ulster Covenant online, www.proni.gov.uk, accessed 30 Apr. 2011; NAI, Census 1911 online, www.census.nationalarchives.ie/, accessed 30 Apr. 2011; the clergyman and his wife also signed the covenant in Belfast.

38 *ST*, 15 Feb., 14 June 1913; *SC*, 21 June 1913; *SI*, 15 Feb., 10 May, 14 June, 25 Oct. 1913; *Notes from Ireland*, 1 Apr., 1 May 1913.

39 *SC*, 29 Nov., 6, 13, 20 Dec. 1913; *ST*, 6 Dec. 1913; *SI*, 6, 13 Dec. 1913; *Notes from Ireland*, 1 Dec. 1913, 1 Jan. 1914; Deignan, *Protestant community*, p. 43; McDowell, *Crisis & decline*, p. 47.

40 Buckland, *Irish Unionism 1*, pp 27–8; Paul Bew, *Ideology and the Irish question: Ulster unionism and Irish nationalism, 1912–1916* (Oxford, 1994), pp 98–100; *SI, SC*, 4, 11, 18, 25 Oct., 1, 8 Nov. 1913.

41 Margaret Ward, 'Conflicting interests: the British and Irish suffrage movements', *Feminist Review*, 50 (1995), 131–2; Rosemary Cullen Owens, *A social history of women in Ireland, 1870–1970* (Dublin, 2005), pp 88–9.

42 *SC*, 16 Mar., 6 July, 7 Sept. 1912.

43 Olga Crichton was born Olga Bestujeff Bieneman *c.*1864 in Brighton, England. She married Alexander Joseph Crichton in 1884; Hugh Montgomery-Massingberd (ed.), *Burke's Irish family records* (London, 1976), p. 290; *Irish Citizen*, 1, 8, 22, 29 June, 6, 13, 20, 27 July, 3, 17 Aug., 23 Nov. 1912; *ST*, 6 July 1912; *SI*, 6 July 1912; *SC*, 3 Aug. 1912. Alexander Crichton was a pioneer of the Irish Agricultural Organisation Society in Sligo and a supporter of home rule; McTernan, *Worthies of Sligo*, pp 274–8; McTernan, *Sligo families*, pp 66–9.

44 *Irish Citizen*, 29 Mar., 28 June, 2, 12, 19 July, 9, 23 Aug., 6 Sept., 18, 25 Oct., 8 Nov. 1913; *ST*, 14, 21, 28 June, 26 July, 2, 16, 23 Aug., 6 Sept., 4 Oct. 1913; *SI*, 2 Aug., 11 Oct. 1913; Rosemary Cullen Owens, *Smashing times: a history of the Irish women's suffrage movement, 1889–1922* (Dublin, 1984), pp 42–73.

45 Wheatley, *Nationalism*, pp 139–41.

46 Cunningham, *Labour*, pp 64–71, 152; Greaves, *ITGWU*, pp 66–7.

47 Greaves, *ITGWU*, pp 69–72.

48 *SC, SI*, 30 Mar. 1912; Wheatley, *Nationalism*, pp 142–3; Cunningham, *Labour*, p. 157; Bishop Clancy, a native of Sooey, Sligo, had opposed the setting up of the ITGWU branch in Sligo and clashed with O'Donnell and Jinks regarding lay control of Sligo AOH in 1906–7; Wheatley, *Nationalism*, pp 140–1; Francis Beirne, *The diocese of Elphin: people, places and pilgrimage* (Dublin, 2000), pp 70–1.

49 *SC, SI*, 24 Feb. 1912; Cunningham, *Labour*, p. 156; *Irish Worker*, 13 Apr. 1912.

50 *SC, SI*, 8, 15, 22 June 1912; Wheatley, *Nationalism*, pp 43–4; Cunningham, *Labour*, pp 188–9; *Irish Worker*, 22 June 1912; Greaves, *ITGWU*, pp 78–9.

51 *SC*, 6 July, 3, 24 Aug. 1912.   52 *SC*, 28 Sept., 23, 30 Nov. 1912.

53 *SI*, 18 Jan. 1913; Greaves, *ITGWU*, p. 83.   54 *SC*, 29 Mar. 1913.

55 *SC, ST, SI*, 22, 29 Mar., 5, 12, 19, 26 Apr., 3, 10 May 1913; *ST*, 31 May 1913; Deignan, *Protestant community*, pp 54–5; Wheatley, *Nationalism*, pp 145–7; Greaves, *ITGWU*, pp 86–7; CI Sligo, Mar.–May 1913 (TNA, CO 904/89–90).

56 *SI*, 6 Sept. 1913.

57 *SC*, 6 Sept., 18 Oct., 1, 8, 15, 22, 29 Nov., 6 Dec. 1913; *SI*, 18 Oct., 8, 15, 29 Nov. 1913.

58 *SC*, 10 Jan. 1914.

59 *SC*, 29 June, 13 July 1912; *SI*, 16 Mar., 29 June 1912; *Notes from Ireland*, 1 Aug. 1912.

60 *SI*, 20, 27 July, 3, 10, 17, 24, 31 Aug., 7 Sept., 12, 19 Oct., 2, 9, 16, 23 Nov., 14 Dec. 1912, 13 Sept., 29 Nov., 20 Dec. 1913.

61 *SI*, 1 Feb. 1913.   62 *SC*, 4, 11, 18, 25 May, 1, 15 June, 20 July 1912.

63 *ST*, 21 Sept. 1912.

64 *SC*, 11 May, 17 Aug., 21 Sept., 14 Dec. 1912; *ST*, 17 Feb., 13 Apr., 4 May, 31 Aug., 1912, 14 June 1913; *SI*, 10 Aug. 1912, 14 June 1913.
65 *SC*, 16, 23, 30 May, 13 June 1914; *SN*, 6 June 1914.
66 *SC*, 1, 22, 29 Nov. 1913, 3 Jan. 1914.   67 *SC*, 10 Jan. 1914.
68 *SC*, 24, 31 Jan., 7 Feb. 1914; *Irish Volunteer* (*IV*), 7 Feb. 1914.
69 CI Sligo, Jan., Mar. 1914 (TNA, CO 904/92).
70 *SC*, 14 Feb., 14, 21 Mar. 1914; *SN*, 14, 21 Feb. 1914; *IV*, 28 Mar. 1914.
71 *SC*, 25 Apr., 2 May, 25 July 1914.
72 *SC*, 14 Mar., 4, 25 Apr. 1914; CI Sligo, Mar., Apr. 1914 (TNA, CO 904/92–3); *IV*, 18 Apr. 1914.
73 *SC*, 2, 9, 23 May 1914; *IV*, 18 Apr., 9, 16, 30 May 1914; *Corran Herald*, v (Aug. 1986), 5, 12.
74 *SC*, 23, 30 May, 6 June 1914; CI Sligo, May, June 1914 (TNA, CO 904/93); Wheatley, *Nationalism*, pp 189–90.
75 *SC*, 30 May 1914; *SN*, 30 May 1914.   76 *SC*, 6, 13 June 1914.
77 *SN*, 18 July 1914; *IV*, 4 July 1914.
78 CI Sligo, July, Aug., Sept. 1914 (TNA, CO 904/94).
79 Charles Gildea (BMH WS 1313, p. 1); Tom O'Grady (BMH WS 917, p. 1); Alec McCabe (BMH WS 277, p. 1); Thady McGowan & Tom Brehony (BMH WS 918, p. 1); Patrick McCannon (BMH WS 1383, pp 3–4); Bernard Meehan (BMH WS 1513, p. 1); McCabe, *Cradling a revolution*; McGee, *The IRB*, p. 355; Denis Carroll, *They have fooled you again: Michael O'Flanagan (1876–1942): priest, republican, social critic* (Dublin, 1993), pp 24–39.
80 *Irish Independent* (*II*), 2, 11, 20, 21, 23 July 1914; *SC*, 30 May, 6 June, 18, 25 July 1914; *SI*, 18, 25 July 1914; *SN*, 25 July 1914.
81 *SC*, 1 Aug. 1914; CI Sligo, July 1914 (TNA, CO 904/94); Crean report, 26 July, 1914 (NLI, Maurice Moore papers, MS 10544/4); Crean's report praised the 'wonderful organising powers of the Rev P.J. O'Grady (PP Keash) who is the leading spirit of the Volunteer movement in Co. Sligo'.
82 *SC*, *SI*, 1 Aug. 1914.
83 Wheatley, *Nationalism*, pp 195–8; *SI*, 1 Aug. 1914.

CHAPTER THREE *'Our place is … on the side of the allies'*

1 Thomas Scanlan MP speaking at Irish Volunteer meeting in Sligo (*SC*, 3 Oct. 1914).
2 *SC*, *SI*, 8 Aug. 1914.
3 Fitzpatrick, *Politics*, pp 53–4; Wheatley, *Nationalism*, p. 203.
4 *SC*, 8 Aug. 1914; Terence Dooley, *The decline of the big house in Ireland: a study of Irish landed families, 1860–1960* (Dublin, 2001), p. 226.
5 *SC*, 15 Aug. 1914; Hillas to Maurice Moore, 9 Aug. 1914 (NLI, Maurice Moore papers, MS 10550); the Hillas family of Doonecoy, Templeboy were large property owners in the barony of Tireragh; McTernan, *Sligo: the light of bygone days, vol. I*, pp 319–20.
6 Seán Ó Cinnéide to Moore, 18 Aug. 1914 (NLI, Maurice Moore papers, MS 10550); Moore to Ó Cinnéide, 20 Aug. 1914 (ibid.).
7 Jinks to Moore, 19 Aug. 1914 (ibid.); McCabe to Hillas, 18 Aug. 1914 (ibid.).
8 Hillas to Moore, 2 Sept. 1914 (ibid.).
9 *SI*, 15 Aug. 1914; CI Sligo, Aug. 1914 (TNA, CO 904/94).
10 *SI*, 27 Feb., 6, 20, 27 Mar., 3 Apr., 1 May 1915.
11 *SC*, 22, 29 Aug., 5 Sept. 1914.   12 *SI*, 19 Sept. 1914; *SC*, 26 Sept. 1914.
13 *SI*, 26 Sept. 1914.   14 *SC*, 26 Sept. 1914.   15 *SI*, 3 Oct. 1914.
16 *SC*, 31 Oct., 7, 14, 21 Nov. 1914.
17 *SC*, 17, 24, 31 Oct. 1914; *IV*, 17 Oct. 1914; Charles McCoy to Moore, 5 Nov. 1914 (NLI, Maurice Moore papers, MS 10550).

18 *IV*, 3 Oct. 1914.

19 *SC*, 21 Nov., 5 Dec. 1914; Nevin to Maurice Moore, 20 Nov., 4 Dec. (NLI, Maurice Moore papers, MS 10550); *National Volunteer*, 12 Dec. 1914.

20 *SC*, 3 Oct. 1914; Wheatley, *Nationalism*, pp 1–2.

21 *SC*, 10, 24 Oct. 1914; *SN*, 10 Oct. 1914.

22 CI Sligo, Oct. 1914 (TNA, CO 904/95); *IV*, 6 Nov. 1914.

23 CI Sligo, Aug. 1914 (TNA, CO 904/94).

24 Wheatley, *Nationalism*, pp 199–203.

25 *SI*, 8 Aug. 1914; *SC*, 15 Aug. 1914.

26 *SI*, 28 Nov. 1914, 13 Mar. 1915; CI Sligo, Nov. 1914 (TNA, CO 904/95).

27 *SC*, 31 Oct., 7 Nov. 1914; *SI*, 21 Nov. 1914.   28 *SC*, *SI*, 8 Aug. 1914.

29 *SC*, *SI*, 19 Sept. 1914.   30 *SC*, *SI*, 12 Sept. 1914; *Sinn Féin*, 19 Sept. 1914.

31 *SI*, 7 Nov., *SN*, 28 Nov. 1914.   32 *SC*, 3 Oct. 1914.

33 *SC*, 21 Nov. 1914; O'Dowd to O'Hara, 24, 31 Oct. 1928 (NLI, O'Hara papers, MS 36440/8).

34 *SI*, 2 Jan. 1915.   35 *SI*, 26 Sept., 7 Nov. 1914.

36 CI Sligo, Sept., Oct. 1914 (TNA, CO 904/94–95).   37 *SI*, 31 Oct. 1914.

38 *SC*, 9, 16 Jan. 1915.   39 *SC*, 23 Jan. 1915.

40 Marie Coleman, *County Longford and the Irish revolution* (Dublin, 2003), pp 36–7; Fitzpatrick, *Politics*, pp 96–7.

41 Wheatley, *Nationalism*, pp 213–16; CI Sligo, Sept.-Dec. 1914 (TNA, CO 904/94–95).

42 *SC*, 7, 21 Nov. 1914; *NV*, 5, 26 Dec. 1914.

43 CI Sligo, Apr. 1915 (TNA, CO 904/96).

44 Moore to Scanlan, 26 Feb. 1915 (NLI, Maurice Moore papers, MS 10550); Scanlan to Moore, 1 Mar. 1915 (ibid.); Hamill to Moore, 15 Mar. 1915 (ibid.).

45 *SC*, 20, 27 Mar., 3 Apr. 1914; *SN*, 27 Mar. 1915; *IV*, 20 Mar. 1915.

46 *SC*, 17 Apr. 1914; *SI*, 10 Apr. 1915.

47 Hamill to Coffey, 7 May 1915 (NLI, Maurice Moore papers, MS 10550); Meredith to Coffey, 7 May 1915 (ibid.); Hamill to Meredith, 15 Apr. 1915 (ibid.); Volunteer battalion lists, 4 May 1915 (ibid.); *IV*, 8, 15, 29 May, 12 June 1915.

48 CI Sligo, Sept., Oct. 1914 (TNA, CO 904/94–5).   49 Coleman, *Longford*, p. 37.

50 CI Sligo, Jan. 1915 (TNA, CO 904/96).

51 *SC*, 12, 26 Sept. 1914; McCoy to Moore, 11 Nov. 1914 (NLI, Maurice Moore papers, MS 10550); *IV*, 17 Oct. 1914; Charles Gildea (BMH WS 1313, pp 1–2).

52 Frank Carty statement [1935] (Department of Defence archives: microfilm, NLI, p 913); Carty was born in 1897, the son of a farmer in Clooncunny, Ballymote.

53 *SC*, 12, 26 Sept. 1914; Patrick McCannon (BMH WS 1383, p. 6); Bernard Meehan (BMH WS 1513, p. 2); Thady McGowan & Tom Brehony (BMH WS 918, p. 1).

54 *SC*, 13 Nov. 1915; Alec McCabe (BMH WS 277, pp 2–3); McCabe, *Cradling a revolution*; *IT*, 6 May 1970; Arrest of Alec McCabe (NAI, Dept. of Education Records, ED 9/26346); Fr Burke/Alec McCabe Enquiry (NAI, Dept. of Education Records, ED 9/25402); Fr Burke had come to the notice of the authorities for speaking against recruiting in November 1914 (NLI, Joseph Brennan papers, MS 26161). He became a chaplain soon afterwards; James McGuinn, *Sligo men in the Great War* (Belturbet, 1994), pp 36–8.

55 *Nationality*, 12 Feb. 1916; Gerard MacAtasney, *Seán Mac Diarmada: the mind of the revolution* (Manorhamilton, 2004), p. 159; McCabe, *Cradling a revolution*; *IT*, 6 May 1970; Alec McCabe (BMH WS 277, pp 2–3).

56 Account of Sligo Volunteers 1915–18 (NLI, J.J. O'Connell papers, MS 22118); Seamus MacGowan was said to have worked on a Labour newspaper in Dublin. William (Billy) Pilkington was from Abbey Street, Sligo and had been attending the Forestry College in Co. Wicklow. This was closed at the outbreak of war and he returned to Sligo and became an apprentice watchmaker in Wehrly Brothers Ltd.

57 *SC*, 24 Apr., 1 May 1915.

58 *SC*, 1, 15, 22, 29 May, 19 June, 7 Aug., 25 Sept., 2 Oct., 30 Nov. 1915.
59 *SC*, 1 May 1915; List of Catholic clergymen reported to government for using anti-recruiting or seditious language, 1914 (NLI, Joseph Brennan papers, MS 26161).
60 *SC*, 19 Dec. 1914, 23 Jan. 1915.
61 *SI*, 20 Feb. 1915.
62 *SC*, 10 Apr. 1915; *SI*, 10, 17 Apr. 1915.
63 *SC*, *SI*, 1 May 1915; CI Sligo, Feb., May 1915 (TNA, CO 904/96–97).
64 CI Sligo, June, Sept., Nov. 1915 (TNA, CO 904/97–98); *SC*, 19 June 1915; *SI*, 19 June, 25 Sept., 2 Oct., 6, 13 Nov. 1915; *SN*, *19* June 1915.
65 *SI*, 27 Feb., 20 Mar., 12 June 1915; McGuinn, *Sligo men*, p. 48.
66 *SI*, 14, 28 Aug. 1915.
67 *SC*, 18, 25 Sept. 1915; *SI*, 25 Sept. 1915; McGuinn, *Sligo men*, pp 52–3.
68 Ben Novick, *Conceiving revolution: Irish nationalist propaganda during the first World War* (Dublin, 2001), pp 21–3; *SI*, 16, 30 Oct., 6, 13, 20 Nov. 1915; *SC*, 6, 13, 27 Nov. 1915; *IT*, 3–9 Nov. 1915; Wheatley, *Nationalism*, pp 230–1.
69 *SC*, 20 Nov., 4 Dec. 1915, 1 Jan. 1916; *IV*, 11 Dec. 1915; *Nationality*, 8 Jan. 1916.
70 Jinks to O'Hara, 7 Jan. 1916 & reply, 8 Jan. 1916 (NLI, O'Hara papers, MS 16826); O'Hara to O/C Kilworth Camp, 8 Jan. 1916 (NLI, O'Hara papers, MS 16448); *SC*, *SI*, *SN*, 29 Jan. 1916.

CHAPTER FOUR *'How is the future of Ireland to be served'*

1 Thomas Scanlan MP speaking at Sligo Borough UIL branch (*SC*, 9 Sept. 1916).
2 Michael Laffan, *The resurrection of Ireland: the Sinn Féin party, 1916–1923* (Cambridge, 1999), p. 121.
3 CI Sligo report on 1916 (TNA, CO 904/120).   4 Carty statement, p. 2.
5 J.M. Wilson's tour of Ireland, Co. Sligo, 24 Feb. 1916 (PRONI, J.M. Wilson papers, D/989/A/9/7).
6 *SI*, 1 Apr. 1916.   7 *SC*, 15 Apr. 1916.   8 *SC*, 15, 22 Apr. 1916; *SI*, 22 Apr. 1916.
9 CI Sligo, Mar. 1916 (TNA, CO 904/100).
10 CI Sligo report on 1916 (TNA, CO 904/120); CI Sligo, Mar. 1916 (TNA, CO 904/100).
11 Carty statement, p. 2; Tom O'Grady (BMH WS 917, p. 2).
12 Patrick McCannon (BMH WS 1383, p. 6).
13 Bernard Meehan (BMH WS 1513, pp 2–3); Patrick McCannon (BMH WS 1383, pp 6–8).
14 John J. Dockery (BMH WS 1312, pp 1–2); Charles Gildea (BMH WS 1313, pp 1–2); Thady McGowan & Tom Brehony (BMH WS 918, p. 2).
15 Alec McCabe (BMH WS 277, pp 3–6); Tom O'Grady (BMH WS 917, pp 2–3).
16 *SC*, *SI*, 6 May 1916.
17 *SC*, *SN*, *SI*, 13, 20, 27 May 1916; List of prisoners deported from Co. Sligo, 1916 (NLI, INAAVDF papers, MS 24364).
18 *SC*, 20 May 1916; Gaughan, *Jeremiah Mee*, pp 48–9.
19 Laffan, *Sinn Féin*, pp 50–6.   20 *SC*, *SN*, 20, 27 May 1916.
21 *SC*, 27 May 1916; *SN*, 1, 8, 15 July 1916.
22 CI Sligo report on 1916 (TNA, CO 904/120).   23 *SC*, 1 July 1916.
24 *SC*, 27 May, 3, 10 June 1916.   25 *SC*, *SI*, 10 June 1916.
26 *SN*, 29 July, 12 Aug. 1916.
27 *SI*, 10 June 1916; List of delegates who attended an executive meeting of the Irish National Aid Association and Irish Volunteers Dependants' Fund in Dublin, 8 Apr. 1917 (NLI, INAAVDF papers, MS 24,339); list of local branches and representatives of the INAAVDF, 1916–1917 (NLI, INAAVDF papers, MS 23,493); list of parishes with amounts collected in each on behalf of the INAAVDF, 1916–1917 (NLI, INAAVDF papers, MS 24,381); Laffan, *Sinn Féin*, pp 66–8; this J.J. Clancy should not be confused with J.J. Clancy, nationalist MP for North County Dublin, 1885–1918.

28 Laffan, *Sinn Féin*, pp 56–62.   29 *SC*, 17 June 1916.
30 *SC*, 10, 17, 24 June, 8, 15, 22 July 1916.   31 *SC*, 17 June 1916.
32 CI Sligo, June 1916 (TNA, CO 904/99).   33 *SN, SC*, 8 July 1916.
34 Minute book of the National Directory of the UIL, 10 Aug. 1904–30 Apr. 1918 (NLI, MS 708).
35 *SN*, 12 Aug. 1916.   36 CI Sligo, July 1916 (TNA, CO 904/99).
37 *SC*, 2, 9 Sept. 1916.   38 *SC*, 4 Nov. 1916.
39 CI Sligo, Sept. 1916 (TNA, CO 904/101).
40 Michael Nevin (BMH WS 1384, p. 1); Account of Volunteers and Sinn Féin in Sligo, n.d. (NLI, O'Connell papers, MS 22,118); Baby Bohan questionnaire, Mar. 1969 (UCDAD, Sighle Humphreys papers, P106/1425); Julia Travers questionnaire, Mar. 1969 (ibid.); CI Sligo, Nov., Dec, 1916 (TNA, CO 904/101); D.A. Mulcahy, a native of Limerick, replaced G.H. Smith as principal of Sligo Technical School in 1912.
41 Laffan, *Sinn Féin*, p. 76.
42 *SC, SI*, 27 Jan. 1917.
43 *SC*, 10 Feb. 1917; CI Sligo, Feb. 1917 (TNA, CO 904/102); Laffan, *Sinn Féin*, pp 77–85; Carty statement, p. 3; Account of Volunteers and Sinn Féin in Sligo, n.d. (NLI, O'Connell papers, MS 22,118); Sarah Bohan questionnaire, Mar. 1969 (UCDAD, Sighle Humphreys papers, P106/1425).
44 *SC*, 10 Feb. 1917.   45 *SC*, 17 Feb., 3 Mar. 1917.
46 *SC*, 24 Mar. 1917; *Nationality*, 17, 24 Mar. 1917.
47 Brighid O'Mullane (BMH WS 450, p. 1); Mary Ann Flynn questionnaire, Mar. 1969 (UCDAD, Sighle Humphreys papers, P106/1425); Baby Bohan questionnaire, Mar. 1969 (ibid.); Julia Travers questionnaire, Mar. 1969 (ibid.); Brighid and Michael J. O'Mullane were born in Sligo, children of a Clare-born RIC man who married a Sligo woman. Brighid became a national organizer for Cumann na mBan. Michael became a teacher in Dublin. He was active in support of Sinn Féin and the Irish Volunteers in County Sligo; McTernan, *Worthies of Sligo*, pp 254–6.
48 List of delegates who attended an executive meeting of the INAAVDF in Dublin, 8 Apr. 1917 (NLI, INAAVDF papers, MS 24339).
49 CI Sligo, May–Dec 1917 (TNA, CO 904/103–104).
50 *SC*, 7 Apr. 1917; *Nationality*, 14 Apr. 1917; *Roscommon Herald* (*RH*), 10 Feb. 1917.
51 *SC, SI*, 14, 21 Apr. 1917; List of those who attended conference (NLI, Count Plunkett papers, MS 11383/1).
52 Laffan, *Sinn Féin*, pp 94–6.
53 Precis of letters seized in Sinn Féin HQRS, 1918 (NLI, MS 10494); CI Sligo, Mar.–July 1917 (TNA, CO 904/102–103).
54 *Nationality*, Apr.–July 1917; *SC*, 9, 23, 30 June 1917.
55 *SC*, 21 July 1917; *SN*, 18 Aug. 1917.
56 Tom O'Grady (BMH WS 917, p. 4); *SC*, 30 June, 14, 28 July 1917; *SI*, 12 May 1917; *SN*, 14 July, 4, 11, 18 Aug. 1917; CI Sligo, May–July 1917 (TNA, CO 904/103).
57 *SC*, 14 July 1917.
58 CI Sligo, Apr., June 1917 (TNA, CO 904/102/103); Coleman, *Longford*, pp 74–6.
59 *SC*, 21 Apr., 1 Sept., 8 Dec. 1917; CI Sligo, May 1917 (TNA, CO 904/103); *Nationality*, 4 Aug. 1917.
60 *SN*, 23 June 1917; *Nationality*, 16 June 1917.   61 *SN*, 30 June 1917.
62 *SC*, 21, 28 July 1917; *Nationality*, 28 July 1917; CI Sligo, June, July 1917 (TNA, CO 904/103).
63 O'Hara to Mahon 19 Aug. 1917 (NLI, O'Hara papers, MS 16826); CI Sligo, Nov. 1917 (TNA, CO 904/104).
64 *RH*, 24 Feb., 1917; *FJ*, 23 Oct. 1917; Jérôme aan de Wiel, *The Catholic Church in Ireland, 1914–1918: war and politics* (Dublin, 2003), pp 191–2; Patrick Murray, *Oracles of God: the Roman Catholic Church and Irish politics, 1922–37* (Dublin, 2000), pp 237–9.
65 *SC*, 15 Sept., 15 Dec. 1917; Thomas Murricane was manager of Rathscanlon creamery, Tubbercurry; Séamus Marren worked in Achonry creamery.

66   *SC*, 15 Sept. 1917.   67 *SC*, 29 Sept., 6 Oct. 1917.
68   *SC*, 25 Aug., 22 Sept., 13, 27 Oct. 1917; *SN*, 6, 13, 20 Oct., 3, 10 Nov., 1 Dec. 1917; CI Sligo,
     Nov. 1917 (TNA, CO 904/104).
69   *SC*, 13 Oct. 1917.
70   Précis of letters seized in Sinn Féin HQRS, 1918 (NLI, MS 10494); *SI*, 5 Jan., 27 Apr. 1918;
     SN. 23 Feb. 1918.
71   *Notes from Ireland*, 23 Feb. 1918.   72 Laffan, *Sinn Féin*, p. 121.
73   Ibid., p. 187.   74 CI Sligo, Sept.–Nov. 1917 (TNA, CO 904/104).

CHAPTER FIVE *1918 – Sinn Féin: 'the only political organisation in the county'*

1   CI Sligo, Oct. 1917 (TNA, CO 904/104).
2   CI Sligo, Dec. 1917 (TNA, CO 904/104); *SC*, 19, 26 Jan. 1918.
3   The constituencies were South Armagh, Waterford City and East Tyrone; Laffan, *Sinn Féin*,
    pp 122–8.
4   McCabe interview, *IT*, 7 May 1970; Novick, *Conceiving revolution*, pp 183–7; Tony Varley, 'A
    region of sturdy smallholders? Western nationalists and agrarian politics during the First
    World War', *Journal of the Galway Archaeological and Historical Society*, 55 (2003), 136–8;
    Fitzpatrick, *Politics*, p. 140; *SN*, 5, 19 Jan., 9, 16 Feb. 1918; *SI*, 16 Feb. 1918; *SC*, 12, 19, 26
    Jan., 2 Mar. 1918; Charles Gildea (BMH WS 1313, p. 3); Bernard Meehan (BMH WS 1513,
    pp 4–5).
5   *SC*, 2, 9, 16, 23 Feb., 9 Mar., 14 Dec. 1918; Gaughan, *Jeremiah Mee*, pp 51–3.
6   Wood-Martin to Gethin, 11 Feb. 1918 (SCL Robinson estate office letter books); Wood-Martin
    to O'Grady, 12 Feb. 1918 (ibid.); Wood-Martin to Harte, 11 Feb. 1918 (ibid.).
7   HC Deb 21 Feb. 1918 vol 103 cc 892–4; Midland & Connaught district intelligence officer
    report, Feb. 1918 (TNA, CO 904/157/1); CI Sligo, Feb. 1918 (TNA, CO 904/105); HC Deb
    1 Aug. 1918 vol 109 cc 587–8.
8   *SN*, 16, 23 Mar. 1918; *IT*, 27 Feb., 2, 16 Mar. 1918.
9   Sinn Féin Standing Committee Minutes (NLI, MSP 3269).
10 *II*, 28 Feb. 1918.   11 *SC*, 2 Mar. 1918.
12 CI Sligo, Feb., Mar. 1918 (TNA, CO 904/105).
13 *SC*, *SN*, *SI*, 2 Mar. 1918; Batt Keaney memoirs, pp 7–8; *New York Times*, 2 Mar. 1918; List
    of operations carried out by 1st Batt. Sligo Bde. 1917–21, n.d. (NLI, O'Connell papers, MS
    22118).
14 Charles Gildea (BMH WS 1313, p. 3).
15 *SC*, 9, 16, 23, 30 Mar., 6, 13, 20, 27 Apr., 6 July 1918.
16 *SC*, 27 Apr., 11, 25 May, 14 Sept. 1918; Gaughan, *Jeremiah Mee*, p. 51.
17 *SI*, 2 Mar. 1918.   18 *SN*, *SI*, *SC*, 30 Mar. 1918.
19 *SC*, 26 Jan., 23 Feb., 30 Mar., 27 Apr. 1918; *SN*, 18 May 1918; CI Sligo, Jan., Feb., Mar. 1918
    (TNA, CO 904/105).
20 *Nationality*, 9, 16 Feb. 1918; *SI*, *SC*, 9 Feb. 1918; *SI*, 16 Feb. 1918.
21 *SC*, 26 Jan., 23, 30 Mar. 1918; *Nationality*, 23 Mar. 1918.
22 CI Sligo, Mar. 1918 (TNA, CO 904/105).
23 *SC*, 6 Apr. 1918.
24 CI Sligo, Apr. 1918 (TNA, CO 904/105); *SC*, 13, 20 Apr. 1918.
25 *SC*, 27 Apr. 1918.
26 *SC*, 13, 20, 27 Apr., 18 May 1918; de Wiel, *Catholic Church*, pp 217, 227–8; Swords, *Achonry*,
    pp 443–5.
27 CI Sligo, May, June 1918 (TNA, CO 904/106).
28 CI Sligo, June 1918 (TNA, CO 904/106).
29 *SC*, 10, 17 Aug. 7; 14, 21 Sept. 1918; *SI*, 14 Sept., 5 Oct. 1918; O'Hara to Murphy, 1 Aug. 1918
    (NLI, O'Hara papers, MS 16826).

30 McGuinn, *Great War*, pp 39–42; *SC sesquicentenary*, p. 43; *SI*, 21, 28 June 1919.
31 J.J. O'Connell was born in Ballina, Co. Mayo and educated at University College Dublin. He spent the years 1912–14 in the United States army and returned to Ireland in 1914. He was interned after the 1916 Rising. His father, J.A. O'Connell, had conducted the inquiry into the 1915 McCabe – Fr Burke incident (NAI, Dept. of Education Records, ED 9/25402).
32 Charles Gildea (BMH WS 1313, p. 3); John P. Brennan (BMH WS 1278, p. 1); this is the same man as Jack Brennan, Tubbercurry IRA, and is referred to as Jack in the O'Malley notebooks; Carty statement, p. 5.
33 CI Sligo, Jan.–Dec. 1918 (TNA, CO 904/102–107).
34 *SC*, *SI* 16, 23 Feb., 13 July 1918; M.C. O'Brien, *Commandant Marren* (Sligo?, n.d.).
35 List of operations 1st Batt. Sligo Bde.; Tom Scanlan (UCDAD, Ernie O'Malley notebooks, P17b/133/9).
36 Bat Keaney memoirs, pp 5–7; *SC*, 9, 16 Mar., 20, 27 Apr. 1918; Micheál O'Callaghan, *For Ireland and freedom: Roscommon's contribution to the fight for independence 1917–1921* (Boyle, 1964), pp 20–4.
37 *SC*, 20, 27 Apr., 4 May 1918.
38 Dorothy Macardle, *The Irish republic* (London, 1968), p. 238.
39 *Nationality*, 11 May 1918; *SC* 13, 27 Apr., 4, 18 May, 1, 29 June 1918; *RH*, 4, 18 May, 1, 8, 15, 29 June 1918.
40 *RH*, 13 Apr. 1918; *SC*, 1 June 1918.
41 *RH*, 13 Apr., 18 May, 8, 29 June, 6 July, 5, 12 Oct. 1918; *SC*, 1 June, 20 July, 10 Aug. 1918; Aideen Sheehan, 'Cumann na mBan, policies and activities' in David Fitzpatrick (ed.), *Revolution? Ireland 1917–1923* (Dublin, 1990), pp 88–90; Margaret Ward, *Unmanageable revolutionaries: women and Irish nationalism* (London, 1983), p. 131; Cumann na mBan convention 1918 (UCDAD, Sighle Humphreys papers, P106/1128); Julia Travers questionnaire, Mar. 1969 (UCDAD, Sighle Humphreys papers, P106/1425); Sarah Bohan questionnaire, Mar. 1969 (ibid.).
42 *RH*, 29 June 1918; *SC*, 8, 15, 22, 29 June 1918.
43 *SC*, 25 May, 1 June 1918; *SN.*, 25 May, 1 June 1918; *SI*, 25 May 1918.
44 *SC*, 22, 29 June 1918; CI Sligo, June 1918 (TNA, CO 904/106).
45 Macardle, *Irish republic*, p. 238; *SC*, *SN*, 17, 24 Aug. 1918.
46 *SC*, 22 June, 20 July, 24 Aug., 14 Dec. 1918; *SN*, 6 July, 12 Oct. 1918; Anderson obit., *II*, 10 Feb. 1973; McTernan, *Worthies of Sligo*, pp 318–20.
47 A census of the membership of the ITGWU, June 1918 (NLI, MS 13,948); ITGWU list of branches, 1909–22 (NLI, MS 7,282); *SC*, 18 May 1918.
48 *SC*, 18 May 1918.
49 *SC*, 19, 26 Oct., 2 Nov. 1918; Michael Laffan, 'Labour must wait: Ireland's conservative revolution' in Patrick J. Corish (ed.), *Radicals, rebels and establishments* (Belfast, 1985), pp 214–15.
50 *SC*, 18 May, 8 June 1918; Novick, *Conceiving revolution*, p. 205.
51 Michael Nevin (BMH WS 1384, p. 2); Harold McBrien (BMH WS 895, p. 1); Martin McGowan (BMH WS 1545, p. 2); John J. Dockery (BMH WS 1312, p. 2); Jim Hever interview, 6 Aug. 1989.
52 *SC*, 15, 22 June 1918; *SN*, *SI*, 15 June 1918.
53 *SC*, 29 June 1918; CI Sligo, June 1918 (TNA, CO 904/106).
54 *SC*, 28 Sept., 5, 19 Oct., 9, 16 Nov. 1918; Secs. south Sligo SF to headquarters, 5, 19 Sept. (Sinn Féin material, SCL); Headquarters to secs. south Sligo Sinn Féin, 20 Sept. 1918 (ibid.); Fr O'Flanagan to P Ó Domhnalláin 11 Oct. 1918 (ibid.); Minutes 19 Sept., 16 Oct., 14 Nov. 1918 (NLI, Sinn Féin Standing Committee minutes, MS P3269).
55 *SC*, 23 Nov., 7 Dec. 1918; Miller, *Church, state and nation*, pp 417–18; CI Sligo, Nov., Dec. 1918 (TNA, CO 904/107).
56 *SC*, *SN*, 23, 30 Nov. 1918.   57 *SI*, 30 Nov. 1918.   58 *SC*, 21, 28 Dec. 1918.
59 *SN*, 21 Dec. 1918; CI Sligo, Dec. 1918 (TNA, CO 904/107).

60 CI Sligo, Dec. 1918 (TNA, CO 904/107).   61 *SN*, 21 Dec. 1918; *SC*, *SI*, 4 Jan. 1919.
62 CI Sligo, Dec. 1918 (TNA, CO 904/107).
63 *SC*, *SC*, 10 Nov., 1 Dec. 1917, 19, 26 Jan., 2, 23 Feb., 10 Aug. 1918; *SN*, 24 Aug. 1918; Matthew Potter, *The municipal revolution in Ireland: a handbook of urban government in Ireland since 1800* (Dublin, 2011), p. 246; Deignan, *Protestant community*, pp 112–6; *SC sesquicentenary*, pp 44–5.
64 *SC*, *SI*, *SN*, 4, 11 Jan. 1919.
65 *SC*, *SI*, *SN*, 18 Jan. 1919; Deignan, *Protestant community*, pp 116–21; Patrick Deignan, 'PR & the Sligo Borough election of January 1919', *History Ireland*, 17:3 (May-June, 2009), 38–9.
66 *SC*, *SI*, *SN*, 25 Jan. 1919.

CHAPTER SIX *'Disloyalty and contempt for the law'*

1 CI Sligo, Apr. 1919 (TNA, CO 904/108).
2 Laffan, *Sinn Féin*, pp 284–5.
3 Joost Augusteijn, *From public defiance to guerrilla warfare: the experience of ordinary volunteers in the Irish War of Independence, 1916–1921* (Dublin, 1996), p. 78; Peter Hart, *The I.R.A. & its enemies: violence and community in Cork, 1916–1923* (Oxford, 1998), pp 62, 71.
4 CI Sligo, Apr. 1919 (TNA, CO 904/108).
5 Jim Hunt (BMH WS 905, p. 1).   6 Michael Nevin (BMH WS 1384, p. 2).
7 *SI*, 17, 24 May 1919; List of operations 1st Batt. Sligo Bde. 1917–21 (SCL); Eugene Gilbride (UCDAD, O'Malley notebooks, P17b/137/30).
8 *SC*, 3 Jan. 1920.   9 *SC*, 28 June, 12 July 1919.
10 AG to acting O/C, Sligo, 6 Dec. 1919 (NLI, O'Connell papers, MS 22118).
11 Pilkington to headquarters, 6 Jan. 1920 (ibid.).
12 Pilkington to AG, 11 May 1920 (ibid.).
13 O'Connell to AG, 25 Sept. 1919 (NLI, Michael Collins papers, Department of Defence archives: microfilm, p 914).
14 Thady McGowan & Thomas Brehony (BMH WS 918, pp 2–3).
15 Pat Hunt interview, 31 May 1986.
16 Sligo Brigade commandant to AG., 4 Apr. 1920 (NLI, Collins papers, Department of Defence archives: microfilm, p 919).
17 Jim Hunt (BMH WS 905, p. 1).   18 *SC*, 7 Dec. 1918.
19 *SC*, 4, 11, 18 Jan., 1, 15 Feb., 22, 29 Mar. 1919; *SI*, 29 Mar. 1919
20 *SC*, *SI*, 8, 15 Mar. 1919; *SN*, 8 Mar. 1919; Tom Scanlon (UCDAD, O'Malley notebooks, P19b/133/32–33).
21 *SC*, 15, 22, 29 Mar. 1919.   22 *SC*, *SI*, 15 Mar. 1919.
23 *SC*, 29 Mar., 5, 12, 19 Apr. 1919; *SI*, 29 Mar. 1919.   24 *SC*, 12, 19 Apr. 1919.
25 *SC*, 29 Mar. 1919.   26 *SC*, 1 Mar., 3, 10, 31 May 1919.   27 *SC*, *SI*, 12 Apr. 1919.
28 *SC*, 28 June, 5, 12 July, 23 Aug. 1919; *SI*, 28 June 1919; CI Sligo, June 1919 (TNA, CO 904/109).
29 Macardle, *Irish republic*, pp 263, 279.   30 *SC*, 4 Oct. 1919; *SN*, 30 Sept. 1919.
31 *SC*, 18, 25 Oct. 1919.
32 John J. Dockery (BMH WS 1312, pp 3–4); Patrick Hegarty (BMH WS 1606, pp 15–19); Jim Hunt (BMH WS 905, pp 1–4); Jim Hunt (UCDAD, O'Malley notebooks, P17b/133/41–2); Patrick Hegarty (UCDAD, O'Malley notebooks, P17b/137/41–44); *SC*, 15, 22, 29 Nov., 6, 13 Dec. 1919; *SN*, 29 Nov. 1919; *SI*, 22 Nov. 1919.
33 CI Sligo, Dec. 1919 (TNA, CO 904/110).
34 Captured documents including Dáil loan material (TNA, CO 904/24).
35 *SC*, 20 Sept. 1919.   36 *SC*, *SN*, 13 Sept. 1919.
37 CI Sligo, Nov. 1919 (TNA, CO 904/110).

38   *SC*, 24 Jan. 1920; *SN*, 17, 24, 31 Jan. 1920; *SI*, 31 Jan. 1920; CI Sligo, Jan. 1920 (TNA, CO 904/111).
39   *SC*, 24 Jan. 1920; *SN*, 21 Feb. 1920; *SI*, 6 Mar. 1920; CI Sligo, Jan., Feb. 1920 (TNA, CO 904/111).
40   Bernard Conway (UCDAD, O'Malley notebooks, P19b/133/75); Joe Sheerin (UCDAD, O'Malley notebooks, P19b/136/23); Patrick McCannon (BMH WS 1383, pp 12–13).
41   *SC*, *SI*, 31 Jan. 1920; *SN*, 24 Jan. 1920; Carty statement, p. 6; CI Sligo, Jan. 1920 (TNA, CO 904/111).
42   *SC*, *SI*, *SN*, 28 Feb. 1920; *SC*, 6, 13 Mar., 3, 10 Apr. 1920; Jim Hunt (UCDAD, O'Malley notebooks, P19b/133/42); Jim Hunt (BMH WS 905, p. 3); Carty statement, pp 6–7.
43   Michael Coleman (UCDAD, O'Malley notebooks, P19b/137/34); John P. Brennan (BMH WS 1278, pp 1–2).
44   *SI*, 6 Mar. 1920.
45   *SC*, 17 Jan., 7, 28 Feb. 1920; *RH*, 29 Jan. 1920; *SN*, 14, 21 Feb. 1920.
46   *RH*, 29 Jan., 15 May 1920; *SI*, 24 Apr. 1920; *Connachtman* (*CM*), 4 June 1920; *SC*, 5 June 1920; Weekly summaries of outrages against the police and returns of recruitment, retirement and dismissal (TNA, CO 904/148–9).
47   Jim Hunt (BMH WS 905, p. 4).
48   Michael Hopkinson, *The Irish War of Independence* (Dublin, 2002), pp 47–8.
49   *SC*, 22 Nov. 1919; *SI*, 27 Sept., 15 Nov. 1919.
50   CI Sligo, Nov. 1919 (TNA, CO 904/110).
51   *SC*, 10 Apr. 1920; AG to O/C Sligo Bde., 9 Apr. 1920 (NLI, O'Connell papers, MS 22118); O/C Sligo Bde. to AG., 11 Apr. 1920 (ibid.); Report on police barracks for Sligo area, 24 Apr. 1920 (ibid.).
52   *SC*, 10, 24 Apr., 15 May 1920; *SI*, 29 May 1920; *RH*, 15, 22 May 1920; *CM*, 24 Apr., 15, 28 May 1920; Thady McGowan & Tom Brehony (BMH WS 918, p. 4).
53   *SI*, 10, 24, 31 July, 14 Aug. 1920; *SC*, 17 Apr., 3, 10, 17, 31 July 1920; *RH*, 24 July, 7 Aug. 1920; *CM*, 9, 23, 30 July 1920; Harold McBrien (BMH WS 895, p. 4).
54   John J. Dockery (BMH WS 1312, p. 3); Thady McGowan & Thomas Brehony (BMH WS 918, pp 3–4); Bat Keaney memoirs, pp 9–10; *SC*, 7, 14, 21 June, 5 July 1919; *SI*, 14 June 1919; CI Sligo, Feb. 1919 (TNA, CO 904/108); Michael Hannon, *Remembering James Hannon*, *Corran Herald*, 33 (2000/2001), 2–3.
55   *SC*, 28 June 1919.
56   *SC*, 5, 12 July, 9 Aug. 1919; CI Sligo, June, July, Aug. 1919 (TNA, CO 904/109–10).
57   Tony Varley, 'Agrarian crime and social control: Sinn Féin and the land question in the west of Ireland in 1920' in Ciaran McCullagh, Mike Tomilson & Tony Varley (eds), *Whose law and order? Aspects of crime and social control in Irish society* (Belfast, 1988), pp 54–75; Fergus Campbell & Kevin O'Shiel, 'The last land war? Kevin O'Shiel's memoir of the Irish revolution, 1916–21', *Archivium Hibernicum*, 57 (2003), 155–200; Campbell, *Land and revolution*, pp 246–57.
58   *SC*, 29 May 1920; *RH*, 15, 29 May, 5 June 1920; Returns of agrarian outrages, May–Dec. 1920 (TNA, CO 904/121).
59   Wood-Martin to Sir Douglas Newton, 31 May 1920 (SCL, Robinson estate letter book, July 1919–July 1920); Thomas O'Donnell from Mahanagh, Gurteen had been very active in SF in south Sligo and was McCabe's election director in 1918. He taught in St Nathy's Diocesan College, Ballaghaderreen 1916–19. He had previously been on the teaching staff at Rockwell College, where he had been a colleague of Eamon de Valera and was said to have been the first person to call the future leader 'Dev'.
60   Wood-Martin to Newton, 31 May 1920 (SCL, Robinson estate letter book, July 1919–July 1920); Wood-Martin to Newton, 5 June 1920 (ibid.); Newton was elected Conservative MP for Cambridge in a 1922 by-election.
61   Wood-Martin to Keogh, 12 June 1920 (SCL, Robinson estate letter book, July 1919–July 1920); Wood-Martin to Newton, 11 Sept. 1920 (ibid.); Wood-Martin to Newton, 26 Feb. 1921 (ibid.).

62 Wood-Martin to Hewetson, 11 December 1920 (ibid.).

63 CI Sligo, July 1920 (TNA, CO 904/112); Returns of agrarian outrages (TNA, CO 904/121); Thomas Neylon, a Catholic, was born in Ennis, Co. Clare in 1874. He was appointed DI in 1910 and was serving in Fermanagh in 1911. In February 1920 he was specially promoted to rank of 1st class DI for good police service. He had been attached to the crime department at RIC headquarters from October 1919 until he was appointed Sligo CI on 15 June 1920.

64 *Irish Bulletin* (*IB*), 17 June 1920; CI Sligo, June 1920 (TNA, CO 904/112).

65 Returns of agrarian outrages (TNA, CO 904/121); CI Sligo, July 1920 (TNA, CO 904/112).

66 Campbell & O'Shiel, 'The last land war?', 157–8.

67 Ibid., 184–6.   68 *SC*, *SN*, *SI*, 14, 21 June 1919.   69 *SC*, 9 Aug. 1919.

70 Peter Hart, *The I.R.A. at war, 1916–1923* (Oxford, 2003), p. 71.

CHAPTER SEVEN *The drift to violence in County Sligo*

1   CI Sligo, June, July 1920 (TNA, CO 904/112).

2   *SI*, 5 June 1920; Eugene Gilbride (UCDAD, O'Malley notebooks, P19b/137/27); Harold McBrien (BMH WS 895, p. 4); Tom Scanlon (UCDAD, O'Malley notebooks, P19b/133/14).

3   Dunnill, 'Summary', p. 9; Thady McGowan & Tom Brehony (BMH WS 918, pp 4–5); CI Sligo, Aug. 1920 (TNA CO 904/112).

4   *SI*, 21 Aug., 18 Sept. 1920; *SC*, 11, 25 Sept. 1920; *RH*, 18, 25 Sept. 1920; *CM*, 3, 17, 24 Sept. 1920; Dunnill, 'Summary', pp 15–16, 19, 24.

5   Richard Abbott, *Police casualties in Ireland, 1919–1922* (Cork, 2000), pp 130–1; W.J. Lowe, 'The war against the R.I.C., 1919–21', *Éire-Ireland*, 37:3–4 (2002), 101–3.

6   CI Sligo, Aug. 1920 (TNA, CO 904/112).

7   Brewer, *RIC*, p. 81; King, *Memorabilia*, p. 23.

8   *RH*, 10, 24 July, 2 Oct. 1920; *SI*, *SC*, 10, 17, 24 July, 28 Aug. 1920; *CM*, 23 July, 20 Aug. 1920; Weekly summaries of outrages against the police (TNA, CO 904/149); Jack Brennan (UCDAD, O'Malley notebooks, P19b/137/20); Dunnill, 'Summary', p. 12.

9   Weekly summaries of outrages against the police (TNA, CO 904/149).

10 *SC*, 11, 25 Sept., 16 Oct. 1920; Warning notices from Nov. 1920 in Dunnill, 'Summary', pp 39–40.

11 *SI*, 17 Jan., 4 Sept. 1920; *SC*, 4 Sept., 2 Oct. 1920. *CM*, 1 Oct. 1920; this is the incident referred to by Peter Hart as 'at least three churches in Clare and at least one in Sligo were burned before the Truce'. Hart, *I.R.A. at war*, p. 239.

12 *SI*, *SC*, 3 July 1920; Jack Brennan (UCDAD, O'Malley notebooks, P19b/137/18–20); Carty statement, p. 7; Tom Scanlon (UCDAD, O'Malley notebooks, P19b/133/29–30); John P. Brennan (BMH WS 1278, p. 4); Florence O'Donoghue, *Sworn to be free: the complete book of IRA jailbreaks, 1918–1921* (Tralee, 1971), pp 108–15.

13 *SI*, 3 July 1920; Jim Hunt (UCDAD, O'Malley notebooks, P19b/133/47); Patrick McCannon (BMH WS 1383, p. 13); Bernard Conway (UCDAD, O'Malley notebooks, P19b/133/74).

14 *SI*, *SC*, *RH*, 31 July 1920; *CM*, 30 July 1920; Tom Deignan (UCDAD, O'Malley notebooks, P19b/133/64); CI Sligo, July 1920 (TNA, CO 904/112).

15 Patrick McCannon (BMH WS 1383, p. 13); Bernard Conway (UCDAD, O'Malley notebooks, P19b/133/74).

16 *SC*, 15 May, 12, 26 June, 31 July, 25 Sept., 9 Oct. 1920; *SI*, 18 Sept. 1920; Thady McGowan & Tom Brehony (BMH WS 918, p. 13); John J. Dockery (BMH WS 1312, pp 4–5)

17 Pat Hunt interview, 31 May 1986.

18 Jim Hunt (UCDAD, O'Malley notebooks, P19b/133/43); Thady McGowan & Tom Brehony (BMH WS 918, p. 6).

19 *SC*, 3 July 1920; *CM*, 30 July 1920.

20 *CM*, 30 July 1920; CI Sligo, June 1920 (TNA, CO 904/112).

21 Hopkinson, *War of Independence*, pp 65–6; F.S.L. Lyons, 'The war of independence, 1919–21' in W.E. Vaughan (ed.), *A new history of Ireland, vi, Ireland under the Union, II: 1870–1921* (Oxford, 2010), pp 244–5; Charles Townshend, *Political violence in Ireland: government and resistance since 1848* (Oxford, 1983), pp 349–51.

22 Hopkinson, *War of Independence*, pp 49–50; Charles MacDermot, 'A summer holiday at Coolavin', *Echoes of Ballaghaderreen*, 22 (2007), 7; Jim Hunt (UCDAD, O'Malley notebooks, P19b/133/41).

23 Dunnill, 'Summary', pp 9–10.

24 William Sheehan, *Hearts and mines, the British 5th Division Ireland, 1920–1922* (Cork, 2009), appendix IX.

25 *SC*, 4, 11 Sept. 1920; *RH*, 14, 21, 28 Aug. 1920; *SI*, 28 Aug. 1920; *CM*, 20 Aug. 1920; John Finn, *Gurteen Co. Sligo: its people and its past* (Sligo, 1994), p. 235; Jim Hunt (UCDA, O'Malley notebooks, P19b/133/58); Tom Deignan (UCDA, O'Malley notebooks, P19b/133/66); Jim Hunt (BMH WS 905, pp 4–6); John J. Dockery (BMH WS 1312, pp 9–10); O'Brien, *Commandant Marren*, p. 11: Watts' body was uncovered by turfcutters in May 1962.

26 Augusteijn, *Public defiance*, pp 17–19; Coleman, *Longford*, p. 122.

27 *CM*, 3 Sept. 1920. *SC*, 4 Sept. 1920; CI Sligo, Aug. 1920 (TNA, CO 904/112); Matt Kilcawley (UCDA, O'Malley notebooks, P19b/136/57–59); Dunnill, 'Summary', p. 13.

28 *SI*, *SC*, 4 Sept. 1920; *RH*, 23 Oct. 1920; Jim Hunt (UCDA, O'Malley notebooks, P19b/133/44–45); Thady McGowan & Tom Brehony (BMH WS 918, p. 5); Jim Hunt (BMH WS 905, pp 6–10); Abbott, *Casualties*, p. 119; MacDermot, *Summer holiday*, 7; T.J. Lavin, 'Some Roscommon actions', *Capuchin Annual* (1970), 406–9.

29 *SI*, *SC*, 14 Aug. 1920; Jack Brennan (UCDAD, O'Malley notebooks, P19b/137/18); Carty statement, p. 8; Thady McGowan & Tom Brehony (BMH WS 918, p. 5); John P. Brennan (BMH WS 1278, pp 5–6); Charles Gildea (BMH WS 1313, pp 4–5).

30 *SC*, 4, 11, 25 Sept. 1920; *SI*, 21, 28 Aug. 1920; *CM*, 20 Aug. 1920; Jack Brennan (UCDAD, O'Malley notebooks, P19b/137/20–21); Carty statement, pp 8–9; CI Sligo, Aug. 1920 (TNA, CO 904/112); Brewer, *RIC*, p. 81; Dunnill, 'Summary', p. 15.

31 *SC*, 2, 9 Oct. 1920; *SI*, 2 Oct. 1920; *CM*, 1, 8 Oct. 1920; Jack Brennan (UCDAD, O'Malley notebooks, P19b/137/21–22); Carty statement, pp 9–11; James Mulholland (UCDAD, O'Malley notebooks, P19b/133/60); John P. Brennan (BMH WS 1278, pp 6–8); Charles Gildea (BMH WS 1313, pp 5–7); Abbott, *Casualties*, pp 128–9; John Kilcoyne, 'Tubbercurry's night of terror recalled', *SC*, 28 Sept. 1985; Jim Herlihy, *Royal Irish Constabulary officers* (Dublin, 2005), p. 68.

32 Dunnill, 'Summary', p. 23.   33 *SC*, 9 Oct. 1920.   34 *SC*, 23 Oct. 1920.

35 *SC*, 16 Oct. 1920.   36 *II*, 16 Oct. 1920.   37 *SI*, 9 Oct. 1920.

38 *An t-Óglach*, 1 Oct. 1920; a similar statement appeared in the 15 Oct. issue.

39 Dunnill, 'Summary', p. 27; *SC*, 30 Oct. 1920.

40 Hopkinson, *War of Independence*, pp 79–84; Fitzpatrick, *Politics*, pp 28–31.

41 *CM*, 15 Oct. 1920; *SC*, 30 Oct., 6 Nov. 1920; *SI*, 30 Oct. 1920; Patrick McCannon (BMH WS 1383, pp 14–19); CI Sligo, Oct. 1920 (TNA, CO 904/113); Dunnill, 'Summary', pp 30–1; Abbott, *Casualties*, pp 138–9; Maureen Waters, 'Sligo, 1919–1922', *Irish Literary Supplement* (Spring 1992), 27; Joe McGowan, *In the shadow of Benbulben* (Manorhamilton, 1993), pp 113–24; Eugene Gilbride (UCDAD, O'Malley notebooks, P19b/137/27–31); Prionnsíos Ó Duigneáin, *Linda Kearns, a revolutionary Irish woman* (Manorhamilton, 2002), pp 28–32; Sergeant Perry was a 51-year-old native of Meath who had served in the RIC at Ballintogher and Bunninadden before transfer to Cliffoney in 1913.

42 *SC*, *SI*, 27 Nov. 1920; Eugene Gilbride (UCDAD, O'Malley notebooks, P19b/137/31–33); CI Sligo, Nov. 1920 (TNA, CO 904/113); Tom Scanlon (UCDAD, O'Malley notebooks, P19b/133/10–11); Dunnill, 'Summary', p. 38; A.P. Smithson (ed.), *In time of peril: leaves from the diary of Nurse Linda Kearns* (Dublin, 1922), pp 15–20; Ó Duigneáin, *Linda Kearns*, pp 36–43.

43 *SC, SI,* 27 Nov. 1920; Ó Duigneáin, *Linda Kearns,* pp 41–2; Matt Kilcawley (UCDAD, O'Malley notebooks, P19b/136/59).

44 Waters, *Sligo, 1919–1922.*

45 Martin B. McGowan (BMH WS 1545, pp 7–8).

46 Michael Coleman (UCDAD, O'Malley notebooks, P19b/133/33): Maurteen Brennan (UCDAD, O'Malley notebooks, P19b/133/5); this is Martin Brennan, Tubbercurry IRA; Tom Deignan (UCDAD, O'Malley notebooks, P19b/137/64); Jack Brennan (UCDAD, O'Malley notebooks, P19b/133/18); Tom Scanlon (UCDAD, O'Malley notebooks, P19b/133/13); John P. Brennan (BMH WS 1278, pp 8–9); Charles Gildea (BMH WS 1313, p. 7).

47 *CM,* 4 Dec. 1920; *SC,* 27 Nov. 1920; Carty statement, pp 11–12; Carty was rescued from Derry jail in Feb. 1921, went to Glasgow where he was again arrested, taken to Dublin and imprisoned in Mountjoy Jail.

48 Charles Gildea (BMH WS 1313, pp 7–8, 13).

49 Dáil Éireann debate, 6 Aug. 1920, http://debates.oireachtas.ie/dail, accessed 23 Mar. 2012.

50 *SC,* 4, 11 Sept. 1920.

51 *RH,* 9 Oct. 1920; *SC,* 4, 11 Sept. 1920; John J. Dockery (BMH WS 1312, pp 4–5); Charles Gildea (BMH WS 1313, p. 4).

52 Harold McBrien (BMH WS 895, p. 6).

53 Hopkinson, *War of Independence,* pp 72–3; Fitzpatrick, *Politics,* pp 179–83; Coleman, *Longford,* pp 122–3; Charles Gildea (BMH WS 1313, p. 8); Patrick McCannon (BMH WS 1383, pp 19–20); Michael Coleman (UCDAD, O'Malley notebooks, P19b/137/33).

54 Tom Scanlon (UCDAD, O'Malley notebooks, P19b/133/9); Patrick McCannon (BMH WS 1383, pp 19–20); Martin B. McGowan (BMH WS 1545, pp 10–11).

55 Jim Hunt (UCDAD, O'Malley notebooks, P19b/133/43).

56 Neal Farry, 'Ballymote during the troubles', *Corran Herald,* 4 (1986), 3, 6.

57 Ó Duigneáin, *Linda Kearns,* p. 26; this mention of Chaffpool should not be taken as evidence that Linda Kearns was at the Chaffpool ambush.

58 Jack Brennan (UCDAD, O'Malley notebooks, P19b/137/23–24); John P. Brennan (BMH WS 1278, p. 9).

59 CI Sligo, Mar. 1921 (TNA CO 904/114).   60 Dunnill, 'Summary', pp 29–30.

61 *CM,* 5 Nov. 1920; *SC,* 6 Nov. 1920.

62 Sergeant Patrick Fallon, a widower, was a native of Galway; McNiffe, Michael, 'Veteran recalls War of Independence', *SC,* 1 Nov. 1985; Pat Hunt interview, 31 May 1986; *CM,* 5 Nov. 1920; *SC, SI, RH,* 6 Nov. 1920; Jim Hunt (UCDAD, O'Malley notebooks, P19b/133/43); Thady McGowan & Tom Brehony (BMH WS 918, p. 6); John J. Dockery (BMH WS 1312, pp 6–7); Farry, *Ballymote,* 3; Dunnill, 'Summary', p. 36; Abbott, *Casualties,* p. 148.

63 *SC,* 4 Dec. 1920; Tom Deignan (BMH WS 894, p. 6).

64 Coleman, *Longford,* pp 186–9; Eve Morrison, 'The Bureau of Military History and female republican activism, 1913–1923' in M. Valiulis (ed.), *Gender and power in Irish history* (Dublin, 2009), p. 61.

65 Brighid O'Mullane (BMH WS 450, pp 12–13); Cal McCarthy, *Cumann na mBan and the Irish revolution* (Cork, 2007), pp 118, 125.

66 Baby Bohan, 'Activities of Cumann na mBan in south Sligo from 1916 to the present day' (UCDAD, Sighle Humphreys papers, P106/1407).

67 Hart, *I.R.A. & its enemies,* pp 257–8; Hopkinson, *War of Independence,* pp 198–9; Morrison, 'Bureau of Military History', pp 90–2; Mai McGowan questionnaire, 1969 (UCDAD, Sighle Humphreys papers, P106/1425); Mary Ann Flynn questionnaire, 1969 (ibid.); Mrs Nell O'Neill questionnaire, 1969 (ibid.); Baby Bohan questionnaire, 1969 (ibid.); Sarah Bohan questionnaire, 1969 (ibid.); Mrs Julia Travers questionnaire, 1969 (ibid.).

68 Coleman, *Longford,* p. 189.

69 Ibid., pp 182–3; McCarthy, *Cumann na mBan,* p. 121; Mrs Julia Travers questionnaire, 1969

(UCDAD, Sighle Humphreys papers, P106/1425); Mary Agnes Bohan questionnaire, 1969 (ibid.).

70 Ó Duigneáin, *Linda Kearns*, pp 23–6.

71 CI Sligo, Oct., Nov., Dec. 1920 (TNA, CO 904/113).

72 CI Sligo, Dec. 1920 (TNA, CO 904/113).

73 Dunnill, 'Summary', pp 37, 43, 48; *SC*, 20 Nov., 25 Dec. 1920.

74 Dunnill, 'Summary', p. 49.   75 Hart, *I.R.A. at war*, pp 66–7.

CHAPTER EIGHT *Stalemate*

1 CI Sligo, Jan. 1921 (TNA, CO 904/114); Dunnill, 'Summary', pp 51, 61; *CM*, 22 Jan., 19 Feb. 1921; Charles Gildea (BMH WS 1313, p. 8).

2 *SC*, 6 Feb. 1921; *CM*, 19 Feb. 1921; *IB*, 18 Feb. 1921; John J. Dockery (BMH WS 1312, pp 7–8); Thady McGowan & Tom Brehony (BMH WS 918, pp 7–8); Jim Hunt (BMH WS 905, pp 11–12); Jack Brennan (UCDAD, O'Malley notebooks, P19b/137/24); Jim Hunt (UCDAD, O'Malley notebooks, P19b/133/43–44); Charles Gildea (BMH WS 1313, pp 8–9); CI Sligo, Jan., Feb. 1921 (TNA, CO 904/114); Dunnill, 'Summary', pp 72–3.

3 Dunnill, 'Summary', pp 65–8; Jim Hunt (BMH WS 905, p. 16).

4 Dunnill, 'Summary', p. 74; W.H. Kautt, *Ambushes and armour, the Irish rebellion, 1919–1921* (Dublin, 2010), p. 248.

5 Dunnill, 'Summary', pp 50–1.

6 *SI*, 26 Feb. 1921; *CM*, 8, 16, 22, 29 Jan., 5, 12, 19 Feb. 1921; *IB*, 1, 15, 22 Jan. 1921.

7 Dunnill, 'Summary', pp 74, 88–90.

8 *SI*, 23 Apr. 1921; *CM*, 21 May, 4 June, 2 July 1921; *RH*, 4 June 1921; *SC*, 30 Apr. 1921; Dunnill, 'Summary', pp 69, 73, 90, 110, 118, 136.

9 Jim Hunt (UCDAD, O'Malley notebooks, P19b/133/52).

10 Dunnill, 'Summary', pp 118, 126, 164–5.

11 Ibid., pp 88–90, 123, 125–6, Appendix 3.

12 *SI*, 26 Feb. 1921; *SC*, 12, 19 Feb., 19 Mar.; *CM*, 12 Feb., 1921; CI Sligo, Feb. 1921 (TNA, CO 904/114); Dunnill, 'Summary', pp 59–62, 68; Coleman, *Longford*, pp 130–1.

13 Charles Gildea (BMH WS 1313, pp 9–10); John P. Brennan (BMH WS 1278, p. 9); CI Sligo, Feb. 1921 (TNA, CO 904/114).

14 *CM*, 19 Mar., 21 May 1921; *SC*, 19 Mar. 1921; Michael Nevin (BMH WS 1384, p. 4).

15 Railway transport officers reports, May 1921 (TNA CO 904/157/2); McNiffe, Michael, 'Veteran recalls War of Independence', *SC*, 1 Nov. 1985.

16 *SC*, 5 Mar., 16 Apr., 21 May, 25 June, 9 July 1921; Charles Gildea (BMH WS 1313, p. 8); CI Sligo, Feb. 1921 (TNA, CO 904/114); Dunnill, 'Summary', Feb.-July 1921.

17 *SC*, 15 Jan. 1921; Thady McGowan (UCDAD, O'Malley notebooks, P19b/133/62); Jim Hunt (BMH WS 905, pp 10–11, 16); CI Sligo, Jan. 1921 (TNA, CO 904/114); Summary of outrages against the police etc., 9 Jan. 1921 (TNA, CO 904/150); Dunnill, 'Summary', p. 51.

18 *SC*, 14 May 1921; Thady McGowan & Tom Brehony (BMH WS 918, pp 10–11); CI Sligo, May 1921 (TNA, CO 904/115); Summary of outrages against the police etc., 6 May 1921 (TNA, CO 904/150); Dunnill, 'Summary', p. 102.

19 *CM*, 21 May 1921; *SC*, 21 May, 25 June 1921; Jim Hunt (BMH WS 905, pp 14–16); Jim Hunt (UCDAD, O'Malley notebooks, P19b/133/45); Dunnill, 'Summary', pp 107–8.

20 Railway transport officers reports, May–July 1921 (TNA, CO 904/157/2).

21 Dunnill, 'Summary', pp 114–16; *SC*, 21 May 1921; Thady McGowan & Tom Brehony (BMH WS 918, p. 14); Jim Hunt (UCDAD, O'Malley notebooks, P19b/133/48–9).

22 Coleman, *Longford*, p. 132.

23 *SI, SC*, 19 Mar. 1921; John J. Dockery (BMH WS 1312, p. 8); CI Sligo, Mar. 1921 (TNA, CO 904/114); Summary of outrages against the police etc., 17 Mar. 1921 (TNA, CO 904/150); Dunnill, 'Summary', p. 80; Abbott, *Casualties*, p. 209; Farry, *Ballymote*, p. 3.

24 Martin McGowan (BMH WS 1545, pp 10–11).

25 *SC*, 9 July 1921; List of operations 1st Batt., Sligo Bde., 1917–21 (NLI, O'Connell papers, MS22118).

26 Letters to Sligo Bde., 14, 18 Feb., 12 Mar., 27 Apr., 12 May 1921 (IMA, Collins papers, A/0747).

27 *SI, CM, SC*, 26 Mar. 1921; Thady McGowan & Tom Brehony (BMH WS 918, pp 9–10); Harold McBrien (BMH WS 895, pp 7–10); Tom Scanlon (UCDAD, O'Malley notebooks, P19b/133/27–9); Jack Brennan (UCDAD, O'Malley notebooks, P19b/137/23); Jim Hunt (UCDAD, O'Malley notebooks, P19b/133/45–6); Tom Deignan (UCDAD, O'Malley notebooks, P19b/133/64–5); CI Sligo, Mar. 1921 (TNA, CO 904/114); King, *Memorabilia*, pp 23–4.

28 Sligo Brigade March activities, 5 Apr. 1921 (UCDAD, Richard Mulcahy papers, P/7A/22); CS to AG, 13 Apr. 1921 (ibid.).

29 Sligo Brigade April activities, 1 May 1921 (UCDAD, Mulcahy papers, P/7A/38); Sligo Brigade May activities, 5 June 1921 (UCDAD, Mulcahy papers, P/7A/19).

30 CS to Pilkington, 6 June 1921 (UCDAD, Mulcahy papers, P7/A/19); O/Cs Sligo battalions to CS, 24 May 1921 (ibid.).

31 Pilkington to CS 2 July 1921 (UCDAD, Mulcahy papers, P7/A/22).

32 O'D to P, 24 May 1921 (UCDAD, Mulcahy papers, P7/A/5); Pilkington to CS, 16 June, QMG to CS, 25 June & CS to Pilkington, 29 June 1921 (UCDAD, Mulcahy papers, P/7A/22).

33 *SI, CM, SC*, 23 Apr. 1921; Michael Coleman (UCDAD, O'Malley notebooks, P19b/137/34); Tom Deignan (UCDAD, O'Malley notebooks, P19b/133/65–6); CI Sligo, Apr. 1921 (TNA, CO 904/115); Summary of outrages against the police etc., 19 Apr. 1921 (TNA, CO 904/150); Dunnill, 'Summary', p. 95; Abbott, *Casualties*, pp 222–3.

34 Patrick McCannon (BMH WS 1383, pp 19–20); McGowan, *Benbulben*, pp 125–7.

35 Dunnill, 'Summary', pp 110, 113.

36 *SI*, 14 May 1921; CI Sligo, Mar., Apr. 1921 (TNA, CO 904/114–15); Patrick McCannon (BMH WS 1383, p. 19); *IB*, 8 Apr. 1921; Pat Hunt interview, 31 May 1986; Dunnill, 'Summary', p. 85.

37 Coleman, *Longford*, pp 132–3, 139–41; Hart, *I.R.A. & its enemies*, pp 292–315.

38 *SI*, 16 Apr. 1921; *CM*, 23 Apr., 7 May 1921; *SC*, 23 Apr., 7 May 1921; CI Sligo, Jan., Apr. 1921 (TNA, CO 904/114–115); Dunnill, 'Summary', pp 92–3; Waters, *Sligo, 1919–1922*, p. 28.

39 Thady McGowan & Tom Brehony (BMH WS 918, p. 8); Jim Hunt (BMH WS 905, pp 12–13); Michael Coleman (UCDAD, O'Malley notebooks, P19b/137/34); Matt Kilcawley (UCDAD, O'Malley notebooks, P19b/137/64); Tom Deignan (BMH WS 894, p. 13).

40 Harold McBrien (BMH WS 895, pp 11–12); Tom Scanlon (UCDAD, O'Malley notebooks, P19b/133/33).

41 Joseph Graham (TNA, Irish Grants Committee (IGC), CO 762/205); George R. Williams (TNA, IGC, CO 762/195).

42 Michael Nevin (BMH WS 1384, p. 4).

43 Sligo Bde. I/O to GHQ I/O, 14 Feb. 1921 (IMA, Collins papers, A/0747); GHQ I/O to Sligo Bde. I/O, 16 June 1921 (IMA, Collins papers, A/0747); Sligo Bde. I/O to GHQ I/O, 9 July 1921 (IMA, Collins papers, A/0747).

44 John J. Dockery (BMH WS 1312, p. 4); Tom Deignan (BMH WS 894, p. 13).

45 *SC*, 16, 30 Apr. 1921; Summary of outrages against the police etc., 15 May 1921 (TNA, CO 904/150); Sligo Bde. activities for April, 1 May 1921 (UCDAD, Mulcahy papers, P/7A/38); Dunnill, 'Summary', p. 106.

46 Maurteen Brennan (UCDAD, O'Malley notebooks, P19b/133/4); CI Sligo, May 1921 (TNA, CO 904/115);.

47 Thady McGowan & Tom Brehony (BMH WS 918, p. 10); CI Sligo, May 1921 (TNA, CO 904/115); Summary of outrages against the police etc., 23 May 1921 (TNA, CO 904/150); Dunnill, 'Summary', p. 113.

48 CI Sligo, June 1921 (TNA, CO 904/115); Summary of outrages against the police etc., 13 June 1921 (TNA, CO 904/150); Dunnill, 'Summary', p. 126.

49 Dunnill, 'Summary', p. 130.
50 *CM*, 23 Apr., 21, 28 May 1921; *SC*, 30 Apr., 18 June 1921; *IB*, 23 June 1921; Dunnill, 'Summary', pp 88, 122.
51 Dunnill, 'Summary', pp 70, 89, 110.
52 *RH*, 4, 18 June 1921; *CM*, 28 May 1921; *IB*, 23 June 1921; Dunnill, 'Summary', p. 96.
53 Dunnill, 'Summary', p. 61. 54 *IB*, 27 June 1921. 55 *SC*, 14 May 1921.
56 *SI*, *SC*, 4 June 1921; CI Sligo, May 1921 (TNA, CO 904/115).
57 Dunnill, 'Summary', p. 118; *SC*, 11 June 1921; *RH*, 11, 18 June 1921; Tom Deignan (UCDAD, O'Malley notebooks, P19b/133/66).
58 CI Sligo, Jan.–June 1921 (TNA, CO 904/114–115); Charles Gildea (BMH WS 1313, p. 7); John P. Brennan (BMH WS 1278, p. 9).
59 Michael Coleman (UCDAD, O'Malley notebooks, P19b/137/35); CI Sligo, Mar. 1921 (TNA, CO 904/114); Dunnill, 'Summary', p. 53.
60 Patrick McCannon (BMH WS 1383, pp 20–1); John J. Dockery (BMH WS 1312, pp 8–9).
61 *SC*, *CM*, 11 June 1921; Jim Hunt (UCDAD, O'Malley notebooks, P19b/133/40); John J. Dockery (BMH WS 1312, p. 8); Pat Hunt interview, 31 May 1986; O'Donoghue, *IRA jailbreaks*, pp 145–52; O'Callaghan, *Roscommon*, pp 99–104.
62 *SC*, 2 July 1921; Michael Nevin (BMH WS 1384, pp 4–5); Tom Scanlon (UCDAD, O'Malley notebooks, P19b/133/11–13); Jack Brennan (UCDAD, O'Malley notebooks, P19b/133/23); Tom Deignan (BMH WS 894, pp 10–12); Charles Gildea (BMH WS 1313, p. 10); *IB*, 6 July 1921; Dunnill, 'Summary', pp 134–5.
63 *SC*, *SI*, 21 May 1921; CI Sligo, May 1921 (TNA, CO 904/115); Sligo Bde. May activities, 5 June 1921 (UCDAD, Mulcahy papers, P/7A/19); Dunnill, 'Summary', p. 110.
64 *SC*, *RH*, *SI*, *CM*, 2 July 1921; Patrick McCannon (BMH WS 1383, pp 20–1); Martin McGowan (BMH WS 1545, pp 12–13); CI Sligo, June 1921 (TNA, CO 904/115); Daniel Waters statement in private possession; Alleged burning of house in County Sligo by auxiliaries (TNA, Irish Office and Irish Branch, HO 351/76); Dunnill, 'Summary', pp 132–3; Abbott, *Casualties*, p. 259.
65 For Mayo, see Hopkinson, *War of Independence*, pp 134–6; Matt Kilcawley (UCDAD, O'Malley notebooks, P19b/137/60).
66 *SI*, *SC*, 23 Apr. 1921; Matt Kilcawley (UCDAD, O'Malley notebooks, P19b/136/60); CI Sligo, Apr. 1921 (TNA, CO 904/115); North Mayo Bde. report, 5 May 1921 (UCDAD, Mulcahy papers, P/7A/18); Dunnill, 'Summary', p. 95.
67 *RH*, 4 June 1921; *CM*, 11 June 1921.
68 *SI*, *CM*, *SC*, 9 July 1921; Matt Kilcawley (UCDAD, O'Malley notebooks, P19b/137/61–63); Maurteen Brennan (UCDAD, O'Malley notebooks, P19b/133/6); CI Sligo, July 1921 (TNA, CO 904/116); *IB*, 6 July 1921; John P. Brennan (BMH WS 1278, pp 11–12); Abbott, *Casualties*, p. 261; John Cowell, *Sligo, land of Yeats' desire* (Dublin, 1989), p. 68; Enniscrone, Kilglass GAA, *One hundred years of an Irish parish, 1890–1990* (Enniscrone, 1990), pp 29–31.
69 Morrisroe of Achonry in *II*, 11 May 1921; Coyne of Elphin in *II*, 7 Feb. 1921.
70 Swords, *Achonry*, pp 463–4; Maurteen Brennan (UCDAD, O'Malley notebooks, P19b/133/4–5); Jim Hunt (UCDAD, O'Malley notebooks, P19b/133/52–3).
71 *SC*, 14 May 1921; Jim Hunt (UCDAD, O'Malley notebooks, P19b/133/51).
72 *SC*, 21 May 1921; CI Sligo, May 1921 (TNA, CO 904/115); Minutes, 10 Apr., 12 May 1921 (NLI, SF Standing Committee minutes, P 3269); John Cowell, *A noontide blazing: Brigid Lyons Thornton: rebel, soldier, doctor* (Dublin, 2005), pp 193–5.
73 Dunnill, 'Summary', pp 125, 131. 74 Ibid., pp 135–6.
75 *SI*, 16 July 1921; CI Sligo, July 1921 (TNA, CO 904/116); Michael Walsh interview, 13 Aug. 1987.
76 *SI*, 16 July 1921; Martin McGowan (BMH WS 1545, p. 13); CI Sligo, July 1921 (TNA, CO 904/116); Summary of outrages against the police etc., 10 July 1921 (TNA, CO 904/150); John J. Dockery (BMH WS 1312, p. 10).

77 Augusteijn, *Public defiance*, table 8, p. 180.
78 I am grateful to Dr Daithí Ó Corráin for these figures.
79 Augusteijn, *Public defiance*, p. 352; Fitzpatrick, *Politics*, p. 230; Hart, *I.R.A. & its enemies*, p. 124; Coleman, *Longford*, p. 133.
80 Harold McBrien (BMH WS 895, p. 11).
81 Tom Deignan (BMH WS 894, p. 13).
82 CS to O/C South Mayo, 25 May 1921 (UCDAD, Mulcahy papers, P7/A/18) quoted in Hopkinson, *War of Independence*, p. 135.

CHAPTER NINE *The republican counter-state in County Sligo*

1   *SC*, 7 Feb. 1920.
2   *SC*, 3 July, 11 Dec. 1920; *CM*, 2 July 1920; Minutes, 27 Apr., 30 June 1920 (SCL, Sligo Corporation minute book); Minister William Cosgrave to Michael Nevin, 18 Jan. 1921 (NAI, Dáil Éireann Local Government (DÉLG), 26/4).
3   *SC*, 18 Dec. 1920; Minutes 1, 15 Dec. 1920 (SCL, Sligo Corporation minute book).
4   Minutes, 5 Jan. 1921 (SCL, Sligo Corporation minute book).
5   *SI*, 6 Feb. 1921; *CM*, 22 Jan., 5 Feb. 1921; *SC*, 22 Jan., 5 Feb. 1921; Michael Nevin (BMH WS 1384, p. 3).
6   Minister to Chief of Inspection, 13 May 1921 (NAI, DÉLG, 26/8).
7   Arthur Mitchell, *Revolutionary government in Ireland: Dáil Éireann, 1919–1922* (Dublin, 1995), pp 125–6; John O'Callaghan, *Revolutionary Limerick: the republican campaign for independence in Limerick, 1913–1921* (Dublin, 2010), p. 93; Macardle, *Irish republic*, appendix 33, pp 910–11.
8   Minutes North Sligo comhairle ceantair SF (NSCCSF), 21 Mar., 4, 11 Apr. 1920 (SCL, NSCCSF minute book).
9   *SC*, 1, 8 May, 5, 12 June 1920; *SI*, 15 May, 5 June 1920, *CM*, 1 May, 11 June 1920; *Milestones & memories: Sligo County Council centenary record: 1899–1999* (Sligo, 2000), pp 20, 82.
10 Letter from bde. adj., 11 June 1920 (SCL, NSCCSF minute book).
11 *CM*, 18, 25 June, 2 July 1920.
12 Mitchell, *Revolutionary government*, pp 157–61; Mary Daly, *The buffer state: the historical roots of the Department of the Environment* (Dublin, 1997), pp 52–3.
13 Mitchell, *Revolutionary government*, pp 158–9.
14 *SC*, 4 Sept. 1920.
15 Daly, *Buffer state*, pp 58–64; Mary Daly, 'Local government and the first Dáil' in Brian Farrell (ed.), *The creation of the Dáil* (Dublin, 1994), p. 129; Coleman, *Longford*, pp 92–6.
16 Minutes, 16 Oct. 1920 (SCL, Sligo County Council minute book, Dec. 1918–Aug. 1922).
17 *RH*, 30 Oct. 1920.   18 *SC*, 13 Nov. 1920.   19 *SI*, 10 July 1920.
20 *SC*, 8, 22, 29 Jan., 5 Mar. 1921; *SI*, *CM*, 5 Mar. 1921.
21 *SC*, 19 Feb., 12 Mar., 16 Apr. 1921.   22 *SC*, 12 Feb. 1921.
23 Mitchell, *Revolutionary government*, p. 234.
24 *SC*, 19 Feb., 2, 30 Apr. 1921; *CM*, 14 May 1921; Dunnill, 'Summary', pp 103–4; Inspector to Chief of Inspection, 23 Oct., 23 Nov. 1921 (NAI, DÉLG, 26/9).
25 CS to Sligo O/C, 16 June 1921 (UCDAD, Mulcahy papers, P7/A/19); Daly, *Buffer state*, p. 89.
26 Cosgrave to Carty and Devins, 1 Nov. 1921 (NAI, DÉLG, 26/9); DÉ Local Government report, 28 Apr. 1922 (UCDAD, Mulcahy papers, P7/A/63); Dáil Éireann debate, 26 Apr. 1922, http://debates.oireachtas.ie/dail, accessed 23 Mar. 2012.
27 *SC*, 2 July 1921; Daly, *Buffer state*, p. 65; Daly, 'Local government', p. 129; *CM*, 22 Jan. 1921.
28 *CM*, 2 Apr. 1921; Inspector to Chief of Inspection, 16 Nov. 1921 (NAI, DÉLG, 26/9).
29 *SC*, 25 June 1921.
30 Minutes, 10, 12 May 1921 (NLI, SF Standing Committee minutes, P 3269).
31 *SC*, 20 Oct., 25 Dec. 1920, 22 Jan. 1921; *CM*, 11 Dec. 1920.
32 *SC*, 5 Mar. 1921; *SI*, 26 Mar. 1921; *CM*, 5 Mar. 1921; Inspector to Chief of Inspection, 23 Oct. 1921 (NAI, DÉLG, 26/9); *Sligo County Council centenary record*, pp 20–1.

33 Minister to Chief of Inspection, 13 May 1921 (NAI, DÉLG, 26/8); *SI*, 16 July 1921.
34 Mitchell, *Revolutionary government*, p. 138.
35 *SC*, 22 Nov. 1919; *SN*, 29 Nov. 1919; James Casey, 'Republican courts in Ireland 1919–1922', *Irish Jurist*, 5 (1970), 321–42; Mary Kotsonouris, *Retreat from revolution: the Dáil courts, 1920–24* (Dublin, 1994), pp 17–27; Campbell & O'Shiel, 'The last land war?', 160–1; Francis Costello, 'The republican courts and the decline and fall of British rule in Ireland', *Eire-Ireland*, 25:2 (1990), 37–9; Jim Hunt (BMH WS 905, p. 4); Dunnill, 'Summary', p. 15.
36 *SC*, 15 May 1920; *CM*, 15 May 1920.
37 *SC*, 29 May, 19 June, 10 July 1920; *CM*, 9 July 1920.
38 *SC*, 29 May 1920; *CM*, 28 May 1920; John P. Brennan (BMH WS 1278, pp 2–3); *RH*, 24 July 1920.
39 Coleman, *Longford*, p. 103; O'Callaghan, *Limerick*, p. 83.
40 *SI*, 14 Aug. 1920; Bradshaw to Stack, 17 Oct. 1921 (NAI, DÉCC, DE 10/57); Kilgannon, *Sligo*, p. 70.
41 *SC*, *SI*, 17 July, 18 Sept. 1920; *CM*, 16 July 1920; *RH*, 25 Sept. 1920.
42 *SC*, 11 Sept. 1920; *CM*, 17 Sept. 1920.
43 *SC*, 4, 18 Sept. 1920; *SI*, 18 Sept., 9 Oct. 1920.
44 *IB*, 14 July 1920; CI Sligo, June, July 1920 (TNA, CO 904/112); Robinson, *Bryan Cooper*, p. 126.
45 Mitchell, *Revolutionary government*, pp 145–6; Coleman, *Longford*, pp 107–8.
46 *CM*, 28 May, 20, 27 Aug., 17, 24 Sept. 1920; *SC*, 29 May, 28 Aug., 18, 25 Sept. 1920; John P. Brennan (BMH WS 1278, pp 2–4); Dunnill, 'Summary', pp 11–12, 19, 21.
47 *SC*, 4 Sept. 1920; *RH*, 2 Oct. 1920.   48 *RH*, 2 Oct. 1920.
49 RM diaries (NAI, CSO Misc Books).
50 Fitzpatrick, *Politics*, pp 149–50; Mitchell, *Revolutionary government*, pp 144–5; Sligo Bde. meeting, 17 July 1920 (NLI, Collins papers, Department of Defence archives, p 911); Martin McGowan (BMH WS 1545, p. 4); Thomas Deignan (BMH WS 894, pp 2–3).
51 *IB*, 21 May, 3, 17 June, 13 July 1920; *CM*, 4, 25 June, 16, 23 July, 20 Aug. 1920; *SC*, 5, 12 June, 3 July, 21 Aug., 11 Sept 1920; *RH*, 15 May, 5 June 1920; *SI*, 29 May, 12 June, 17 July 1920; Dunnill, 'Summary', pp 11, 68.
52 *RH*, 2 Oct. 1920; *SC*, 31 July 1920; *CM*, 30 July, 6, 20 Aug. 1920; *IB*, 26 June, 27 Aug. 1920; Charles Gildea (BMH WS 1313, p. 8); Sligo Bde. meeting, 17 July 1920 (NLI, Collins papers, Department of Defence archives, p 911); Dunnill, 'Summary', p. 12; Mitchell, *Revolutionary government*, p. 153; *SC*, 11 Sept. 1920.
53 *SC*, *SI*, 9 July 1921; CI Sligo, July 1921 (TNA, CO 904/116); Dunnill, 'Summary', p. 138.
54 Mitchell, *Revolutionary government*, pp 210–11; *SI*, 9 Oct. 1920.
55 *RH*, *SI*, 9 Oct. 1920; O'Donnell to Stack, 5 Oct. 1921 (NAI, DÉCC, DÉ10/58); ibid., Registrar South Sligo District Court to Stack, 15 Nov. 1921; ibid., Stack to Registrar, 8 Dec. 1921.
56 CI Sligo, Dec. 1920, Feb., Apr. 1921 (TNA, CO 904/113–15); *SI*, 9 Apr. 1921.
57 Dáil Éireann debates, 18 Aug. 1921, http://debates.oireachtas.ie/dail, accessed 23 Mar. 2012.
58 South Sligo district court, 14 Mar. 1918 (NAI, DÉCC, DE 6/4131); Boles to Stack, 2 Jan. 1922 (NAI, DÉCC, DE 10/58).
59 Campbell & O'Shiel, 'The last land war?', 184–6.

CHAPTER TEN *Martial law for Sligo?*

1 Dunnill, 'Summary', p. 142; CI Sligo, July 1921 (TNA, CO 904/116).
2 CI Sligo, July 1921 (TNA, CO 904/116); *SC*, 1 Oct. 1921.
3 *SC*, 10 Sept., 22 Oct. 1921; Devins had not faced an election, having been unopposed in the 1921 election.

4 Mitchell, *Revolutionary government*, pp 300–1; *SC*, 20, 27 Aug., 27 Oct., 17 Sept. 1921.
5 *SC*, 16, 23, 30 July 1921; Dunnill, 'Summary', pp 145–6.
6 Letters to and from Bradshaw (IMA, Truce liaison material, LE 4/16A).
7 Report on union amalgamation, 13 Feb. 1922 (NAI, DÉLG 26/9).
8 Inspector to Chief of Inspection, 23 Oct. 1921 (NAI, DÉLG 26/9); Minutes, 22 Feb. 1919
   (SCL, Sligo County Council minute book, Dec. 1918–Aug. 1922).
9 *CM*, 22 Oct. 1920; Minutes, 16 Oct. 1920 (SCL, Sligo County Council minute book, Dec.
   1918–Aug. 1922).
10 Minutes, 9 July 1921 (SCL, Sligo County Council minute book, Dec. 1918–Aug. 1922); *CM*,
   9, 16, 23 July 1921.
11 Inspector to Chief of Inspection, 23 Oct. 1921 (NAI, DÉLG 26/9); Minutes, 27 Aug. 1921
   (SCL, Sligo County Council minute book, Dec. 1918–Aug. 1922).
12 Tom Garvin, *1922: the birth of Irish democracy* (Dublin, 1996), pp 77–83; Daly, *Buffer state*, p.
   75; *SC*, 27 Nov. 1920, 9 Apr. 1921.
13 *CM*, 2, 9 Apr. 23, 30 July 1921.
14 Minister to Sec. Sligo County Council, 26 Sept. 1921 (NAI, DÉLG 26/9).
15 *SI*, 17, 24 Sept., 22 Oct. 1921; *SC*, 13 Aug., 3 Sept., 19 Nov. 1921.
16 Circular department of Loc. Gov., 17 Nov. 1921 (NAI, DÉLG 26/9); O/C 5th Batt. North
   Mayo Bde., IRA to Loc. Gov. Dept., 2 Nov. 1921 (ibid.); McGrath to Chief of Inspection, 6
   Feb. 1922 (ibid.); *SI*, 21 Jan. 1922.
17 *SC*, 3 Dec., 10 Dec. 1921; Inspector to Chief of Inspection, 13 Dec. 1921 (NAI, DÉLG 26/9);
   Supplementary report on union amalgamation, 13 Feb. 1922 (ibid.).
18 *SC*, 6 Aug. 1921.
19 Extracts from Tubbercurry RDC minutes, 8 Aug. 1921 (NAI, DÉLG 26/7); Inspector's report
   on Tubbercurry RDC meeting, 8 Aug. 1921 (ibid.).
20 *SC*, *SI*, 1 Oct. 1921; Minutes, 24 Sept. 1921 (SCL, Sligo County Council minute book, Dec.
   1918–Aug. 1922); *Sligo County Council centenary record*, p. 40.
21 AG to Minister, 14 Oct. 1921 (NAI, DÉLG 26/9).
22 *SI*, *SC*, 15 Oct. 1921.
23 Gilligan to Cosgrave, 14 Oct. 1921 (NAI, DÉLG 26/9); Inspector to Chief of Inspection, 23
   Oct. 1921 (ibid.).
24 Mitchell, *Revolutionary government*, p. 306.   25 *SI*, 3, 31 Dec. 1921.
26 Mitchell, *Revolutionary government*, pp 312–13; Macardle, *Irish republic*, p. 492.
27 Dunnill, 'Summary', p. 177.
28 Inspection report, T. Burke to GHQ, 17 Oct. 1921 (IMA, Collins papers, A/0747).
29 DI Russell, 24 Sept. 1921 (TNA, Truce breaches, CO 904/155); ibid., Fintan Murphy, 26
   Sept. 1921; Dunnill, 'Summary', p. 166.
30 Inspection report, T. Burke to GHQ, 17 Oct. 1921 (IMA, Collins papers, A/0747).
31 Carty statement, pp 14–15.
32 Report on republican police force, 24 Feb. 1922 (NAI, DJ, Payment of brigade police officers,
   H97/3); *SC*, 17 Sept. 1921; *SC*, 15 Oct. 1921; *SI*, 10 Sept., *SC*, *SI*, 3 Dec. 1921.
33 McCabe to Stack, 24 Nov. 1921 (NAI, DÉCC, DÉ 11/219a).
34 Mitchell, *Revolutionary government*, pp 305–6; Casey, 'Republican courts', 210–11 & 330–1;
   Farry, *Sligo, 1914–1921*, p. 291; Kotsonouris, *Retreat*, pp 51–60; Stack to TDs, 13 Sept. 1921
   (UCDAD, Mulcahy papers, P7/A/24).
35 Bradshaw to Stack, 17 Oct. 1921; Stack to Bradshaw, 20 Oct. 1921 (NAI, DÉCC, DE 10/57);
   North Sligo District Court, 10 Jan. 1922 (NAI, DÉCC, DE 6/4118); Western Wholesale Co.
   Ltd v Tolan (NAI, DÉCC, DE 6/4161).
36 Registrar to Stack and McCabe to Stack, 15 Nov. 1921 (NAI, DÉCC, DE 10/58); Registrar to
   Stack, 30 Dec. 1921 (ibid.); Stack to Fr Henry, 8 Dec. 1921 (ibid.); Stack to Registrar, 8 Dec.
   1921 (ibid.).
37 Stack to Registrar, 17 Sept., 10 Oct. 1921 (NAI, DÉCC, DE 10/58); Registrar to Stack, 4 Oct.
   1921 (ibid.).

38 *SI*, 1 Oct. 1921; McAllister to Minister, 17 Apr. 1923 (NAI, DÉCC, DE 14/63).
39 *CM*, 17 Sept. 1921.
40 Alleged truce breaches by the IRA (TNA, Truce breaches, CO 904/155).
41 Kotsonouris, *Retreat*, p. 53; Mitchell, *Revolutionary government*, p. 305.
42 *SI*, 8 Oct. 1921.   43 *SI*, 29 Oct. 1921.   44 Casey, 'Republican courts', 337.
45 *RH*, 18, 25 Feb., 1 Apr. 1922; *SC*, 4, 25 Feb., 4 Mar. 1922; *SI* 28 Jan., 4 Mar. 1922; *CM*, 18 Feb., 4 Mar., 15 Apr. 1922; D.H. O'Donnell report, 10 Mar. 1922 (NAI, DÉCC, DE 11/219b).
46 *SI*, 11 Feb., 11 Mar. 1922; *RH*, 18 Mar. 1922.
47 Mitchell, *Revolutionary government*, pp 314–15.
48 File including statements of marines and reply from IRA Liaison Officer, 22 Aug. 1921 (TNA, Truce breaches, CO 904/155); Dunnill, 'Summary', p. 150.
49 DI Russell, 3 Oct. 1921 (TNA, Truce breaches, CO 904/155); Dunnill, 'Summary', p. 163.
50 DI Russell, 13 Sept. 1921 (TNA, Truce breaches, CO 904/155).
51 Reports Sligo 545, 552 (TNA, Police reports, CO 904/150).
52 Dunnill, 'Summary', pp 179–80.
53 Mitchell, *Revolutionary government*, pp 312–13; S.M. Lawlor, 'Ireland from truce to treaty: war or peace? July to October 1921', *IHS*, 22:85 (1980), 55; *SC*, 29 Oct. 1921.
54 Report, 19 Oct. 1921 (TNA, Truce breaches, CO 904/155); CI Sligo, Sept. 1921 (TNA, CO 904/116); Dunnill, 'Summary', pp 152, 171.
55 Dunnill, 'Summary', p. 170.
56 Mitchell, *Revolutionary government*, pp 310–11; Robert Beattie statement, 16 May 1928 (TNA, IGC, Robert Beattie 1066, CO 762/66); Dunnill, 'Summary', pp 158, 162, 164, 165, 169–72; Claims by M.C. Kevins, Christopher Smith, John R. Gorman, John Reynolds, Ballymote, Nov. 1922 (NAI, DF, Belfast boycott, F 311/8–12); *SI*, 15 Oct. 1921; Kevins to Hennigan, 11 Feb. 1925 (NAI, DF, Belfast boycott, F 837/4).
57 Dunnill, 'Summary', p. 173.   58 Ibid., p. 156.
59 *SC*, 13 Aug. 1921; *CM*, 27 Aug., 8 Oct. 1921.   60 *SC*, *CM*, 3 Sept. 1921.
61 The premises were those of Richard T. Kerr-Taylor (TNA, IGC, Richard T. Kerr-Taylor 747, CO 762/66), raided twice, Thomas Hunt (TNA, IGC, Thomas Hunt 3661, CO 762/202) also raided twice and Charles Graham (TNA, IGC, Charles Graham 1477, CO 762/90).
62 *SC*, 19 Nov. 1921.
63 Minister for Defence to CS, 18 Nov. 1921 & CS to AG, 19 Oct. 1921 (UCDAD, Mulcahy papers, P/7A/33); Gurteen Batt. report, 27 Oct. 1921 (ibid.).
64 Gurteen Batt. report, 21 Nov. 1921 (ibid.); AG to OC Sligo Bde., 8 Nov. 1921 (ibid.).
65 *CM*, 3 Dec. 1921; *SC*, 8 Apr. 1922.
66 SF Tuairisc na Rúnaithe, Ard-Fheis 1921 (NLI, Barton papers, MS 8786/2); the *Irish Independent* reported 34 affiliated clubs in Sligo in September, *II*, 24 Oct. 1921.
67 Macardle, *Irish republic*, p. 492; Tom Garvin, 'Unenthusiastic democrats: The emergence of Irish democracy' in Ron Hill & Michael Marsh (eds), *Modern Irish democracy: essays in honour of Basil Chubb* (Dublin, 1993), pp 11–15; Garvin, *1922*, pp 40–4.

CHAPTER ELEVEN *'Let it be war'*

1 Michael Nevin speaking at Sligo Corporation meeting (*SC*, *SI*, *CM*, 31 Dec. 1921).
2 Michael Hopkinson, *Green against green: the Irish Civil War* (Dublin, 1988), p. 34.
3 *SC*, 10 Dec. 1921.   4 *CM*, 10, 17 Dec. 1921.
5 *SC*, 10 Jan. 1922; Hopkinson, *Green against green*, pp 36–9; Garvin, 'Unenthusiastic democrats', pp 9–23.
6 *CM*, 17, 24 Dec. 1921, 21 Jan. 1922.   7 *CM*, 14 Jan. 1922; *SC*, 31 Jan. 1922.
8 Maurteen Brennan (UCDAD, O'Malley notebooks, P19b/133/7); Joseph Curran, *The birth of the Irish Free State, 1921–1923* (Alabama, 1980), p. 170; Ernie O'Malley, *The singing flame* (Dublin, 1978), pp 51–2.

9   *SC, SI, CM*, 31 Dec. 1921.
10 *SI*, 7 Jan. 1922; *RH*, 21 Jan. 1922; Dáil Éireann private sessions, 16 Dec. 1921 & Dáil Éireann debate on Treaty, 4 Jan. 1922, http://debates.oireachtas.ie/dail, accessed 23 Mar. 2012.
11 *RH, CM, SC*, 7 Jan. 1922.   12 *SC, SI*, 7 Jan. 1922; *SC, RH*, 14 Jan. 1922.
13 Murray, *Oracles*, pp 40, 69.   14 *Western People (WP)*, *SI, RH*, 7, 14 Jan. 1922.
15 Hopkinson, *Green against green*, p. 35.
16 *SC, SI*, 7 Jan. 1922; Minutes, 31 Dec. 1921 (SCL, Sligo County Council minute book, Dec. 1918– Aug. 1922).
17 *WP, RH, SC*, 14 Jan. 1922.   18 *CM*, 4 Feb. 1922; *II*, 28 Jan., 1, 3 Feb. 1922.
19 Hopkinson, *Green against green*, p. 56; *CM, SC*, 25 Feb. 1922.
20 Dunnill, 'Summary', p. 192; *SI*, 28 Jan., 4 Feb. 1922.
21 *SC, CM*, 11 Mar. 1922; *RH*, 28 Jan., 25 Feb. 1922.
22 *SI*, 21 Jan. 1922.   23 *SC*, 1 Apr. 1922.
24 Tom Scanlon (UCDAD, O'Malley notebooks, P17b/133/26, 30); Hopkinson, *Green against green*, pp 79–81; Tim Pat Coogan, *Michael Collins* (London, 1990), p. 343; *SC, SI*, 11 Feb. 1922.
25 *SC, SI*, 4 Feb. 1922.   26 *SC*, 18 Feb., 11 Mar. 1922.
27 *SI*, 11 Feb. 1922; *CM*, 25 Feb. 1922; *RH*, 4 Mar. 1922.
28 *RH*, 13 Jan., 11 Feb. 1922; *SC, CM*, 18, 25 Feb. 1922; in Aug. 1923 some of this stolen money was repaid to the Provincial Bank of Ireland (£802) and the Bank of Ireland (£2,203) and acknowledged in the *Irish Independent* of 3 Aug. 1923.
29 *RH*, 11 Mar. 1922; *SC*, 18 Mar., 20 May 1922; *SC, RH*, 13 May 1922.
30 Hart, *I.R.A. at war*, pp 236–9; O'Callaghan, *Limerick*, p. 203.
31 *RH*, 29 Apr., 6, 27 May, 3, 17 June 1922; *SI*, 22 Apr. 6, 20 May, 17 June 1922.
32 *RH*, 6 May 1922.   33 *RH*, 17 June 1922.
34 *RH*, 20 May, 3 June 1922; *CM, SC*, 3 June 1922; *WP*, 24 June 1922.
35 *SC*, 24 June 1922; *CM*, 1 July 1922.   36 *SC, CM, RH, WP*, 4 Mar. 1922.
37 Macardle, *Irish republic*, p. 612.
38 *RH*, 8 Apr., 3 May 1922; Tom Scanlon (UCDAD, O'Malley notebooks, P17b/133/15).
39 *RH*, 8 Apr. 1922; *SC*, 8, 29 Apr. 1922.
40 Army council members (UCDAD, Moss Twomey papers, P69/144); Florence O'Donoghue, *No other law* (Dublin, 1986), pp 220–4. Hopkinson, *Green against green*, pp 68–73.
41 Reports on railway raids, 25 Apr. 1922 (UCDAD, Mulcahy papers, P7/A/63); *SC*, 1, 15 Apr. 1922.
42 Hopkinson, *Green against green*, p. 90; *SC*, 6 May 1922; Tom Scanlon (UCDAD, O'Malley notebooks, P17b/137/39–40); Charles Gildea list of activities.
43 Tom Scanlon (UCDAD, O'Malley notebooks, P17b/133/15); *RH*, 3 June 1922.
44 O'Donoghue, *No other law*, pp 250, 252; Maryann Gialanella Valiulis, *Portrait of a revolutionary: General Richard Mulcahy* (Dublin, 1992), p. 141; Hopkinson, *Green against green*, pp 83–4; Tom Scanlon (UCDAD, O'Malley notebooks, P17b/133/15); Matt Kilcawley (UCDAD, O'Malley notebooks, P17b/137/66).
45 *RH*, 11 Mar. 1922; *SC*, 18 Mar. 1922; Tom Scanlon (UCDAD, O'Malley notebooks, P17b/133/26); Charles Gildea list of activities; Hopkinson, *Green against green*, pp 62–6.
46 *RH*, 18 Mar. 1922; *SI, CM*, 25 Mar. 1922; *SC, SI*, 1 Apr. 1922.
47 Cunningham, *Labour*, pp 105, 160; *Voice of Labour*, 25 Feb. 1922; Arthur Mitchell, *Labour in Irish politics* (Dublin, 1974), pp 153–5; *CM*, 4, 25 Mar., 1 Apr., 27 May 1922; *SC*, 4, Mar., 1 Apr. 1922; *Voice of Labour*, May-June 1922.
48 Hopkinson, *Green against green*, pp 75–6.
49 *SI*, 1, 8 Apr. 1922; *SC*, 8 Apr. 1922.
50 *RH, CM*, 8 Apr. 1922; *SC, SI, RH*, 15 Apr. 1922; Telegram from Nevin to Griffith with draft of typescript reply from Griffith, with ms. corrections by him, 12 Apr. 1922 (NLI, Kathleen Mac Kenna Napoli papers, MS 22,759).

51 Interviews with Batt Keaney (8 Oct. 1988, 30 Aug. 1990); Paddy Hegarty (UCDAD, O'Malley notebooks, P17b/137/49); *SI*, 15 Apr. 1922; Extract from publicity file (IMA, Some events leading up to the Civil War, Collins papers, A 0790); Tom Deignan (UCDAD, O'Malley notebooks, P17b/133/73); Tom Scanlon (UCDAD, O'Malley notebooks, P17b/133/16); ibid., 137/40; Maurteen Brennan (UCDAD, O'Malley notebooks, P17b/133/8); Calton Younger, *Ireland's Civil War* (London, 1968), pp 260–4.
52 Carty statement, p. 16.   53 *SI*, 22 Apr. 1922; *Free State*, 22 Apr. 1922.
54 *SI*, *RH*, 22 Apr. 1922; *SC*, *SI*, 29 Apr. 1922; the 22 April 1922 issue of the *Connachtman* is also missing from the file in SCL.
55 *RH*, 6 May 1922; *RH*, *SC*, 13 May 1922.   56 *SC*, *WP*, *RH*, 10 June 1922.
57 *SC*, 29 May 1922.   58 *CM*, 29 Apr. 1922; *WP*, 13, 20 May 1922; *RH*, 13, 20 May 1922.
59 Hopkinson, *Green against green*, pp 97–100.   60 *CM*, *SC*, 27 May 1922.
61 *SC*, *RH*, 13 May 1922; *SC*, *WP*, *RH*, 3 June 1922.   62 *CM*, *SC*, *SI*, *RH*, 10 June 1922.
63 *CM*, 10, 14 June 1922.
64 *RH*, 29 Apr., 10 June 1922; *WP*, *CT*, 10 June 1922; Michael Gallagher, 'The pact general election of 1922', *IHS*, 21:84 (1979), 159.
65 *SI*, 2, 10 June 1922; *CM*, 10, 14 June 1922; *SC*,10, 17 June 1922; *RH*, 17 June 1922.
66 Hopkinson, *Green against green*, p. 109.   67 *SC*, *SI*, *CM*, *RH*, 17 June 1922.
68 *CM*, 14 June 1922; *SC*, 17 June 1922.   69 *SI*, *SC*, 24 June 1922.
70 *SI*, 10 June 1922; *CM*, 14 June 1922; *SC*, 17 June 1922.
71 *SC*, 17, 24 June, 1 July 1922; *RH*, 24 June 1922; *II*, 21 June 1922.
72 Michael Gallagher (ed.), *Irish elections 1922–44: results and analysis* (Limerick, 1993), p. 10; Gallagher, 'Pact election', 404–21; *SC*, *SI*, 24 June 1922; Hopkinson, *Green against green*, pp 110–11.
73 *SC*, 11 Mar., 1 Apr. 1922; Minutes, 21 July 1922 (SCL, Sligo County Council minute book, Dec. 1918–Aug. 1922). Martin Roddy, a native of Breeogue, Coolera, had worked in the British Civil Service in London before returning to Sligo. He was co-opted to Sligo RDC in 1920; McTernan, *Worthies of Sligo*, pp 401–5.
74 *CM*, *SC*, 24 June 1922.

CHAPTER TWELVE *'Pressing back the forces of disorder'*

1 Mulcahy to Mac Eoin, 19 Oct. 1922 (UCDAD, Mulcahy papers, P7/B/74).
2 Hopkinson, *Green against green*, pp 127–31.
3 *SC*, *SI*, *CM*, 8, 15 July 1922; Report on capture of Collooney Market House, July 1922 (UCDAD, Seán Mac Eoin papers, P151/152); Maurteen Brennan (UCDAD, O'Malley notebooks, P19b/133/34); Carty statement, pp 15–17; Diary of activities 1st Brigade 3WD from 30 June, 1922 (UCDAD, Twomey papers, P69/33/27); Diary of activities 4th Brigade, 3WD to 30 Nov. 1922 (UCDAD, Twomey papers, P69/33/17); Joe Baker, *My stand for freedom* (Westport, 1988), pp 42–4.
4 *SC*, *SI*, *CM*, 8 July 1922; Western Command report, 6 July 1922 (UCDAD, Mulcahy papers, P7/B/106); Western Command reports, 6 July 1922 (IMA, Radio & Phone Reports, CW/R/1); Diary of activities 1st Brigade 3WD from 30 June, 1922 (UCDAD, Twomey papers, P69/33/27); MacNeill to O/C 4WD, 2 July 1922 (UCDAD, Twomey papers, P69/33/50).
5 *SC*, *SI*, *CM*, 8, 15 July 1922; Diary of activities 1st Brigade 3WD from 30 June 1922 (UCDAD, Twomey papers, P69/33/27); Western Command war news, 14 July 1922 (UCDAD, Mac Eoin papers, P151/158); Tom Scanlon (UCDAD, O'Malley notebooks, P19b/133/18); Report by Mac Eoin, 15 July 1922 (UCDAD, Mulcahy papers, P7/B/106); Maurteen Brennan (UCDAD, O'Malley notebooks, P19b/133/35); Carty statement, pp 18–19; Younger, *Civil War*, pp 353–4.

6   *SC*, *SI*, *CM*, 22 July 1922; Diary of activities 1st Brigade 3WD from 30 June 1922 (UCDAD,
    Twomey papers, P69/33/27); Tom Scanlon (UCDAD, O'Malley notebooks, P19b/133/19);
    Younger, *Civil War*, pp 358–61; Eoin Neeson, *The Civil War, 1922–23* (Dublin, 1989), pp
    182–4; Murray, *Oracles*, p. 69.

7   *SC*, *SI*, *CM*, 22 July 1922; Report by Mac Eoin, 15 July 1922 (UCDAD, Mulcahy papers,
    P7/B/106); Diary of activities 4th Brigade, 3WD to 30 Nov. 1922 (UCDAD, Twomey papers,
    P69/33/17); Younger, *Civil War*, pp 354–8; King, *Memorabilia*, pp 27–8; *CM*, 30 Aug. 1924.

8   Carty statement, pp 19–20; Maurteen Brennan (UCDAD, O'Malley notebooks, P19b/133/
    34).

9   Diary of activities 4th Brigade, 3WD to 30 Nov. 1922 (UCDAD, Twomey papers, P69/33/17);
    SC, *SI*, *CM*, 29 July, 5 Aug. 1922; Hopkinson, *Green against green*, pp 158–9.

10 Western Command memo, office of CS, July 1922 (UCDAD, Mulcahy papers, P7/B/73).

11 Diary of activities 1st Brigade 3WD from 30 June 1922 (UCDAD, Twomey papers,
    P69/33/27); Reports I/O 3WD, 5, 8 & 22 Aug. 1922 (IMA, Western Command papers,
    CW/Ops/7c); Tom Scanlon (UCDAD, O'Malley notebooks, P19b/133/17); *SC*, 5 Aug. 1922.

12 Western command intelligence report, 4 Aug. 1922 (IMA, Western Command papers,
    CW/Ops/7c).

13 Western command intelligence reports, 4, 11, 21, 22 Aug. 1922 (ibid.).

14 Henry to O/C 3WD, 17 Nov. 1922 (IMA, Western Command papers, CW/Ops/7b).

15 Brian MacNeill to Liam Lynch, 2 Aug. 1922 (UCDAD, Twomey papers, P69/33/49).

16 CS to O/C 3WD, 9 Nov. 1922 (UCDAD, Twomey papers, P69/33/46); Adj. Western
    Command to CS, 17, 25 Jan. 1923 (UCDAD, Twomey papers, P69/31); Letter to Director of
    Engineering GHQ, 16 Dec. 1922 (IMA, Captured Documents, Lot No. 232).

17 Diary of activities 1st Brigade 3WD from 30 June 1922 (UCDAD, Twomey papers,
    P69/33/27).

18 Carty statement, pp 20–1; Diary of activities 4th Brigade, 3WD to 30 Nov. 1922 (UCDAD,
    Twomey papers, P69/33/17).

19 *SC*, *SI*, 2 Sept. 1922; Manager Sligo, Leitrim & Northern Counties Railway to Minister for
    Defence, 27, 28 July 1922 (UCDAD, Mulcahy papers, P7/B/73); Assistant QM Western
    Command to CS, 31 July 1922 (ibid.); Sligo, Leitrim & Northern Counties Railway (IMA,
    Dept. Defence files, A7160).

20 General position of the army, Aug. 1922 (UCDAD, Mulcahy papers, P/7B/29); CS to Mac
    Eoin, 7 Aug. 1922 (UCDAD, Mulcahy papers, P7/B/73); Mac Eoin to CS, 10 Aug. 1922
    (ibid.); CS to Mac Eoin, 14 Aug. 1922 (ibid.).

21 Diary of activities 1st Brigade 3WD from 30 June 1922 (UCDAD, Twomey papers,
    P69/33/27); Mac Eoin to CS and C-in-C to Mac Eoin, 4 Sept. 1922 (UCDAD, Mulcahy
    papers, P/7B/73).

22 Farrelly to Mac Eoin, 11 Sept. 1922 (UCDAD, Mulcahy papers, P7/B/74); Mac Eoin to C-
    in-C, Lawlor to Mac Eoin 12 Sept. 1922 (ibid.).

23 Statement by Vol. James Carr, n.d. (IMA, Western Command papers, CW/Ops/7c); Report
    from Ballymote I/O, 13 Sept. 1922, Report from Tubbercurry Adj., 14 Sept. 1922 (ibid.); *SC*,
    SI, *CM*, 16, 23 Sept. 1922; Carty statement, pp 21–3; Diary of activities 4th Brigade, 3WD to
    30 Nov. 1922 (UCDAD, Twomey papers, P69/33/17); Peadar Ó Flanagáin, 'Brigadier-
    General Joe Ring', *Cathair na Mart*, 7:1 (1987), 14–20.

24 Western Command Operation Order No. 1, n.d. (UCDAD, Mac Eoin papers, P151/212);
    Hopkinson, *Green against green*, p. 215; Younger, *Civil War*, p. 461; *SC*, *SI*, 23 Sept. 1922; Tom
    Scanlon (UCDAD, O'Malley notebooks, P19b/133/22–24); *SC*, *SI*, 23 Sept. 1922; Report
    I/O 3WD, 20 Sept. 1922 (IMA, Western Command papers, CW/Ops/7c).

25 Michael Tierney, *Eoin MacNeill: scholar and man of action, 1867–1945*, ed. F.X. Martin
    (Oxford, 1980), pp 312–13.

26 McGowan, *Benbulben*, p. 134; I/O Western Command, 21 Sept. 1922 (IMA, Western
    Command papers, CW/Ops/7c); *SC*, *SI*, *CM*, 23, 30 Sept. 1922; Athlone to C-in-C, 18 Sept.

1922 (UCDAD, Mulcahy papers, P7/B/73); ibid., O'Doherty, Ballyshannon to HQRS, 20 Sept. 1922; O/C 3WD to CS, 8 Dec. 1922 (UCDAD, Twomey papers, P69/33/43); Diary of activities 1st Brigade 3WD from 30 June 1922 (UCDAD, Twomey papers, P69/33/27); *Poblacht na hÉireann War News*, 22, 27 Jan. 1923; *Poblacht na hÉireann* (Scottish edition), 30 Sept., 7 Oct. 1922; O'Farrell, *Mac Eoin*, pp 88–9.

27 Diary of activities 1st Brigade 3WD from 30 June 1922 (UCDAD, Twomey papers, P69/33/27); O/C 3WD to CS, 28 Nov. 1922 (UCDAD, Twomey papers, P69/33/45); Hopkinson, *Green against green*, pp 212–17.

28 Report from Boyle, 4 Nov. 1922 (IMA, Western Command papers, CW/Ops/7b).

29 Weekly appreciation of situation, 6 Nov. 1922 (IMA, Western Command papers, CW/Ops/7b).

30 Maurteen Brennan (UCDAD, O'Malley notebooks, P19b/133/36).

31 Diary of activities 4th Brigade, 3WD to 30 Nov. 1922 (UCDAD, Twomey papers, P69/33/17); *SI*, *SC*, 14 Oct. 1922.

32 Phone message from Mac Eoin, 24 Oct. 1922 (UCDAD, Mulcahy papers, P7/B/74); Reports Officer 3WD to Reports Officer Western Command, 7 Nov. 1922 (UCDAD, Mulcahy papers, P7/B/114); Henry to OC 3WD, 17 Nov. 1922 (IMA, Western Command papers, CW/Ops/7b).

33 C-in-C to Mac Eoin, 19 Oct. 1922 (UCDAD, Mulcahy papers, P7/B/74).

34 *SC*, *SI*, 21 Oct. 1922; Daily Operations Report, 20 Nov. 1922 (IMA, Western Command papers, CW/Ops/7(b); *SC*, 18 Nov. 1922; Diary of activities 1st Brigade 3WD from 30 June 1922 (UCDAD, Twomey papers, P69/33/27).

35 *SC*, *SI*, *CM*, 11 Nov. 1922; Carty statement, p. 24.

36 Daily operations report, 17 Nov. 1922 (IMA, Western Command papers, CW/Ops/7b).

37 CS to O/C 3WD, 9 Nov. 1922 (UCDAD, Twomey papers, P69/33/48); Diary of activities 4th Brigade, 3WD to 30 Nov. 1922 (ibid., P69/33/17).

38 Diary of activities 4th Brigade, 3WD to 30 Nov. 1922 (UCDAD, Twomey papers, P69/33/17); Conroy telephone message, 30 Nov. 1922 (IMA, Western Command papers, CW/Ops/7b); Daily operations report, 27 Dec. 1922 (ibid.); Report by I/O Sligo, 30 Nov. 1922 (IMA, Donegal Command papers, CW/Ops/6); Reports, 15 & 18 Dec. 1922 (IMA, Western Command papers, CW/Ops/7c); Carty statement, p. 24.

39 *SC*, *SI*, 16 Dec. 1922; O/C 1st Brigade to O/C 3WD, 10 Dec. 1922 (UCDAD, Twomey papers, P69/33/32); Letter to prisoner J. Quinn, 17 Dec. 1922 (UCDAD, Mulcahy papers, P7/B/75); Adj. Sligo to Adj. 3WD, 14 Dec. 1922 (IMA, Western Command papers, CW/Ops/7c); Report on attack on Sligo town hall, 18 Dec. 1922 (UCDAD, Mac Eoin Papers, P151/183).

40 *SC*, *SI*, 13, 20 Jan. 1923; 1st Brigade 3WD diary of activities for fortnight ended 15 Jan. 1923 (UCDAD, Mulcahy papers, P7/B/91); Adj. 3WD to Western Command, 27 Feb. 1923 (IMA, Western Command papers, CW/Ops/7a); Daily operations report, 12 Jan. 1923 (IMA, Western Command papers, CW/Ops/7b); Burning of Sligo railway station (IMA, Dept. Defence files, A8125).

41 Report by Sligo I/O, 1 Dec. 1922 (IMA, Donegal Command papers, CW/Ops/6); 3WD strengths, Nov. 1922 (IMA, Western Command papers, CW/Ops/7b).

42 Report on north-west Sligo area, 29 Dec. 1922 (UCDAD, Mulcahy papers, P7/B/75).

43 O/C 3WD to CS, 10 Dec. 1922 (UCDAD, Twomey papers, P69/33/39).

44 Hopkinson, *Green against green*, p. 228.

45 Ibid., pp 230–2; Matt Kilcawley (UCDAD, O'Malley notebooks, P17b/137/69); Carty to Deasy, 6 Feb. 1923 (NLI, Ernie O'Malley papers, MS 10973).

46 Hopkinson, *Green against green*, p. 182; Murray, *Oracles*, p. 75.

47 Thomas Scanlon (UCDAD, O'Malley notebooks, P19b/133/17); Matt Kilcawley (UCDAD, O'Malley notebooks, P17b/137/67).

48 *II*, 12, 13 Feb. 1923; *SC*, 17 Feb. 1923.

49 *SC*, 24 Feb. 1923; Hopkinson, *Green against green*, p. 185.

50 Army order No. 4, Reorganisation of commands (IMA, General routine orders).
51 1st Brigade diary of activities for fortnight ended 31 Jan. 1923 (IMA, Western Command papers, CW/Ops/7a).
52 Donegal Command report, 21 Apr. 1923 (IMA, Dept. Defence files, A/8083); Operation Order No. 2, Operation in Dromore West area, n.d. (IMA, Donegal Command papers, CW/Ops/6); Report on operations, 27 Apr. 1923 (ibid.); Report on operations, 25 Mar. 1923 (ibid.); Report on operations, 14 Apr. 1923 (ibid.); 4th Brigade diary of activities for fortnight ended 15 Feb. 1923 (IMA, Western Command papers, CW/Ops/7a); Adj. 3WD to O/C Western Command, 16 Apr. 1923 (UCDAD, Twomey papers, P69/30).
53 4th Brigade diary of activities for fortnight ended 15 Feb. 1923 (IMA, Western Command papers, CW/Ops/7a); *SC*, 3 Feb., 7 Apr. 1923.
54 1st Brigade diary of activities for fortnight ended 31 Jan. 1923 (IMA, Western Command papers, CW/Ops/7a); Reports, 19, 27 Mar. 1923 (IMA, Donegal Command papers, CW/Ops/6o); *SC*, 27 Jan., 3 Feb., 31 Mar. 1923; *SC*, 17 Mar. 1923.
55 *SC*, 27 Jan., 3, 10 Feb., 7, 28 Apr. 1923; Thomas Scanlon (UCDAD, O'Malley notebooks, P19b/133/36); No. 1 Brigade diary of activities for fortnight ended 15 Mar. 1923 (UCDAD, Twomey papers, P69/30).
56 Report Mac Eoin to CS, 19 Apr. 1923 (UCDAD, Mac Eoin Papers, P151/200).
57 Operation report, 14 Apr. 1923 (IMA, Claremorris Command papers, CW/Ops/4d); Reports, 27 Apr. & 31 May 1923 (IMA, Donegal Command papers, CW/Ops/6n); Report on Irregular activities, 24 Apr. 1923 (UCDAD, Mac Eoin Papers, P151/200); Claremorris Command fortnightly report, 2 June 1923 (IMA, Dept. Defence files, A8079).
58 Report on Western Command, 17 Mar. 1923 (UCDAD, Twomey papers, P69/30); CS IRA to Adj. Western Command, 12 Mar. 1923 (ibid.); CS to O/C Western Command, 23 Mar. 1923 (ibid.).
59 Thomas Scanlon (UCDAD, O'Malley notebooks, P19b/133/25); Pilkington to CS, 15 June 1923 (UCDAD, Twomey papers, P69/30/7).
60 Claremorris Command reports, May–June 1923 (IMA, Dept. Defence files, A8079); Donegal Command reports, Apr.–July 1923 (IMA, Dept. Defence files, A8083).
61 *WP*, 29 July 1922; *RH*, 5 Aug. 1922; *SC*, 29 July, 5 Aug. 1922.
62 *SC*, 28 Oct. 25 Nov. 1922; *WP*, 28 Oct. 1922; *RH*, 14 Oct., 30 Sept., 21 Oct., 18 Nov., 23, 30 Dec. 1922.
63 Armed robberies at Bunninadden, Co. Sligo (NAI, DJ H5/856).
64 *SI*, *SC*, 7 Apr. 1923; Murder of Mrs Catherine McGuinness (NAI, DJ, H5/700).
65 *SC*, 29 July 1922; *RH*, 12 Aug., 14, 28 Oct. 1922.
66 Civic Guard, general distribution (NAI, DJ, H99/29); *RH*, 4 Nov. 1922; *SI*, 28 Oct. 1922.
67 Civic Guards monthly reports, July 1923 (IMA, Dept. Defence, A8454); Civic Guard (NAI, DJ, H99/125).
68 *SI*, *SC*, 14 Apr. 1923; *Iris an Ghárda*, 7 May 1923.
69 Civic Guards monthly reports, July 1923 (IMA, Dept. Defence, A8454).
70 *RH*, 19 Aug., 9 Sept. 1922; *SC*, 26 Aug. 1922.
71 *SC*, 30 Sept., 7 Oct. 1922, 13 Jan. 1923; *RH*, 30 Dec. 1922, 26 May 1923.
72 Kotsonouris, *Retreat*, pp 93–4; Garvin, *1922*, p. 171; *SI*, 4, 11 Nov., 30 Dec. 1922, 24 Feb., 3 Mar., 7 Apr. 1923; *RH*, 11 Nov., 30 Dec. 1922, 17 Feb. 1923; *SC*, 3, 10 Feb. 1923; *Iris an Ghárda*, 1923.
73 Niamh Brennan, 'A political minefield: Southern loyalists, the Irish Grants Committee and the British government, 1922–31', *IHS*, 30:119 (1997), 406–20; McDowell, *Crisis & decline*, pp 137–62; Farry, *Aftermath*, pp 177–201.
74 Palmer J. McCloughrey (TNA, IGC, CO 762/63).
75 John Lougheed (TNA, IGC, CO 762/137); Illegal seizure of lands of John Lougheed, Riverstown (NAI, DJ, H5/1091).
76 *RH*, 13, 20 May 1922; Protection of lands at Bunninadden (NAI, Dept. Defence, A3642);

Damage to property of C. Phibbs, Doobeg, Bunninadden (NAI, DJ, H5/215); Charles Phibbs (TNA, IGC, CO 762/70); Einion Thomas, 'From Sligo to Wales: the flight of Sir Charles Phibbs', *History Ireland*, 12:1 (2004), 9–10.

77 Jessica Hunter (TNA, IGC, CO 762/51).
78 *RH*, 14 Apr. 1923; *SI*, 21 Apr. 1923; Farry, *Chronicle*, p. 224.
79 J. Walpole-Boyers (TNA, IGC, CO 762/202).
80 Joseph Graham (TNA, IGC, CO 762/205).
81 George R. Williams (TNA, IGC, CO 762/195).
82 Annie Brennan (TNA, IGC, CO 762/108); some Auxiliaries left without settling their accounts.
83 Edith Anderson (TNA, IGC, CO 762/62); T.E. Guthrie (TNA, IGC, CO 762/40); Joseph Graham (TNA, IGC, CO 762/205); P.J. McCloughery (TNA, IGC, CO 762/63).
84 McDowell, *Crisis & decline*, p. 120.
85 Farry, *Aftermath*, pp 115–30.
86 Baby Bohan, 'Activities of Cumann na mBan in south Sligo from 1916 to the present day' (UCDAD, Sighle Humphreys papers, P106/1407); Mai McGowan questionnaire, 1969 (UCDAD, Sighle Humphreys papers, P106/1425); Baby Bohan questionnaire, 1969 (ibid.); Mrs Julia Travers questionnaire, 1969 (ibid.); Sarah Bohan questionnaire, 1969 (ibid.); Sinéad McCoole, *No ordinary women: Irish female activists in the revolutionary years* (Dublin, 2003), Appendix 2; McCarthy, *Cumann na mBan*, pp 176–7.
87 *SC*, 1, 8, 29 Apr., 14 Oct. 1922, 13, 20 Jan. 1923; McCarthy, *Cumann na mBan*, pp 176–7; Ward, *Unmanageable revolutionaries*, p. 173.
88 Casualty figures were compiled from reports in local newspapers, 3WD reports in Moss Twomey papers, Western Command correspondence in Richard Mulcahy papers, Operation and Intelligence files in the Irish Military Archives as well as the incomplete but useful Roll of Deceased Personnel in the latter archive.

CHAPTER THIRTEEN *Revolution?*

1 Irish statute book online, http://www.irishstatutebook.ie/1926/en/act/pub/0003/, accessed 3 May 2012.
2 *RH*, 8 Mar. 1924.

Select bibliography

PRIMARY SOURCES

A. MANUSCRIPTS

Armagh

Archdiocese of Armagh, Records Centre
Fr O'Kane Papers: Charles Gildea material.

Bedford

Bedfordshire and Luton Archives and Records Service, Bedford

Capt. A.L. Dunnill, 'A summary of events during the period in which the 1st Battalion
Bedfordshire & Hertfordshire Regiment was stationed in Ireland, 1920, 1921, 1922'.

Belfast

Public Record Office of Northern Ireland

J.M. Wilson papers.

Dublin

University College Dublin, Archives Department

Sighle Humphreys papers.
Seán Mac Eoin papers.
Richard Mulcahy papers.
Ernie O'Malley notebooks.
Moss Twomey papers.

National Library of Ireland

Michael Collins papers.
Maurice Moore papers.
J.J. O'Connell papers.
O'Hara papers.
Count Plunkett papers.
United Irish League, minute book of the National Directory.
Joseph McGarrity papers.
Barton papers.
Kathleen Mac Kenna Napoli papers.
Joseph Brennan papers.

Count Plunkett papers.
Brighid O'Mullane papers.
Ernie O'Malley papers.
Official diary, William Herbert Bodley, R.I.C. officer, at Dublin Depot, Portlaw, Co. Waterford, Ballymote, Co. Sligo and Gorey, Co. Wexford, 1912–17.
Irish National Aid Association and Volunteer Dependants' Fund papers.
A précis of about two thousand letters, seized by police in a raid on Sinn Féin headquarters, 1918.
Sinn Féin: minute book of the standing committee. Jan. 1918–May 1919; June 1919–Mar. 1922.
Irish Transport and General Workers' Union census, June 1918.
Irish Transport and General Workers' Union list of branches, 1909–22.
J.J. Clancy, Sligo, correspondence, 1918–20.
William O'Brien collection.
Sligo branch Irish Transport and General Workers' Union material.

National Archives of Ireland

Records of the Clerks of the Crown and Peace, County Sligo.
Resident Magistrates diaries (CSO Misc Books).
Department of Education records.
Dáil Éireann records.
Records of the Dáil Éireann Courts (Winding Up) Commission.
Dáil Éireann Local Government records.
Department of Finance files.
Department of Justice files.
Department of the Taoiseach general files.

Irish Military Archives

Bureau of Military History witness statements.
Civil War Operation and Intelligence Files: Claremorris, Donegal & Western Commands.
Radio and phone reports.
Daily press survey.
Captured documents.
Department of Defence files.
Michael Collins papers.
Roll of deceased personnel.
Deceased members of the defence forces.
Special Infantry Corps material.
Truce liaison material.
Internment prisoner location books.
Free State Army Census, Dec. 1922.

Grand Lodge of Freemasons Archive

Membership registers, Lodges 20 & 165.

London

National Archives of the United Kingdom

Colonial Office papers.
Home Office papers.
War Office papers.

Sligo

Sligo County Library

Sligo County Council minute books.
Sligo Corporation minute books.
Sligo County Home and hospital committee minute books.
Sligo Union Board of Guardians minute books.
Dromore West Board of Guardians miscellaneous records.
North Sligo comhairle ceantair Sinn Féin minute book, Feb.–July 1920.
Hennessy, S., 'The life and career of John Jinks' (typescript).
Gray family, Ballynalough, statement re republican activities, 1920.
Harlech Masonic Lodge, list of attendance at meetings, 1918, 1919.
Sligo Constitutional Club register of candidates, 1905–29.
Robinson estate office letter books.
Letter concerning battle in Collooney between republican and Free State forces by
    'Lillie' [Lily H. Martin, Rathrippon, Collooney].
Letter describing activities of Black and Tans in Tubbercurry in Oct. 1920 by Bridget
    Gilmartin.
Dominic Benson, letter from Mountjoy Jail, 1923.
Batt Keaney memoir.
Joseph A. Ballantyne: A record of his War of Independence service, 1916–22.
Cash account book 4th Battalion, Sligo Brigade, IRA, Sept. 1921–Apr. 1922.
Old lined copybook (minus cover) outlining various aspects of IRA structure in west
    Sligo during the Civil War.

B. OFFICIAL RECORDS

Dáil Éireann. Parliamentary Debates.
Dáil Éireann. Private Sessions of Second Dáil.
Census of Ireland, 1911.
House of Commons, 1914, Judicial statistics, Ireland, 1912.
Saorstát Éireann. Census of population, 1926.

C. NEWSPAPERS AND PERIODICALS

An tÓglach   *Iris an Ghárda*
Daily Bulletin   *Nationality*
Éire   *Notes from Ireland*
Free State   *Poblacht na hÉireann*

Poblacht na hÉireann (Scottish edition)   *Roscommon Herald*
Poblacht na hÉireann War News   *Sligo Champion*
Sinn Féin   *Sligo Independent*
Connachtman   *Sligo Nationalist*
Daily Sheet   *Sligo Times*
Irish Bulletin   *Voice of Labour*
Irish Citizen   *Watchword of Labour*
Irish Volunteer   *Weekly Summary*
Leitrim Observer   *Western People*
National Volunteer

D. PRINTED PRIMARY MATERIAL

Gaughan, J. Anthony (ed.), *Memoirs of Constable Jeremiah Mee, R.I.C.* (Dublin, 1975).
Kilgannon, Thady, *Almanac for north Connaught* (Sligo, 1905).
——, *Directory of County Sligo* (Sligo, 1907).
——, *Sligo and its surroundings* (Sligo, 1926).
Mac Goilla Choille, Breandán (ed.), *Intelligence notes, 1913–1916* (Dublin, 1966).
Smithson, A.P. (ed.), *In times of peril: leaves from the diary of Nurse Linda Kearns* (Dublin, 1922).

SECONDARY SOURCES

E. PUBLISHED WORKS

aan de Wiel, Jérôme, *The Catholic Church in Ireland, 1914–1918: war and politics* (Dublin, 2003).
Abbott, Richard, *Police casualties in Ireland, 1919–1922* (Cork, 2000).
Augusteijn, Joost, *From public defiance to guerrilla warfare: the experience of ordinary volunteers in the Irish War of Independence, 1916–1921* (Dublin, 1996).
Augusteijn, Joost (ed.), *The Irish revolution, 1913–1923* (New York, 2002).
Baker, Joe, *My stand for freedom* (Westport, 1988).
Beirne, Francis (ed.), *The diocese of Elphin: people, places and pilgrimage* (Dublin, 2000).
Bew, Paul, *Ideology and the Irish question: Ulster unionism and Irish nationalism, 1912–1916* (Oxford, 1994).
Boyce D.G. (ed.), *The revolution in Ireland, 1879–1923* (Basingstoke, 1988).
Breathnach, Diarmuid & Máire Ní Mhurchú, *Beathaisnéis: 1882–1982, vol. I* (Dublin, 1986).
—— *Beathaisnéis: 1882–1982, vol. II* (Dublin, 1990).
Brennan, Niamh, 'A political minefield: Southern Loyalists, the Irish Grants Committee and the British Government, 1922–31', *IHS*, 30:119 (1997), 406–20.
Brewer, John D., *The Royal Irish Constabulary: an oral history* (Belfast, 1990).
Buckland, Patrick, *Irish unionism 1: the Anglo-Irish and the new Ireland, 1885–1922* (Dublin, 1972).

Bull, Philip, 'The United Irish League and the reunion of the Irish Parliamentary Party, 1898–1900', *IHS*, 26:101 (1988), 51–78.

Campbell, Fergus, *Land and revolution: nationalist politics in the west of Ireland, 1891–1921* (Oxford, 2005).

Campbell, Fergus & Kevin O'Shiel, 'The last land war? Kevin O'Shiel's memoir of the Irish revolution (1916–21)', *Archivium Hibernicum*, 57 (2003), 155–200.

Campbell-Perry, V.W. Bro. R.H., 'A glimpse of freemasonry in Sligo 1767–1951', *The Lodge of Research transactions for years 1949–57* (Dublin, 1959), 34–43.

Carroll, Denis, *They have fooled you again: Michael O'Flanagan (1876–1942) priest, republican, social critic* (Dublin, 1993).

Casey, James, 'Republican courts in Ireland, 1919–1922', *Irish Jurist*, new series, 5 (1970), 321–42.

—— 'The genesis of the Dáil Courts', *Irish Jurist*, new series, 9 (1974), 326–38.

Coleman, Marie, *County Longford and the Irish revolution* (Dublin, 2003).

Conlon, Lil, *Cumann na mBan and the women of Ireland, 1913–1925* (Kilkenny, 1969).

Coogan, Tim Pat, *Michael Collins* (London 1990).

Costello, Francis, 'The republican courts and the decline and fall of British rule in Ireland', *Eire-Ireland*, 25:2 (1990), 36–55.

Cowell, John, *Sligo, land of Yeats' desire* (Dublin, 1989).

Cullen Owens, Rosemary, *Smashing times: a history of the Irish women's suffrage movement, 1889–1922* (Dublin, 1984).

—— *A social history of women in Ireland, 1870–1970* (Dublin, 2005).

Cunningham, John, *Labour in the west of Ireland: working life and struggle, 1890–1914* (Belfast, 1995).

Curran, Joseph M., *The birth of the Irish Free State, 1921–1923* (Alabama, 1980).

Daly, Mary A., 'Local government and the first Dáil' in Brian Farrell (ed.), *The creation of the Dáil* (Dublin, 1994), pp 123–36.

—— *The buffer state: the historical roots of the Department of the Environment* (Dublin, 1997).

Deignan, Padraig, *The Protestant community in Sligo, 1914–49* (Dublin, 2010).

—— 'The importance of fraternities and social clubs for the Protestant community in Sligo from 1914 to 1949', *Corran Herald*, 44 (2011/12), 9–15.

—— 'PR & the Sligo Borough election of January 1919', *History Ireland*, 17:3 (May–June, 2009), 38–9.

Dooley, Terence, *The decline of the big house in Ireland: a study of Irish landed families, 1860–1960* (Dublin, 2001).

Duffy, Seán (ed.), *Atlas of Irish history* (2nd ed., Dublin, 2000).

Enniscrone, Kilglass GAA, *One hundred years of an Irish parish, 1890–1990* (Enniscrone, 1990).

Farry, Michael, *Sligo, 1914–1921: a chronicle of conflict* (Trim, 1994).

—— *The aftermath of revolution: Sligo, 1921–23* (Dublin, 2000).

Farry, Neal, 'Ballymote during the troubles', *Corran Herald*, 4 (May 1986), 1–3, 6, 11.

Finn, John, *Gurteen Co. Sligo: its people and its past* (Sligo, 1994).

Fitzpatrick, David, *Politics and Irish life, 1913–1921: provincial experience of war and revolution* (Dublin, 1977).

—— 'The geography of Irish nationalism, 1910–1921', *Past and Present*, 78 (1978), 113–44.

—— (ed.), *Revolution? Ireland, 1917–1923* (Dublin, 1990).

Gallagher, Michael 'The pact general election of 1922', *IHS*, 21:84 (1979), 404–21.

—— (ed), *Irish elections, 1922–44: results and analysis* (Limerick, 1993).

Garvin, Tom, *The evolution of Irish nationalist politics* (Dublin, 1981).

—— *Nationalist revolutionaries in Ireland* (Oxford, 1987).

—— *1922: the birth of Irish democracy* (Dublin, 1996).

Glór Shligigh, Conradh na Gaeilge comóradh caoga bliain, 1893–1943 (Sligo, 1943).

Greaves, C. Desmond, *The Irish Transport and General Workers' Union: the formative years, 1909–1923* (Dublin, 1982).

Hannon, Michael, 'Remembering James Hannon', *Corran Herald*, 33 (2000/1), 2–3.

Hart, Peter, *The I.R.A. & its enemies: violence and community in Cork, 1916–1923* Oxford, 1998).

—— *The I.R.A. at war, 1916–1923* (Oxford, 2003).

—— 'The geography of revolution in Ireland, 1917–1923', *Past and Present*, 155 (1997), 142–73.

Hegarty Thorne, Kathleen, *They put the flag a'flyin: the Roscommon Volunteers, 1916–1923* (Oregon, 2005).

Herlihy, Jim, *Royal Irish Constabulary officers: a biographical and genealogical guide, 1816–1922* (Dublin, 2005).

Hill, Ronald J. & Michael Marsh (eds), *Modern Irish democracy: essays in honour of Basil Chubb* (Dublin, 1993).

Hopkinson, Michael, *Green against green: the Irish Civil War* (Dublin, 1988).

—— *The Irish War of Independence* (Dublin, 2002).

Jackson, Alvin, 'Irish unionism 1870–1922' in George D. Boyce & Alan O'Day (eds), *Defenders of the union: a survey of British and Irish unionism since 1801* (London, 2001), pp 115–36.

Kautt, W.H., *Ambushes and armour: the Irish rebellion, 1919–1921* (Dublin, 2010).

Kelly, M.J., *The Fenian ideal and Irish nationalism, 1882–1916* (Woodbridge, 2006).

Keogh, Dermot, *The Vatican, the bishops and Irish politics, 1919–1939* (Cambridge, 1986).

King, Cecil A., *Memorabilia, musings on sixty-odd years of life as a newspaper man* (Ballyshannon, 1989).

Kotsonouris, Mary, *Retreat from revolution: the Dáil courts, 1920–24* (Dublin, 1994).

Laffan, Michael, 'Labour must wait: Ireland's conservative revolution' in Patrick J. Corish (ed.), *Radicals, rebels and establishments* (Belfast, 1985), pp 203–22.

—— *The resurrection of Ireland: the Sinn Féin party, 1916–23* (Cambridge, 1999).

Lavin, T.J., 'Some Roscommon actions', *Capuchin Annual* (1970), 406–9.

Lawlor, S.M., 'Ireland from truce to treaty: war or peace', *IHS*, 22:85 (1980), 49–64.

Lowe, W.J., 'The war against the R.I.C., 1919–21', *Éire-Ireland*, 37:3–4 (2002), 79–117.

Lyons, F.S.L., *The Irish Parliamentary Party, 1890–1910* (London, 1951).

—— 'The War of Independence, 1919–21' in W.E. Vaughan (ed.), *A new history of Ireland*; VI, *Ireland under the union 1870–1921* (paperback ed., Oxford, 2010), chapter 11.

Macardle, Dorothy, *The Irish Republic* (paperback ed., London, 1968).

MacAtasney, Gerard, *Seán Mac Diarmada: the mind of the revolution* (Manorhamilton, 2004).

McCabe, Alec, 'Cradling a revolution', *An tÓglach* (Christmas 1962), 7–8.

—— Interview by Dermot Mullane, *Irish Times*, 6 & 7 May 1970.

McCarthy, Cal, *Cumann na mBan and the Irish revolution* (Cork, 2007).

McCoole, Sinéad, *No ordinary women: Irish female activists in the revolutionary years* (Dublin, 2003).

MacDermot, Charles, 'A summer holiday at Coolavin', *Echoes of Ballaghaderreen*, 22 (2007), 7.

McDowell, R.B., *Crisis and decline: the fate of the southern unionists* (Dublin, 1997).

McGee, Owen, *The IRB: the Irish Republican Brotherhood, from the Land League to Sinn Féin* (2nd ed. Dublin, 2007).

McGowan, Joe, *In the shadow of Benbulben* (Manorhamilton, 1993).

McGuinn, James, *Sligo men in the great war* (Belturbet, 1994).

McNiff, Liam, *A history of the Garda Síochána* (Dublin, 1997).

McNiffe, Michael, 'Veteran [Pat Hunt] recalls War of Independence', *SC*, 1 Nov. 1985.

McTernan, John C., *Historic Sligo* (Sligo, 1965).

—— (ed.), *Sligo GAA – a centenary history 1884–1984* (Sligo, 1984).

—— *In Sligo long ago* (Sligo, 1998).

—— *Worthies of Sligo* (Sligo, 1994).

—— *Olde Sligoe* (Sligo, 1995).

—— (ed.), *Sligo: sources of local history.* Sligo, 1994.

—— 'The Tubbercurry "conspirators"', *Corran Herald*, 43 (2010/2011), 72–73.

—— *Sligo: the light of bygone days, Volume I: Houses of Sligo and associated families, Volume II: Sligo families* (Sligo, 2009).

Maume, Patrick, 'Parnell and the I.R.B. oath', *IHS*, 29:115 (1995), 363–70.

Milestones & memories : Sligo County Council centenary record: 1899–1999 (Sligo, 2000).

Maye, Brian, *Arthur Griffith* (Dublin, 1997).

Miller, David W., *Church, state and nation in Ireland, 1898–1921* (Dublin, 1921).

Mitchell, Arthur, *Labour in Irish politics* (Dublin, 1974).

—— *Revolutionary government in Ireland: Dáil Éireann, 1919–22* (Dublin, 1995).

Moffitt, Miriam, *The Church of Ireland community of Killala and Achonry* (Dublin, 1999).

Montgomery-Massingberd, Hugh (ed.), *Burke's Irish family records* (London, 1976).

Morrison, Eve, 'The Bureau of Military History and female republican activism, 1913–1923' in Maryann Gialanella Valiulis (ed.), *Gender and power in Irish history* (Dublin, 2009), pp 59–83.

Murphy, W.M., *The Yeats family and the Pollexfens of Sligo* (Dublin, 1971).

Murray, Patrick, *Oracles of God: the Roman Catholic Church and Irish politics, 1922–37* (Dublin, 2000).

Neeson, Eoin, *The Civil War in Ireland, 1922–23* (Cork, 1966).

Ní Liatháin, Íde, *The life and career of P.A. McHugh, a north Connacht politician, 1859–1909: a footsoldier of the party* (Dublin, 1999).

Novick, Ben, *Conceiving revolution: Irish nationalist propaganda during the First World War* (Dublin, 2001).

O'Brien, M.C., *Commandant Marren* (Sligo?, n.d. [*c.*1930]).

Ó Broin, Leon, *Revolutionary underground: the story of the Irish Republican Brotherhood, 1858–1924* (Dublin, 1976).

O'Callaghan, John, *Revolutionary Limerick: the republican campaign for independence in Limerick, 1913–1921* (Dublin, 2010).

O'Callaghan, Micheál, *For Ireland and freedom: Roscommon's contribution to the fight for independence, 1917–1921* (Boyle, 1964).

O'Donoghue, Florence (ed.), Diarmuid Lynch, *The I.R.B. and the 1916 insurrection* (Cork, 1957).

—— *Sworn to be free: the complete book of IRA jailbreaks, 1918–1921* (Tralee, 1971).

—— *No other law* (Dublin, 1986).

O'Dowd, Mary, 'Sligo', in Anngret Simms & J.H. Andrews (eds), *Irish country towns* (Dublin, 1994), pp 151–3.

Ó Duigneáin, Prionnsíos, *Linda Kearns, a revolutionary Irish woman* (Manorhamilton, 2002)

Ó Duibhir, Ciaran, *Sinn Féin: the first election, 1908* (Manorhamilton, 1993).

O'Farrell, Padraic, *The Séan Mac Eoin story* (Cork, 1981).

Ó Flanagáin, Peadar, 'Brigadier-General Joe Ring', *Cathair na Mart*, 7:1 (1987), 5–20.

O'Malley, Ernie, *The singing flame* (Dublin, 1978).

Potter, Matthew, *The municipal revolution in Ireland: a handbook of urban government in Ireland since 1800* (Dublin, 2011).

Reid, Steven, *Get to the Point at County Sligo golf club* (Naas, 1991).

Robinson, Lennox, *Bryan Cooper* (London, 1931).

Rumpf, E. & A.C. Hepburn, *Nationalism and socialism in twentieth-century Ireland* (Liverpool, 1977).

Ryan, Louise & Margaret Ward (eds), *Irish women and the vote: becoming citizens* (Dublin, 2007).

Scholes, Andrew, *The Church of Ireland and the third Home Rule Bill* (Dublin, 2010).

Sheehan, Aideen, 'Cumann na mBan, policies and activities' in David Fitzpatrick (ed.), *Revolution? Ireland, 1917–1923* (Dublin, 1990), pp 88–97.

Sheehan, William, *Hearts and mines: the British 5th Division in Ireland, 1920–1922* (Cork, 2009).

Sligo Champion centenary number (Sligo, 1936).

Sligo Champion sesquicentenary supplement (Sligo, 1986).

Steele, Karen, *Women, press, and politics during the Irish revival* (Syracuse, 2007).

Thomas, Einion, 'From Sligo to Wales; the flight of Sir Charles Phibbs', *History Ireland*, 12:1 (2004), 9–10.

Tierney, Michael, *Eoin MacNeill: scholar and man of action, 1867–1945*, ed. F.X. Martin (Oxford, 1980).

Townshend, Charles, 'The Irish Republican Army and the development of guerrilla warfare, 1916–1921', *English Historical Review*, 94 (1979) 318–45.

—— *The British campaign in Ireland, 1919–1921* (Oxford, 1975).

—— *Political violence in Ireland: government and resistance since 1848* (Oxford, 1983).

Valiulis, Maryann Gialanella, *Portrait of a revolutionary: General Richard Mulcahy* (Dublin, 1992).

Varley, Tony, 'Agrarian crime and social control: Sinn Féin and the land question in the west of Ireland in 1920' in Ciaran McCullagh, Mike Tomilson & Tony Varley (eds), *Whose law and order? Aspects of crime and social control in Irish society* (Belfast, 1988).

—— 'A region of sturdy smallholders? Western nationalists and agrarian politics during the First World War', *Journal of the Galway Archaeological and Historical Society*, 55 (2003), 127–50.

Ward, Margaret, *Unmanageable revolutionaries: women and Irish nationalism* (London, 1983).

—— 'Conflicting interests: the British and Irish suffrage movements', *Feminist Review*, 50 (1995), 127–47.

Waters, Maureen, 'Sligo, 1919–1922', *Irish Literary Supplement* (Spring 1992), 27–8.

Wheatley, Michael, *Nationalism and the Irish Party: provincial Ireland, 1910–1916* (Oxford, 2005).

Williams, T.D. (ed.), *The Irish struggle, 1916–26* (London, 1966).

Younger, Calton, *Ireland's Civil War* (London, 1968).

F. INTERNET RESOURCES

Census of Ireland 1901, 1911, NAI: http://www.census.nationalarchives.ie/
Ulster Covenant online, PRONI: http://www.proni.gov.uk/
Dáil Éireann debates: http://debates.oireachtas.ie/dail/

Interviews

Michael Burgess	15 Oct. 1991.
Pat Hunt	31 May 1986 & 3 Aug. 1987.
Bat Keaney	8 Oct. 1988 & 30 Aug. 1990.
Thomas Kilcoyne	14 Aug. 1986.
John Sweeney	26 July 1986.
Michael Walsh	13 Aug. 1987.

Index